THE BIG
RIPOFF

THE BIG RIPOFF

HOW BIG BUSINESS AND BIG GOVERNMENT STEAL YOUR MONEY

TIMOTHY P. CARNEY

WILEY

John Wiley & Sons, Inc.

Published by John Wiley & Sons, Inc., Hoboken, New Jersey.
Published simultaneously in Canada.

For general information on our other products and services or for technical support, please contact our Customer Care Department within the United States at (800) 762-2974, outside the United States at (317) 572-3993 or fax (317) 572-4002.

Wiley also publishes its books in a variety of electronic formats. Some content that appears in print may not be available in electronic books. For more information about Wiley products, visit our web site at www.wiley.com.

Library of Congress Cataloging-in-Publication Data:

Carney, Timothy P., 1978–
  The big ripoff : how big business and big government steal your money /
by Timothy P. Carney.
      p. cm.
  Includes bibliographical references.
  ISBN-13: 978-0-471-78907-9 (cloth)
  ISBN-10: 0-471-78907-0 (cloth)
  1. Business and politics—United States. 2. Corporations—United
States—Political activity. I. Title.
  JK467.C39 2006
  322′.30973—dc22
                                                     2006009327

Printed in the United States of America.

10 9 8 7 6 5 4 3 2 1

I dedicate this book
to my parents,
my brothers, my wife,
and our baby.

Contents

Foreword

imothy P. Carney may be the best political reporter among the outstanding young men and women who worked for me starting with
the redoubtable John Fund in 1981. Tim was a fabulous political
handicapper, who was nearly perfect in forecasting the outcome of the 2002
midterm elections for the *Evans-Novak Political Report*. But I had not appreciated his skills as an investigative reporter until I read this extraordinary book.

Most reporters who describe themselves with the investigative adjective
really are making a deeper new furrow in a well-ploughed journalistic field.
But *The Big Ripoff* definitely ploughs new ground. Carney exposes in detail
a scandal that has been largely ignored. I think he should be put in the category of Upton Sinclair more than a century ago, and shares with him the
designation of *muckraker*. That term was applied to Sinclair and others by
President Theodore Roosevelt as a term of opprobrium.

With the passage of time, Roosevelt's reputation has swollen out of pro-
portion. He is venerated as an icon by all kinds of Republicans, and is universally praised by Democrats as well. But if he were alive, I am sure he
would be castigating Carney as a muckraker. Carney makes clear in this
book that Teddy Roosevelt is a part of the problem—the unholy alliance of
big government and big business, overriding partisan considerations.

That alliance is nothing new. Alexander Hamilton, deified as a founding
father, was the first architect of corporate welfare (as Carney points out

here), and was shameless about it. But the full extent of that alliance and what it means in losses to American taxpayers and entrepreneurs has not been addressed until this book.

What is involved here is really much more than a "big rip-off." Newspaper stories about outrageous pork barrel projects are commonplace. What Carney has done is put together individual instances of corporate welfare into a coherent pattern that constitutes a genuine national scandal. "Corporate welfare," he writes, "is the transfer of wealth from taxpayers to huge corporations. A sizable portion of government spending is for corporate welfare programs, of which there are dozens. The mind-set underlying corporate welfare is that of the central planner, who puts more trust in the wisdom of politicians and favored industry giants than in consumers and investors. The politicians and the big businesses win out, while the customers, entrepreneurs, and especially the taxpayers all lose."

Upton Sinclair was a socialist, and investigative reporters—finding fault with what they see in America—tend to come from the Left. But Tim Carney is no leftist. He is part of a group of iconoclastic young journalists, congressional aides, and political operatives in Washington who generally are labeled as conservatives. Tim was trained at the conservative National Journalism Center and, after working for me, began this book with a grant from the Phillips Foundation, headed by conservative publisher Tom Phillips and its board of trustees, including myself.

But Carney and his young colleagues are unlike the "conservatives" who lead the Republican Party and who are tied to the culture of corporate welfare. The truth, as exposed convincingly in *The Big Ripoff,* is that this is a bipartisan affliction transcending party and ideological lines.

The problem has expanded as the federal government has grown in the half century that I have been in Washington. With its growth have come the giant "law" firms, with 300 or more practitioners deeply involved in the government programs that enrich their clients. They are the princes of lobbyists in Washington and keep intact the system that Carney describes.

Milton Friedman, the Nobel laureate economist, long has expressed pessimism about any serious rewriting of the Internal Revenue Code. He attributes this to the symbiotic relationship between lobbyists and lawmakers. The lobbyists desire complexity in the Code that guarantees their fees. The lawmakers who support that complexity are financed with contributions from the lobbyists. It is all perfectly legal and undermines any serious reform. There is nothing the lobbyists like better than a tax bill that finds them scurrying all over Capitol Hill to complicate tax law.

The only serious effort to curb welfare reform that I have seen in my time in Washington came in 1981, the first year of Ronald Reagan's presidency when all reforms seemed possible. The Gramm-Latta spending reduction and the Conable-Hance tax reduction were about to be passed when Budget Director David Stockman told me of his plans to take on corporate welfare next. It never happened. The pressures inside the Republican Party and the Reagan administration to maintain the status quo were too great.

The reason for this can be found in Friedman's symbiotic relationship. The contributors to the Republican Party who benefit from corporate welfare are represented not only by the burgeoning law firms but also by the trade associations that have grown exponentially during the past half-century. Many have moved their headquarters from Chicago or New York to Washington in order to influence legislation and government. They are not interested in less government but want government directed to serve their private interests.

Democrats who ordinarily pounce on any Republican opening are loath to attack on this issue. The law firms and trade associations are carefully stocked with Democrats. As Carney makes clear, this is a bipartisan game. It is just that the Republicans seem more hypocritical in their sponsorship of these schemes.

Carney reveals the intricate schemes for Washington's transferring wealth, including the Enron scandal. That dreadful episode offers an object lesson for businessmen eagerly seeking the embrace of big business. Carney writes: "While government may never quit trying to solve every problem, businessmen might be able to take a lesson from the Enron tale. Enron was built on subsidies, gaming complex and artificial rules, and banking on environmental regulations. This formula may work for a while, but ask Ken Lay today: It will catch up with you."

But there is no sign that businessmen have heard a warning signal from Enron. The country needs a white knight to take Tim Carney's text and preach it to the nation. Carney concludes that "the blame . . . rests on the politicians, who unlike CEOs are supposed to answer to all the people." After reading this book, the country ought to be looking harder.

Robert D. Novak

Washington, DC
April 2006

Acknowledgments

I owe thanks to dozens of individuals and organizations for their aid and help with this book.

This book never would have happened without the two fellowships that gave me the time and support to research, write, and finish it. The Phillips Foundation Journalism Fellowship was the origin of this book and provided the occasion for most of the work of writing the book. The Competitive Enterprise Institute's Warren T. Brookes Journalism Fellowship gave me not only material support, and an office and a desk, but also intellectual support, criticism, and motivation.

I also must thank the bosses and editors I have had in Washington: Tom Winter, whose grammatical nagging and paternal support are slowly making me into a better writer; Terry Jeffrey, who taught me that wherever there is money and power, there is bound to be something worth reporting on; and Bob Novak, whose example of hard work, contrariness, and doggedness will always serve as an inspiration. I am grateful, too, for the National Journalism Center, where I received my first training as a reporter and researcher.

My agent Teresa Hartnett and my editor Pamela Van Giessen are the midwives of this work, responsible for its coming into the world.

Dozens of sources, contacts, and experts helped me with every chapter. They are too numerous to name, but I gratefully remember all their help.

Chris Manger ably assisted me as an intern over the sweltering DC summer, and this book is better for his help.

Of course, I owe thanks to my family and friends, who always serve as my editors, censors, interlocutors, and proofreaders. Special thanks go to my brother/tenant/roommate Mike who also served on some days as my only human contact. Also I am grateful for the support of my now-wife Katie, whose love (and faith in providence) shone forth on the day she agreed to marry a writer with no book contract. My brothers Brian and John, my always-supportive mother, and my tolerating father were also crucial for this work.

THE BIG
RIPOFF

1

The Big Ripoff

The Greatest Trick the Devil Ever Pulled

This is a book about how the regular guy gets ripped off. But this book is different from most of the others: It is not about the victims as much as it is about the perpetrators.

This book doesn't focus on the regular guy's or gal's struggle. This book peers into the proverbial smoke-filled room where the ripoffs are planned and executed and shows you—the regular guy or gal—what goes on in that room. This book shows that the two most powerful characters in America— big business and big government—are in cahoots. You are their target.

Big business has too much power in Washington, according to 90 percent of Americans in a December 2005 poll. In the same survey, 85 percent said political action committees (PACs) had too much pull, while 74 percent said the same about lobbyists.[1] Campaign finance numbers and everyday headlines give Americans good reason to suspect that business is up to *something* in Washington.

In the 2004 elections, PACs, mostly representing big businesses or industries, donated over $300 million to political races.[2] In 2000, companies spent over $1.4 billion on lobbyists. In 2002, the average winning congressional candidate spent just under $1 million, with nearly half coming from PACs. A Senate seat cost about $5 million on average, with about a quarter of that amount coming from PACs.

Every week, headlines reveal some scandal involving politicians, lobbyists, corporate cash, and allegations of bribes. CEOs get face time with senators, cabinet secretaries, and presidents. Lawmakers and bureaucrats take laps through the revolving door between government and corporate lobbying. Whatever goes on behind closed doors between the CEOs and the senators or the lobbyists and the lawmakers can't be good or the doors would not be closed.

Just what is big business doing with all this influence? How is it that government is its partner?

There are many assumptions about big business's agenda in Washington. In 2003, one author asserted, "When corporations lobby governments, their usual goal is to avoid regulation."[3] This statement reflects the conventional wisdom. Historian Arthur Schlesinger articulated a similar point, but from the perspective of the government. Schlesinger wrote that "Liberalism in America [the progression of the welfare state and government intervention in the economy] has been ordinarily the movement on the part of the other sections of society to restrain the power of the business community."[4]

The standard assumption seems to be that government action protects ordinary people by restraining big business, which, in turn, wants to be left alone.

The facts point in an entirely different direction:

- Enron was a tireless advocate of strict global energy regulations supported by environmentalists. Enron also used its influence in Washington to keep laissez-faire bureaucrats *off* the federal commissions that regulate the energy industry.
- Philip Morris has aggressively supported heightened federal regulation over tobacco and tobacco advertising. Meanwhile, the state governments that sued Big Tobacco are now working to protect those same large cigarette companies from competition and lawsuits.
- A recent tax increase in Virginia passed because of the tireless support of the state's business leaders, and big business has a long history of supporting tax hikes.
- General Motors provided critical support for new stricter clean air rules that boosted the company's bottom line.

Most important, in these and hundreds of similar cases, the government action that helps big business hurts consumers, taxpayers, less established businesses, and smaller competitors. Following closely what big business does in Washington reveals a very different story from conventional wisdom.

Yes, big business has enormous influence in Washington. Yes, the fruits of the business-government intimacy often harm the "little guy," But, no, big business's usual goal is not to "avoid regulation." Nor is government regulation, taxation, or welfare usually aimed at "restrain[ing] the power" of big business.

The truth—as the stories in this book demonstrate—is that big business lobbies for and profits from big government policies that ripoff consumers, taxpayers, and entrepreneurs. Moreover, government is happy to comply.

The Big Myth

The myth is widespread and deeply rooted that big business and big government are rivals—that big business wants small government.

A 1935 *Chicago Daily Tribune* column argued that voting against Franklin D. Roosevelt was voting for big business. "Led by the President," the columnist wrote, "New Dealers have accepted the challenge, confident the people will repudiate organized business and give the Roosevelt program a new lease on life."[5] However, three days earlier, the president of the Chamber of Commerce and a group of other business leaders met with FDR to support expanding the New Deal.

The day after George W. Bush's inauguration in 2001, columnist Paul Krugman assailed the GOP. "The new guys in town are knee-jerk conservatives; they view too much government as the root of all evil, believe that what's good for big business is always good for America and think that the answer to every problem is to cut taxes and allow more pollution."[6] At the same time, "big business" just across the river in Virginia was ramping up its campaign for a tax increase, and Enron was lobbying Bush's closest advisors to support the Kyoto Protocol on climate change.

Months later, when Enron collapsed, writers attributed the company's corruption and obscene profits to "anarchic capitalism,"[7] and asserted that, "the Enron scandal makes it clear that the unfettered free market does not work."[8] In fact, Enron thrived in a world of complex regulations and begged for government handouts at every turn.

When President Bush helped defeat a congressional bill for strict new regulation of tobacco in 2004, Democratic Senator Tom Harkin charged that the president had "concurred with big tobacco."[9] In fact, Philip Morris openly and actively supported the bill that the president had opposed.

In 2004, an anti-Bush protest group that called itself "Billionaires for Bush," sporting false names such as "Phil T. Rich" and "Lucinda Regulations," tried to reinforce the conventional view that the rich (read: big business) and the Republicans are good friends. Big business and the filthy rich, however, are hardly staunch opponents of tight regulations, as evidenced by the money that the "Billionaires" received from actual billionaires who were certainly not for Bush.

When commentators *do* notice business looking for more federal regulation, they mark it up as an aberration.

When a *Washington Post* reporter noted in 1987 that airlines were asking Congress for help, she commented, "Last month, when the airline industry found itself pursued by state regulators seeking to police airline advertising, it looked for help in an unlikely place—Washington."[10] In truth, airline executives had been behind federal regulations of their industry for decades and had aggressively opposed deregulation.

That *Post* reporter was not the first journalist to be shocked by the airline industry's flirtation with government. A *Chicago Tribune* story in 1975 quoted top airline executives pleading for the preservation of strict federal regulations of airlines. The headline betrayed the writer's shock, "What's this? Airline chief wants continued control."[11] But airline executives had been in on the regulatory regime from the beginning.

In 1984, the National Association of Manufacturers (NAM) rated the members of Congress on their voting records, with a high score meaning the congressman was pro-manufacturer. Democratic Congressman James Jones scored higher than Republican Newt Gingrich, while Democrat Dan Rostenkowski, the leading tax hiker of the day, scored above average. Commentator Walter Olson declared, "NAM has broken with its old reputation as a bastion of laissez faire."[12]

But two years earlier, *Washington Post* reporter David Broder told this story: "When reporters left the headquarters of the Chamber of Commerce of the United States yesterday morning, after a news conference in which its president claimed that business is '10-to-1 against' President Reagan's tax increase bill, a strange sight greeted them. On the sidewalk was a publicity man from the National Association of Manufacturers with a handout claiming that 'the vast majority of American business leaders' favor passage of the bill 'as quickly as possible.' "[13]

While the president of the Chamber opposed the tax hike, about half of the board and its chairman favored higher taxes. Assumptions about business and taxes remained unchanged 11 years later. When the U.S. Chamber of

Commerce supported Bill Clinton's tax increase in 1993, columnists Rowland Evans and Robert Novak wrote about, "the switch of the U.S. Chamber, long an impassioned advocate of the free market."[14] At the same time, Republican Congressman John Boehner said the Chamber, "has refused to be what it had been in the past, a firebrand, principled organization."

And so it goes that every time a regulation is defeated, its proponents claim a victory for big business and a loss for the little gal. Every time commentators see a big business favoring higher taxes or greater regulation, they note it as an oddity.

The big myth is alive and well.

Ulterior Motives

"The greatest trick the devil ever pulled," said Kaiser Soze in the film *The Usual Suspects,* "was convincing the world he didn't exist." In a similar way, big business and big government prosper from the perception that they are rivals instead of partners (in plunder). If we don't see that big business lobbies for big government out of self-interest, we might assume that they are doing so out of altruism and thus put more stake in their argument than it deserves.

If a coal company argues against government limits on carbon dioxide emissions, any listener ought to consider the company's vested interests, as well as any legitimate points the company makes. But what about when Enron lobbied *for* the Kyoto Protocol—a treaty aimed at curbing global warming?

In 2002, after some journalists reported that Enron, like environmentalists, wanted Kyoto ratified, Timothy Noah, a *Slate* columnist, responded: "But the mere fact that Enron stood to benefit financially from the Kyoto Treaty, and therefore was pushing energetically for its passage, doesn't in itself constitute an argument against the Kyoto Treaty."[15]

Noah is correct. Just because Enron liked Kyoto doesn't make the Protocol bad. But it still matters that Enron, which would profit from Kyoto, was a loud lobbyist for its ratification.

Many people argue against regulations and higher taxes. Part of the conservative and libertarian arguments on these issues are that federal regulations often do little or no good for the environment, the worker, or whomever they are supposed to protect, while imposing heavy costs by driving up prices, driving up taxes, driving down wages, or creating shortages.

Sometimes, the regulation proponents engage in a debate weighing the costs and the benefits. Sometimes, however, the pro-regulation side just impugns the motives and the character of their opponents—a tactic used on all sides in every Washington scuffle. When George W. Bush opposes a new environmental rule, some green advocates simply say that Bush is evil, hates trees, and wants kids to drink more arsenic. This caricature is not very believable, in part because it ascribes no credible *motive* to the antiregulation forces.

A more common and more politically useful charge is that Bush receives campaign contributions from—and is personally friendly with—companies that stand to lose from a green regulation, and so he opposes the regulation. This charge is usually enough to at least cast doubt on antiregulatory arguments. Timothy Noah's rebuttal, however, is apropos here: Pointing out that Bush's supporters stand to gain from rolling back or blocking a regulation is not an argument in and of itself against the rollback.

Examining ulterior motives—be they pro or con—is a legitimate undertaking for the media. Proposed regulations are often deeply complex (as are the problems they address), and they carry immense uncertainty and countless possible unintended consequences. It might truly be impossible for the average reporter, reader, congressional representative, or voter to really understand all the arguments in favor of or in opposition to a proposed rule. Frankly, most people have better things to do with their time. On most policy issues, people are best served not by reading the cryptic proposed regulations and studying the underlying science but by listening to the experts and deciding whom they trust most. In that case, the ulterior motives matter.

Which brings us back to Enron and its support of Kyoto: We should consider how Enron would have profited from the implementation of the Kyoto Protocol and examine whether such business practices would be good or bad for us. Higher prices for coal and oil would be good for Enron and bad for us. More third-world, coal-fired power plants would be good for Enron and (if we believe carbon dioxide emissions are harmful) bad for us. This was Enron's business plan under Kyoto.

Full Disclosure

While we are discussing corporate money and ulterior motives, I want to fully disclose my affiliations. I wrote this book during two consecutive fellowships. The first fellowship was from the Phillips Foundation, a private foundation based on individual contributions that primarily fund the work of young journalists such as myself.

My second fellowship was a Warren T. Brookes Journalism Fellowship from Competitive Enterprise Institute (CEI). Competitive Enterprise Institute is a free-market think tank in Washington, DC, and, like most nonprofits in this town, it is funded in part by corporate donations—a fact that pro-regulation forces bring up most times a CEI spokesperson argues against government intrusion. I have not had contact with CEI donors: They have not reviewed my manuscript or contributed to the book. I have tried to remain ignorant about the identities of CEI's funders. As a result, I don't know if I discuss any of them in this book, but if I do, it is probably not in a flattering light.

It would be fair if you, or a critic, kept in mind that I have taken money from people who have taken money from corporations or corporate foundations, but I promise that not a word in this book, or a word omitted from this book, was influenced by any corporation. You also ought to consider two other points:

1. While my patrons are free-market advocates, the other side in the debate over regulation and big government also receives corporate funds. Many of the corporations that fund regulation advocates stand to profit directly from big government intrusion.

2. My arguments and reporting deserve to be considered on their own merits, even if you have some skepticism about the organizations that have funded my research. This applies across the board: Even after we discover that Enron stood to profit from Kyoto, or General Motors stood to profit from clean air laws, we still ought to listen to their arguments in favor of these regulations, and to the arguments of the groups they fund. While ulterior motives ought to be considered, the merits of the argument ought to have the most weight.

All that said, I primarily have a vested interest in this subject matter as a consumer, a taxpayer, and an independent working man.

How You Suffer

So Enron and General Motors get rich from regulations and big government, why should you care? Because government action doesn't *create* wealth—it *redistributes* it. This means Enron's government-aided profits come from somewhere—you.

That companies would profit from a particular policy does not matter in itself. Profit is not immoral. In fact, when undertaken with ethics and fair play, profit is a noble pursuit with many beneficial side effects for individuals and society. The problem comes when businesses try to make a profit by lobbying to take away your freedom and your money to their nearly sole benefit.

Whenever the government makes a new mandate, tax, or prohibition, we all sacrifice a little bit of our freedom. Sometimes it may be a worthy trade. Funds are needed for police, firefighters, or national defense, for instance. Maybe you think that the police do a lousy job or that our military is too big or too adventurous, but unless these functions are to be abolished altogether, we must accept some tax burden. This means we must give up control over some of our money.

If a state government requires that all high school football players wear pads and helmets on the field, a little freedom is lost because choice is stripped from the game. In this case, though, the freedom lost is a freedom to do something we probably wouldn't want to do anyway: play helmetless football against a team wearing helmets. We don't really complain about this sort of government intrusion on our freedom.

But if the government starts restricting our freedom to benefit somebody else—somebody we don't think deserves it—we ought to be upset because the restrictions have a real cost. Government action makes us poorer and less free. On a strictly economic level, government action almost always reduces the net wealth of society.

Government can't *create* wealth. If the government is giving a bonus to Boeing, the money is coming from somewhere. Usually, it comes from you, without your knowledge or specific consent. In the most direct cases of corporate welfare, the government taxes you and hands your tax dollars to some corporation. Maybe the corporation will use that money to hire people, and so the government and the corporation will argue that this redistribution of wealth "created" jobs. But this assumes that if you had not handed that money over to the taxman you would have wasted it. Comic writer Dave Barry ridiculed this line of reasoning: "When government spends money, it creates jobs; whereas when money is left in the hands of taxpayers, God only knows what they do with it. Bake it into pies, probably. Anything to avoid creating jobs."

Of course, if you paid less in taxes, you might take your family on vacation, buy some new books, send your children to a better college, or go out to dinner. All Americans would do the same. That would create jobs—jobs that would provide products and services that we want.

Businesspeople, small and big, respond to incentives. If people want ice cream, a businessman or businesswoman will sell ice cream—not because he or she is nice, but because he or she knows people will spend money on ice cream. This creates a happy situation—if there's something people want, as long as they are willing and able to spend money on it, sooner or later someone will sell it.

But when government takes your money and spends it for you, you suddenly lose that power. Suppliers begin responding to what government wants instead of to what you, the consumer, want. When the government takes steps to enrich some big business with your money, you lose twice—you are poorer thanks to taxes, and your voice matters less in the marketplace.

Regulations are similar. Business obeys the almighty dollar, which, in turn, means that it obeys the consumer. A businessperson dedicates time and money to answering consumer demands. But when government starts regulating, business has two masters—the people and the bureaucrats. Also, regulation tends to drive up prices. Regulation bears three costs: prices go up, your choice is restricted, and you lose your voice.

Finally, regulations and taxes might keep you out of business entirely or drive you out of business if you are an entrepreneur.

Despite all these burdens, some regulations are worth the costs. We pay more in airfare because the government requires that pilots be licensed, but if that significantly reduces crashes, we're willing to make that sacrifice. The economic costs of making the marketplace less efficient are often worthy sacrifices for noneconomic gains.

But many regulations and wealth transfers are just ripoffs.

Don't Hate the Player, Hate the Game

Who is the real bad guy?

Wal-Mart, for example, takes millions and millions of dollars in favors from the government. The retail giant, like many other big stores, often receives special exemptions from paying the taxes that you or other businesses have to pay. Frequently, governments will pave Wal-Mart's driveways, give them free land, and take care of housing and training the company's employees. All of these government favors make you poorer and Wal-Mart richer.

But should we really blame Wal-Mart?

If you were about to set up a corner store, and the mayor, eager to develop Main Street came up to you and said, "Joe (or Joanna) Smith, the city owns the lot at the corner of 11th and Main, would you like it for free?" Would you say, "No, your honor, I'll pay full market price for that lot so that the good people of this town get their money's worth"? Maybe you would. Maybe you wouldn't be able to sleep at night if the town raised taxes to pay for benefits that you got.

But when John Bull launches his corner store on 10th and Main, and he *accepts* the mayor's offer, you're in trouble. Operating on lower overhead, Bull can probably undercut your prices. Suddenly, your altruism starts looking like bad business.

If you're a noble chap or lass, you might say, "I'd rather lose money the honest way than make money by taking it from the people." But your wife or husband and your children, consigned now to eating rice and lentils every night, might not agree. And what about your investors? What about your brother-in-law who invested half of his savings in your store? Do you console him by saying, "Buddy, your investment may not return any money to you, but I took a moral stand, which has value beyond riches"? I doubt this would make your brother-in-law feel better about losing his money.

Wal-Mart owes as much to its shareholders as the corner-store owner owes to his brother-in-law/investor. If politicians are so eager to lure in Wal-Mart that they offer them every favor they can think of, should Wal-Mart be blamed for not turning it down? It is a tricky question, and one this book does not try to answer. You have to ask yourself what you would do in the same situation. Free money is tough for even the most stalwart ethicist to decline.

Business faces another conundrum in the unholy alliance with government: Politics is not their game. Businesspeople know business. They don't necessarily know politics. Accordingly, many of them deal with politicians and bureaucrats a little uneasily. If a policy question arises, and a businessperson has to choose between battling politicians or working with them, he or she will often work with them. When playing politics, a businessperson is playing on foreign turf.

But staying out of politics is not an option—as some companies have learned the hard way. In the late 1990s, the federal government took on Microsoft, with Congress calling hearings on its business practices and prosecutors hunting down antitrust violations. In March of 1998, one congressional staffer exclaimed the software company had it coming: "The industry had an attitude that government should do what it needs to do but leave us alone. . . . Their hands-off approach to Washington will come back to haunt them."[16] It was a common criticism of Microsoft by lawmakers and bureaucrats: The company leaders were *so* arrogant that they only cared about making software and didn't even try to play politics. Imagine that.

But Bill Gates learned his lesson. After having to sit through a scolding of a Senate Judiciary Committee hearing, Gates wrote, "It's been a year since I was in D.C. I think I'm going to be making this trip a lot more frequently from now on." America Online CEO Stephen Case read the landscape clearly and said, "it's increasingly clear the industry's future is less about technology and more about policy."[17]

And so business has no choice but to play the political game, which includes hiring the best lobbyists. Case's comment reveals another cost to the regular guy and gal that this big business-big government marriage provides: Companies choose investing in good lobbyists over creating better products. Where a better product helps both the company and you, the consumer who uses it, a better lobbyist helps only the company and the lawmaker who then gets the lobbyist's love and gratitude. But lobbyists don't give us better products, new technology, life-saving drugs, or advanced medical devices. Lobbyists don't make iPods, create more efficient appliances, or get your flight to Orlando on time.

This whole arrangement creates a vicious circle. When more lobbyists come to town, they ask for more favors. This gets government involved in new areas. As government's power and reach grows, businesses need to care even more about Washington, and so on.

It also creates what Catholics would call an "occasion of sin." Why do companies spend billions on lobbyists and give millions to candidates?

Businesses are willing to spend billions on politics because there is so much at stake. A regulation that hurts a competitor is invaluable. A taxpayer-funded loan can make or break a huge deal. One clause of one sentence in a regulation can be the difference between huge profits and huge losses. The most effective campaign finance reform or the most effective lobbying reform would be to make the seats of power less lucrative, and in turn to make access to politicians less valuable.

If, at times, this book sounds like an attack on big business, it is not intended to be. It is an attack on certain *practices* of big business. In the parlance of contemporary hip-hop, "don't hate the player, hate the game." Most of the stories in this book depict business cleverly playing by the crooked rules of politics and end with you being ripped off. The blame lies with those who wrote the rules.

The Lesson

Reducing the power of the government over business would alleviate some corruption and level the playing field. In a smaller government environment, Joe and Joanna Smith wouldn't be ripped off quite so much. Businesses will always do whatever they can to make money. If they have government available as a tool, they will use it. Government and business working together, as this book shows you, make a very dangerous coupling—almost like a drug dealer and an addict.

This book shows you the nature of this addiction and how it harms regular people the most. Many will read these stories and feel frustrated, wondering how they can possibly fight a system where the players are so entrenched, wealthy, and resource rich. But as Alcoholics Anonymous says: The first step to recovery is to admit that you have a problem. This book uncovers the problem.

PART I

FRIENDS IN
HIGH PLACES

Adlai Stevenson ran against Dwight Eisenhower in 1956 promising to "take the government away from General Motors and give it back to Joe Smith." Such is often the theme of insurgent political campaigns in America: The opposing candidate is the stooge for big business, while *our* guy, in the words of Al Gore in 2000, is the gladiator for "the people, not the powerful."

Maybe "General Motors" and "the powerful" just have a winning streak going, because they keep getting what they want from Washington. More likely, though, both candidates in any big race are friendly with big business. Regardless of who the president is or which party is in control, big business has always had friends in high places. Presidents from George Washington to George W. Bush (yes, even Teddy Roosevelt and Franklin D. Roosevelt) have allied with big business.

Democrats make their living attacking Republicans as the party of big business. Republicans have been campaigning since at least 1994 as the champions of small business. The facts suggest otherwise. Exit polls, campaign finance data, election results, and a couple of telling anecdotes in the next chapters show that *both* parties are equally the party of big business, and both parties eventually expand the power and size of the government.

History books tell us that Teddy Roosevelt was the scourge of big business, and his Bull Moose wing of the GOP overthrew the robber barons who had reigned during the Gilded Age. A closer look at the Progressive Era, however, unearths continued big business influence that resulted in vast expansions of federal power. Woodrow Wilson, Herbert Hoover, and Franklin D. Roosevelt followed the same pattern: increase government and help big business.

The next two chapters demonstrate just how big business resembles a cockroach that can survive a nuclear bomb. In times of peace and war, in times of plenty and poverty, in times of Republican control and Democratic control, big business gets its way—and its way is not laissez-faire.

We are taught to believe the New Deal reined in big business and that the Democratic Party's policies cause corporate America to tremble. This myth helps big business and big government get their way even more. These chapters debunk this myth and set the groundwork for demonstrating just what big business is doing in Washington and just what big government is doing to our economy.

2

The Parties of Big Business

Corporate America Loves Republicans and Democrats—Republicans and Democrats Love Big Business

The New York City sky was perfectly blue, and the Great Lawn splendidly green on an August Sunday morning in Central Park. The humidity would not rear its head for a few hours, and the 80-degree air felt perfect. It was an ideal day for a game of lawn croquet.

Decked in varied attire (men in white tie or seersucker, and women in ball gowns and tiaras or tennis whites and pearl necklaces), the Billionaires for Bush enjoyed some croquet and badminton while sipping champagne. The group, one could imagine, gathered some attention, especially when passersby noticed their signs, which read, "Taxes are not for everyone" and "Widen the income gap."

The revelers were not truly billionaires. Nor, as you might have guessed, were they for Bush. They were drama students and protestors in New York during the Republican National Convention to make a point. Bush's policies, they implied through sarcasm and entertainment, benefited the rich at the expense of everyone else.

On the score of pure theater, the Billionaires for Bush do a great job. Reporters love to write about them, and local residents are far more receptive to these quieter, more congenial protestors than to the typical angry antiwar marcher finding new vulgar wordplays on the president's name. But when it comes to accurately assessing the political situation, the Billionaires are not much better than some angry Oberlin student claiming that Bush plotted 9/11—it's hyperbole with little basis in truth.

The idea that the very wealthy are Republican (and the corresponding implication that everyone else who is not wealthy is a Democrat) goes unchallenged in the media. Everyone knows that. Well, maybe everybody but Herb and Marion Sandler.

The Sandlers are very rich. They have run their thrift bank (a lending institution that takes in savings deposits and lends out mortgages), Golden West Financial, so well that *Forbes* magazine called it "perhaps [the United States'] best financial company." Golden West, by early 2004, had $80 billion in assets.[1] The Sandlers' combined net worth is over $2 billion.

But they are not greedy. Herb told *Forbes,* "If our dreams come true, we'll give every last dollar away." In 2004, the Sandlers worked toward that end by giving $13 million to the campaign to defeat George W. Bush and other Republicans. The Sandlers gave $8.5 million to Citizens for a Strong Senate, a 527 group (as they are known for the section in the tax code that covers them) that spent about $20 million trying to get Democrats elected to the upper chamber. They also gave $2.5 million to MoveOn.org, perhaps the most famous of the 527s.[2]

Marion gave $19,000 to Democratic candidates for Senate in the 2004 cycle, and $25,000 to the Democratic Senate Campaign Committee. She gave $11,000 to Democratic House contenders and $35,000 to the Democratic Congressional Campaign Committee.

In addition to six-figure gifts to three other anti-Bush groups, Herb and Marion Sandler sent a $500 check to Billionaires for Bush.

The $500 check is small, but the irony is great: Two financial tycoons worth billions spend their riches to condemn George W. Bush as the candidate of the rich.

The cliche that the GOP is the party of the rich turns out to be more illusion than reality. The vast majority of political cash from billionaires goes to Democrats. Voters who self-identify as upper class voted for Gore over Bush. The wealthiest counties, by two different measures, both supported Kerry. The five wealthiest states all gave their electoral college votes to Kerry. Other measures, however, suggest that the rich *do,* in fact, favor Republicans. Asserting one party is the party of the rich requires ignoring half of the data.

On the related but slightly different question of big business's political leanings, the question is similarly ambiguous. The political action committees (PACs) run by businesses give more to Republicans than to Democrats. However, the most prodigious PAC last election split its money evenly, and the most partisan PACs are all on the Democratic side. Both the data as a whole and some telling anecdotes smash the myth that big business loves the Right. Chuck Schumer and Hillary Clinton, liberal Democrats, garner more money from Wall Street and realtors than do any other lawmakers. Real estate and lawyers, the top two industries in terms of donations to politicians, give more to Democrats than to Republicans.

Billionaires for Kerry

The Sandlers, who spent millions to defeat Bush, are not a rare breed.

Hedge-fund king George Soros, worth $7.2 billion, famously spent $23.5 million on his anti-Bush crusade in 2004. Peter Lewis, president of Progressive insurance company (worth $1.9 billion), spent just less than $23 million against Bush in 2004. Steve Bing inherited $600 million from his father's business building luxury apartments and is now a movie producer. Bing reportedly once checked into the Hotel Bel-Air in Los Angeles and stayed for nine years.[3] He spent $13.9 million against Bush in 2004.

Those men, all billionaires or multimillionaires thanks to corporate success, were the top four contributors to 527s in the 2004 campaign. Number five, realtor Bob Perry, spent over $8 million in *favor* of Bush. Number six, developer and owner of the San Diego Chargers, Alex Spanos, spent $5 million to help the president.

The primary effect of the McCain-Feingold campaign finance laws was to drive political donors away from the parties (who could no longer accept "soft money") and toward these 527 groups. At well over a half-billion dollars, the 527s raised and spent more than either the Kerry or the Bush campaign. For rich people looking to influence the 2004 elections, 527s were the place to be. (As a point of comparison, the most generous donor directly to campaigns and parties in 2004 gave less than a half-million dollars—one fortieth of Soros's largesse.)

The top four donors to 527s in 2004—and the only donors to spend in the eight figures on that election—all gave exclusively to pro-Democrat groups. Of the top 25 individual donors—all billionaires or multimillionaires—15 of them gave to pro-Democrat groups, and 10 gave to Republican-supporting groups. From this elite group of super-rich donors, the Democratic side got $108.4 million, compared to the Republican side's $40 million. Soros and Lewis together spent more to defeat Bush than the 10 most prolific Republican fat cats *combined* spent to support him.

This dynamic was not particular to 2004 and the anti-Bush fever. In 2002 (before McCain-Feingold and the explosion of the 527s), Haim Saban, entertainment mogul and CEO of Saban Capital Group (net worth $2.8 billion), topped the donor list with $9.4 million—every dime to Democrats. Second place was another media mogul Fred Eychaner, president of Newsweb Corporation. Eychaner also gave exclusively to Democrats. Steve Bing was third in 2002. In fact, the top nine donors all gave exclusively to Democrats. Number 10, Roland Arnall of Ameriquest Capital, gave 65 percent to Republicans and 35 percent to Democrats.

The top 25 donors in 2002 gave $4.5 million to Republicans, but $51.5 million to Democrats. Democrats had 20 donors who gave more than $1 million: Republicans had four.

In 2000, the story was much the same. Daniel Abraham, head of Slim-Fast, headed the list with $1.6 million. Right behind him was Bernard Schwartz of Loral, with $1.4 million. They both gave exclusively to Democrats. The top five all gave only to Democrats, with number six, Carl Lindner, giving just over half of his $1.2 million in gifts to Democrats. In 2000, you had to go down to number 13 to find a loyal Republican donor. While the Democrats had five people who gave in the seven figures, not a single donor gave a million dollars to the Republican Party in 2000.

Measured by the standard of the biggest individual spenders in politics, Democrats are undeniably the party of the rich, although the metric is a bit incomplete because it appears that rich Democrats are more likely to spend their money on politics than are rich Republicans. Other ways of measuring the political leanings of the rich turn up mixed results.

The richest Americans (as opposed to those who spend the most on politics) lean toward the Republican Party, though not nearly to the degree that the top donors lean toward the Democrats. The political spending of the top corporate PACs certainly favors Republicans, but Democrats get more contributions from individuals in top American companies such as Goldman Sachs and Time Warner.

The general theme that emerges from the different analyses is that in general, richer people and bigger businesses favor Republicans, but the businesses and executives who are most interested in politics side with Democrats—a point that goes to the heart of this book and the big ripoff, as we shall see.

You would not know that the results were so mixed, however, by listening to the public discussion of big business and big money in politics. In 2004, AFL-CIO President John Sweeney sounded the Democrats' typical class-warfare refrain, telling his union rank and file, "It's a choice between a president who looks out for working families [Kerry] or a president who looks out only for his corporate cronies [Bush]."[4] In the fall of 2005, Democratic National Chairman Howard Dean made the same jab at Senate Majority Leader Bill Frist. "Frist spends most of his time looking out for his own financial interests and for Republican big business cronies," Dean said.[5] Former Clinton aide and *Crossfire* cohost Paul Begala stayed on message that the GOP was the party of the rich. In a typical counter-factual applause line, Begala said, "If I liked rich people, I would become a Republican."[6] Begala is, in fact, a rich person himself, owning a five-bedroom, 4.5-bathroom house on a cul-de-sac in tony McLean, Virginia, assessed at $1.3 million.[7]

Just weeks earlier, Begala had gone on another *Crossfire* tirade, hammering home the similar theme, "George W. Bush is of the rich, by the rich, and for the rich. He has governed strictly for the rich. [APPLAUSE]. It has been a kleptocracy for the rich under George W. Bush." Begala continued, "They're stealing everything that is not nailed down and giving it to the rich."[8]

Such is the theme of many Democratic attacks, but the claim does not hold up to the facts.

The Richest of the Rich

Bill Gates, president and founder of Microsoft, sits atop the *Forbes* 400 list of the richest Americans, with a net worth in 2005 of $51 billion at the tender age of 49.[9] Politically, he is a fence sitter. Since the 2000 election, Gates has given more than $46,000 to Republicans and $17,000 to Democrats. Most of his GOP cash is to state Republican parties. When it comes to candidates for federal office, Gates favors Democrats $17,200 to $12,200. But that includes gifts such as $1,000 to Vermont Democratic Senator Pat Leahy, who never faced a serious opponent in 2004, or $2,000 to Arizona Republican John McCain, who similarly ran without a real challenge. Counting only gifts to candidates in competitive races, Gates favored Democrats two to one.

Warren Buffett is the second richest American, and he does not share Gates' political ambivalence. While he has given $4,600 to two Republican congressmen since 2000, he has given over $50,000 to Democrats in that same time. In 2004, Buffett also gave his time and his prestige, joining the Kerry campaign as an economic advisor.

Trailing Buffett's $40 billion is Paul Allen, former Microsoft colleague of Gates, who is worth $22.5 billion. Since 2002, when Republicans took control of all arms of government, Allen has slightly favored the GOP, giving $15,000 to Republicans and $12,000 to Democrats. Before that, though, he was a steadfast Democrat, giving over $150,000 to Democrats and nothing to Republicans in the run-up to the 2000 election.

Number four on the richest list is a Republican, Michael Dell, who has given more than $400,000 to Republicans this decade, and only about $12,000 to Democrats. Number five, Larry Ellison, also is a Republican donor. Numbers 6 through 10 are all Waltons, of Wal-Mart fame and fortune, and they lean toward Republicans, though not exclusively. The Waltons have given over $25,000 to Arkansas's Democratic Senator Blanche Lincoln since her first race in 1998, slightly more than they donated to Republican Senator Tim Hutchinson of Arkansas during his stint in the Senate.

Many of the richest Americans are Republican but the picture is mixed and varied: The most politically active billionaires are uniformly Democrats, but what about those who are only barely politically active? How do rich people *vote*?

Ballots are anonymous, and so it is impossible to look at a Bush vote or a Kerry vote and tell if a rich man or a poor man cast it. But by looking at rich towns, counties, and states, and comparing those areas' election results, we can detect a pattern—and it is not the one Paul Begala and Howard Dean would have us believe.

Jackson Hole is the Aspen of Wyoming—the western playground of the rich. Harrison Ford owns an 800-acre ranch near Jackson Hole, Wyoming, complete with two helicopters and a private jet. In fact, he is the local search and rescue pilot, and has twice saved hikers in danger. Sandra Bullock also hangs her hat in Jackson Hole. Among the less famous (but no less wealthy) denizens of Jackson are World Bank president James D. Wolfensohn, former Columbia Pictures president and CEO Alan Hirschfield, Vice President Dick Cheney, Christy Walton (the wealthiest of the Wal-Mart family) and

West Virginia Senator John D. Rockefeller IV. In fact, Standard Oil heir and the senator's grandfather John D. Rockefeller Jr. was one of the earliest settlers of this year-round playground for the ultra-wealthy.[10]

Measured according to the Internal Revenue Service's data on average adjusted household gross income, Teton is the nation's wealthiest county.[11] It was also the only county in Dick Cheney's home state to vote for John Kerry.[12]

Other top rich counties, according to the IRS, were also tinted blue on the election map. Kerry stronghold Fairfield County, Connecticut, is the runner-up to Teton County by the IRS's count, and liberal utopia Marin County, California, which voted three to one for Kerry, is in third place. Of the top 10 counties by this measure (average adjusted household gross income), six voted for Kerry.

The Census Bureau uses a different standard to measure the richest counties (median household income, for counties with populations of at least 250,000), but comes up with similar results. Fairfax County, Virginia, home to the 4.5 bathrooms of Paul Begala (who claims not to like rich people), is the wealthiest county in America according to the Census Bureau's measure. The electorate in Fairfax County voted 54 percent for Kerry, while the rest of Virginia voted about 45 percent for him. That means Kerry fared 20 percent better in wealthy Fairfax than in the rest of the state.

Of the states (including the District of Columbia) with the highest per capita income, according to the Bureau of Economic Analysis, Kerry won all of the top 7, and 8 of the top 10. However, examining voting results and income by municipality can be misleading. Washington, DC, has many rich people, as the immaculate townhouses in Georgetown and palaces on the cliffs above the Potomac River suggest, but it also has poverty. To claim Washington, DC, is a "rich" city is to ignore most of the population. For example, Bush did best in Ward Three, the district's wealthiest ward, pulling in 19 percent compared to his 9 percent citywide.

Exit polls, which focus on individual voters, show a similarly complex story. CNN's exit polls for the past three election cycles have asked voters their income, and shown how voters earning over $100,000 have voted.[13] In 2004, Bush won 58 percent of this demographic, compared to 52 percent of the whole country. In 2000, he won 54 percent of six-figure earners (a sample that comprised 15 percent of the electorate) compared to 48 percent of the total popular vote. But that year, CNN also asked voters to self-identify by class. Four percent called themselves "upper class." Of that group, Gore won big, 56 percent to 39 percent. This would imply that "rich folk" vote Republican, but "really rich folk" vote Democratic.

Exit polls have their flaws, however. Voters may not be entirely honest about their vote or their income. The 2004 elections highlighted the problems with such surveys as early exit polls led most Americans to believe that John Kerry would be president.

Democrat John Kerry, it turns out, is the wealthiest lawmaker in Washington, worth at least $160 million before his presidential bid, thanks to his wife's catsup fortune. The second and third richest senators were Democrats, too, Herb Kohl of Wisconsin (he owns a furniture store chain and the Milwaukee Bucks basketball team) and Jackson Hole regular Jay Rockefeller of West Virginia, whose name says it all. While the richest senators are Democrats, the Senate millionaires' club (about 40 strong) is nearly evenly split between the parties.[14]

So, rich people break down evenly along party lines, but what about big business?

Dollars for Donkeys

With thousands waiting for him on the National Mall days before his inauguration, President-Elect Bill Clinton triumphantly arrived at the Lincoln Memorial—by bus. The mode of arrival was meant to send a populist message. The East Coast WASPs of the George H. W. Bush administration were leaving, and Bubba from Arkansas was in charge now.

"Our bus," Clinton explained about the vehicle he used both on the campaign and on his big trip to Washington, "was a way of saying to the people of America, 'We want you to be in control, we don't want to be out of touch with you, we don't want to be a long way from you. We want you to believe that this is your government just as much as it's your country.' "[15]

The mood of the inaugural events seemed to carry the same regular-person aura. "Republicans had all those big cars and fancy dresses," Democratic Congresswoman Patsy Schroeder said at one ball, "and they walked around looking hoity-toity."[16]

But behind the populist facade was money—lots of it. At about $25 million, Bill Clinton's first inauguration was hardly a middle-class affair. The four-day affair that began with a humble bus ride ended with black-tie Hollywood-studded galas throughout the district. One columnist (a perhaps-envious conservative) wrote of the affair, "Americans, I dare say, gave up their cherished right to mock the pomp and pretensions of British royalty, thanks to the excesses of this week's coronation—oops—inauguration events."[17]

The *Washington Post* Style Section tried to cover the more exclusive parties of the weekend—the ones you needed $1,500 and an invitation to attend. One article, under the headline "Dinners Fit For a Republican: What's a Few Furs Among Friends?" began with the question: "If somebody throws a party and rich people come, famous people—fur-coated people!— and the TV cameras can't get footage of them going in, going out or eating . . . did the furs exist? And what about the edible flowers in the salad?"

The writer commented on the efforts by Clinton staff to keep the press away. "Last night the new Washington royalty threw four inaugural dinners. They were big. They were official. They were pricey ($1,500 a ticket). And if the press handlers had their way, little more would be known. Reporters? Just cordon them off in lobbies or across the street!"

"Which leaves us with the other questions of the night: Who could be inside? Mafia dons? Illegal aliens? Special interests?"[18]

To answer that question, the Style Section reporters ought to have taken the advice of their colleague Bob Woodward, and "followed the money." One guest at the more elite inaugural events was Dwayne Andreas, chairman of Archer Daniels Midland, the largest agribusiness in the country. "I'm here because I was invited," he told a reporter. Andreas was invited, one might surmise after reviewing the inaugural committee's financial records, because he donated $100,000 to the inauguration. He was not alone.[19] The populist face of the event made it a fitting place for a Bud. Anheuser-Busch, the largest brewer in the world, also underwrote the inaugural festivities to a tune of $100,000. Given Clinton's famous lack of punctuality, Federal Express's (motto: "The World on Time") $100,000 likely drew some chuckles. The shift from "stodgy" to "chic" made sense given the $100,000 each from Guess, Inc., and The Limited. And Indonesian businessman James Riady with ties to China's People's Liberation Army—well, nobody ever quite figured out what he was trying to accomplish with *his* $100,000. Other big givers included Enron, Apple, AT&T, Duracell, Pfizer, and Salomon Brothers.

The new president—the man of the people—was just as tight with corporate America as were the Connecticut WASP Republicans before him. Soon, baffled journalists were writing about the coziness between Clinton and the business community. "Clinton's Unlikely Boosters" ran one typical magazine headline in March. "For many in Washington," the article about Clinton's proposed tax increase began, "the most surprising reaction to President Clinton's economic plan was the U.S. Chamber of Commerce's hearty applause."[20] A few weeks later, another headline declared, "GOP Right, Chamber in Bitter Feud; Clinton Victories Part Old Allies."[21]

The writers' only error in noting the Clinton-business alliance was implying there was something odd about it. Especially off base was the implication that the more conservative Republicans were particularly close to the business community. Analyzing hard data shows that both parties are the parties of big business and that politicians on the far right are just as much pariahs to business as the radicals on the far left.

Leader of the PAC

Which is the party of big business? As with the political leanings of rich individuals, discerning big business's political stance is a tricky matter. Depending on which set of data you examine, you come up with a different answer to the question.

Defining *big business* in this case is not simple, but one place to begin may be the U.S. Chamber of Commerce. The Chamber, like most corporations, has a PAC. Their PAC collects donations from its members and its officers and then contributes to political campaigns. Most of the Chamber's PAC money, fitting with the conventional wisdom, goes to Republicans.

In fact, in 1998, Congressman Charlie Stenholm of Texas was the only Democrat to receive cash from the Chamber. The $10,000 the Chamber's PAC gave to Republican candidates dwarfed the $548 to Stenholm. In 2000, Democrats' share of Chamber cash rose from 5 percent to 8 percent. In 2002, it crawled upward again to 10 percent. Democrats more than doubled their portion of the Chamber's pot in 2004 by hauling in $40,000 of the PAC's $170,000 (about 24 percent). If the first 11 months of 2005 are any indication, this ratio is holding steady.

The leadership of the Chamber leans strongly toward Republicans, but during the Clinton administration, and especially at the beginning, when Democrats also controlled Congress, the Chamber welcomed the Democratic president warmly, supporting Clinton's tax increase. Looking at the PACs of individual corporations and trade associations, the picture is similar.

The PAC that spent the most on the 2004 election was the National Association of Realtors at $3.79 million. The realtors split their donations almost evenly—52 percent to Republicans and 47 percent to Democrats.

PACs tend to favor incumbents heavily, which suggests that business is more interested in aligning with whoever is in power than with political philosophy. The realtors' contributions ratio matched the ratio of Republicans to Democrats in Congress. In contested races, the realtors favored Republicans.

Big labor PACs are far more prodigious givers in general than big business, and labor gives almost exclusively to Democrats. The second largest *business* PAC in 2004 was the National Auto Dealers Association, which spent $2.60 million—three-fourths of it going to the GOP. The National Beer Wholesalers, at $2.32 million, also sided with the GOP by a three-to-one ratio.

But the most partisan of the top business PACs in 2004 was the Association of Trial Lawyers of America, which gave 93 percent of its $2.18 million to Democrats.

In addition to PAC money, big business money comes in the form of donations from executives and employees of corporations. The Center for Responsive Politics (funded by George Soros) compiles campaign contributions on its web site. It breaks down campaign cash by "sector" and "industry." Examining the behavior of different parts of the economy is telling. The Center for Responsive Politics lists 13 sectors including "labor," "ideology/single issue," and "other." That leaves 10 business sectors. George W. Bush pulled in more donations from 8 of those 10 sectors, with Kerry leading among "lawyers and lobbyists" and "communications/electronics."

The Center for Responsive Politics further breaks sectors down into industries, and at that level, Democrats have an advantage. The top industry giving to members of Congress in 2004 was lawyers, who gave $85.7 million, nearly $70 million to Democrats. Real estate was the second highest giving industry, and individual realtors gave most of their money (55 percent) to Democrats (even while the chief PAC in that industry slightly favored Republicans).

In the first two quarters of 2005, lawyers gave nearly twice as much in contribution as the real estate industry, with 64 percent of this amount going to Democrats. The top three industries in the first half of 2005 all gave more money to Hillary Clinton than to any other lawmaker.

What better embodies big business than Wall Street? In the 2004 cycle, the top four senatorial beneficiaries of the "securities and investment" industry (not counting John Kerry, whose presidential run makes him incomparable in fund-raising to other senators) were all Democrats. Fifth place belonged to liberal Republican Arlen Specter of Pennsylvania. Wall Street's favorite senator was Clinton's fellow New Yorker, Chuck Schumer.

Senator Charles E. Schumer may be the prime case to blow apart the myth that "pro-business" means conservative or free market. The senior senator from New York, Schumer is one of the Democrats' best fund-raisers. For 2006, he is the chairman of the Democratic Senate Campaign Committee, which is responsible for helping Democrats get elected to Congress's upper chamber.

In his first term in the Senate, Schumer raised more money from Wall Street ($3.5 million) than did any other lawmaker in either party. Schumer was also the favorite lawmaker of the real estate industry, pulling in $1.8 million. He has received millions more from other industries.

Schumer is also one of the most liberal officials in Washington. The liberal Americans for Democratic Action gave him a 98 percent lifetime rating. The American Conservative Union gave him 6 percent. The National Taxpayers Union has given him an F every year in the Senate. That means the liberals love him, and the conservatives and antitax activists hate him.

Schumer has carried his success in raising funds over to his new job of getting Democrats elected to the Senate. The Democratic Senatorial Campaign Committee (DSCC) raised more than its Republican counterpart in 2005. Going into 2006, the DSCC had $25 million in its coffers, more than twice the amount of its counterpart the National Republican Senatorial Committee (NRSC). In 2005, Schumer's committee raised $44 million compared to the NRSC's $35.5 million.[22]

Not counting presidential candidates, Schumer ranked in the top three lawmakers for gifts from architects, the liquor industry, commercial banks, the dairy industry, software, subcontractors, and textiles. Who was the tobacco industry's favorite senator? It was not conservative Kentucky Republican Jim Bunning who faced a tough reelection in 2004. It was Chuck Schumer.

Meshing Schumer's liberalism with his friendship with big business is difficult to do without closer examination of big business's agenda. As we see repeatedly throughout this book, big business likes big government and the politicians who make government so big, irrespective of their party.

A Socialist and a Libertarian Walk into a Fund-Raiser . . .

It was three o'clock in the morning on Good Friday, and the House of Representatives was full. Every member was seated, and silent. Curious spectators packed the galleries, some decked in evening gowns and some in white tie, all craning their heads, listening for a word from the woman's mouth. But she sat silent. The clerk, seeing she was present, called out more loudly, "Miss Rankin!" With no response, the clerk continued with the roll. Congressman "Uncle Joe" Cannon approached the lady from Montana, Congresswoman Jeanette Rankin. "Little woman," he said, "you cannot afford not to vote."

A second time, the clerk called the roll, listing the names of those who had not yet voted. Again, he called on Miss Rankin. Again, she sat silent. As every eye focused on her, she stood, unsteady, swaying from side to side. The only woman in the House, and the first ever elected to that chamber, Rankin did not say "Aye" or "Nay" as every other member had. Instead, breaking with custom and House rules, she delivered her maiden speech. "I want to stand by my country," she said, as tears came to her eyes, "but I cannot vote for war." She began sobbing. Now the clerk came up to her and asked, "Do you intend to vote 'No'?" She nodded her head to affirm, and walked off.[23]

This tearful pacifist vote confirmed what many believed about women in 1917—that they were more emotional than rational, even in positions of public trust. Rankin's first vote, against entering World War I, would not be her last pacifist vote. On December 8, 1941, Rankin would cast the lone vote against entering World War II, the day after Japan bombed Pearl Harbor.

Both times, Rankin would pay for her vote with her job. In 1918, she lost her party's primary, and in 1942, Rankin declined to seek reelection, and her brother Wellington lost his Senate bid.

In 2002, some thought Barbara Lee might be in a similar plight. On September 14, 2001, on a rainy day in the nation's capital, Congresswoman Lee of California cast the lone vote against House Joint Resolution 64, which authorized military force, "against those responsible for the recent attacks launched against the United States."[24]

On the same day, a member on the other side of the aisle took his own lonely stand. Representative Ron Paul of Texas proposed his response to 9/11: The Antiterrorism Act of 2001, H.R. 2896, appropriated no funds, created no new agencies, and granted the government no new powers. In fact, it did the opposite. Paul's bill would declare, "that no Federal agency shall prohibit a pilot, copilot, or navigator of an aircraft, or any law enforcement personnel specifically detailed for the protection of such aircraft, from carrying a firearm." Paul intended to fight terrorism by getting the federal government out of the way of cops and private citizens. His bill never even received a hearing in subcommittee.

Also on that day, Lee joined a figurative club whose chairman would be Ron Paul: the House lone dissenter caucus. Between 1997 and 2004, the House of Representatives held 4,657 roll call votes. In 172 of those votes, including Lee's antiwar vote, only one member voted no. Ron Paul was that one member 107 of the 172 times.[25]

Paul was on the losing end of votes on the Telemarketing Fraud Protection Act (411 to 1), the Mammography Quality Standards Reauthorization bill (401 to 1), the Unsolicited Commercial Electronic Mail Act (427 to 1), the Shark Finning Prohibition Act (390 to 1), an amendment to subject "low-speed electric bicycles" to the Consumer Product Safety Act (401 to 1), and the Americans Spirit Fraud Prevention Act (422 to 1). In other words, Paul doesn't want Congress taking new measures to limit fraud, regulate bikes, limit spam, regulate mammograms, or stop shark finning.

Paul votes against nearly every spending bill brought to the House floor, on the grounds that they all spend too much or fund agencies that should not exist.

For her part, Lee is extraordinary not only as a firm opponent of war but also as an advocate of some of the most far-reaching social welfare legislation to ever collect dust in the file cabinets of the House clerk. Most notable is her "A Living Wage, Jobs For All Act of 2005." This bill would have Washington guarantee every single American a "decent job," "freedom from monopolies," "decent housing," job training, and health care. In short, Lee would have the federal government provide everyone in America with everything they need.[26]

On November 5, 2002, Barbara Lee won reelection with 82 percent of the vote. Some ascribe her success to the far-left leanings of her Oakland district, but that would be unfair to the dozens of business PACs that spent nearly $60,000 to help get her reelected. Ron Paul won easily, too, with 68 percent of the vote. While the voters were nearly as favorable to Paul as to Lee, the businesses were not: Paul gathered less than $15,000 in PAC money.

The case study of Barbara Lee and Ron Paul is illustrative and provides good if anecdotal evidence that big business supports politicians who support more intrusive government. The true situation refutes the claims of the Billionaires for Bush and others who would have us believe that conservatives are for big business and liberals are defenders of the little person.

The Billionaires for Bush satire web site contains this paragraph:

For much of the 20th century, democratic notions like "opportunity for all" and "public services" dominated American public policy, seriously threatening the privileges of wealth all Billionaires depend on. Government taxed the rich, regulated corporations, protected the environment and the average person felt increasingly entitled to share in America's prosperity. Ordinary people were educated for free and over 50 media companies helped give them a balanced picture of what the government and corporations were up to. They were dark days.[27]

The advisors and staff for the Billionaires use pseudonyms to make their point. "Phil T. Rich," "Hal E. Burton," and "Robin D. Poor" are three. The public relations director for Billionaires for Bush goes by "Lucinda Regulations."

It is in this last name that we begin to see one of the assumptions underlying the Billionaires for Bush message—regulations curb big business and the ultra-rich while protecting small businesses and the poor. This claim is simply false, and there is an abundance of evidence disproving it throughout this book. The Paul versus Lee analysis can serve as Exhibit A that billionaires and big business have little desire to "Lucinda Regulations."

Both Paul and Lee are on the far end of their respective party's ideological spectrum. Lee is practically socialist in her policies. She believes that the government should control the economy and radically redistribute wealth to provide basic needs for all. Paul is fairly called a libertarian. He believes that federal government should, in almost every case, let businesses and individuals do as they please. He favors deregulation and low taxes.

Both members sit on the Financial Services Committee, a coveted panel whose members garner the attention of bankers, accountants, and insurers, which makes comparing them even more apt. Paul is a doctor, Lee a nurse. In 2004, Paul ran unopposed, and so raised very little money. This makes 2002 the best point of comparison between the two.

If the assumptions of Billionaires for Bush are correct, Paul, who opposes regulation, favors tax cuts, and opposes welfare programs should be beloved by business, while Lee should be loathed. The numbers point in the opposite direction.

Both members, naturally, receive PAC money from the finance, insurance, and real estate sectors, as defined by OpenSecrets.org. Lee, however, gets a lot more. In 2002, PACs in the financial sector gave her $31,903 while giving Paul a grand total of $2,500. Except for the construction and defense sectors, PACs from every sector gave more to Lee than to Paul. Opensecrets.org reports that Lee got $58,903 from business PACs in 2001 and 2002, compared to the $14,500 Paul received from all business PACs—that's more than a four-to-one difference.

The picture is similar for donations from individuals. In 2002, Lee received more money than Paul from lawyers, the real estate industry, actors and singers, commercial bankers, printers and publishers, and health professionals. Among specific industries with significant donations to him, only construction services and general contractors gave more to Paul than to Lee.

Paul, it should be noted, ended up raising more money than Lee, but most of Paul's money was from retired individuals throughout the country who appreciate his dedication to limited government.

When we compare the archliberal Lee to the libertarian Paul, we see that Lee pulled in more business PAC money by a three-to-one ratio. The firms affected by the committee work of these two—financial companies—favored Lee nearly 15 to 1. Nearly every industry gave more to Lee than to Paul.

Having It Both Ways

Exit polls say that the rich vote Republican, but the very rich vote Democrat. The three richest Americans split their donations between parties but favor Democrats. The rest of the top 10 favor Republicans. All of the biggest individual donors to politicians are Democrats. The three richest senators are Democrats, but the Senate millionaires club is evenly split between the parties.

The U.S. Chamber of Commerce has historically given more money to Republicans, but now it is splitting its cash more evenly. Most PACs favor Republicans, but the top-spending PACs straddle the fence or favor Democrats.

Individuals working in most sectors of the economy give more money to Republicans, but the most generous sectors favor the Democrats. Wall Street's favorite senators are Democrats, including liberal icons Hillary Clinton and Charles Schumer.

Congress's fiercest advocate of deregulation and low taxes has trouble getting big business money, while one of the most socialist representatives has far more success.

The theme that emerges is that the richest and most politically active of the rich tend to be Democrats. The second tier tends to be Republican. Overall, it seems that the rich have good friends in both parties. American history shows that indeed they do.

3

The History of
Big Business

. . . Is the History of Big Government

William Faulkner was new to western Pennsylvania, hence his near-deadly mistake. In the summer of 1792, the army officer (not the twentieth century author with the same name) was unfamiliar with the political and social environment of Washington County. New to the frontier, Faulkner ill-advisedly rented out a part of his building, where he and his family lived, to John Neville, a tax collector.[1]

Aside from the savage Indians who were known to rape and pillage frontier counties, such as Washington, tax collectors were the most hated forms of human life in the region. Neville set up his office in Faulkner's building, and then placed an advertisement in the *Pittsburgh Gazette* calling for anyone in the county with a whiskey still to come and register it with him, at his new address. This way he could properly assess the federal distilled spirits tax.

A few days later, the locals loyally appeared at the address—just not to register their stills. Dressed and painted as Indians, they quickly went to work breaking down the doors to Faulkner's house. They intended to tar and feather Faulkner—perhaps kill him—for his cooperation with the whiskey excise tax. Faulkner, luckily, was away from home that night, but when the agitators later found him on the road, they threatened him at knifepoint. Faulkner promptly evicted Neville.

That same month a more respectable assembly met nearby, and after two days unanimously voted that the whiskey excise tax was "unjust" and "oppressive." They posted their proclamation throughout the county. The Whiskey Rebellion had started. The rebels, fighting to the death to avoid the whiskey tax, were not the giant barons of the whiskey industry. As historian Thomas P. Slaughter notes about excise taxes in England, "Large distillers of alcoholic beverages actually favored an excise on their products because of its prejudice in favor of efficient production. They helped write and revise legislation; during the seventeenth century they were also responsible for collecting the tax."[2]

The story was similar in the United States. Indeed, the rebels who raided Faulkner's house were largely poor farmers who distilled whiskey for their own consumption or limited distribution. The more civilized rebels who passed proclamations were their local frontier political leaders.

Back East in civilized Philadelphia, Secretary of the Treasury Alexander Hamilton advised President George Washington to arrest those men publicly opposing the whiskey excise—both Faulkner's evening visitors and those who publicly and peacefully proclaimed against the excise—and to "exert the full force of the law against the offenders, with every circumstance that can manifest the determination of government to enforce its execution."[3]

Washington arrested the violent rebels, and a couple of years later the president went further and took Hamilton's hard line. In 1794, George Washington deployed U.S. soldiers to western Pennsylvania and put down the Whiskey Rebellion. By imposing and enforcing the whiskey excise tax, Washington struck an early victory for federal government power—and for Alexander Hamilton.

Consolidating power into the federal government and increasing its role in the economy was Hamilton's chief aim as treasury secretary. Hamilton also created a national property tax (which led to another rebellion, this one in New England). He introduced tariffs on imports and founded the system of central banking. In other words, Alexander Hamilton was the first champion of big government in the United States.

How, then, is this the same man renowned as "the creator of American capitalism"?[4] Historian Ron Chernow phrases this description more precisely: "Hamilton didn't create America's market economy so much as foster the cultural and legal setting in which it flourished."[5] Is it possible for a big government politician to be a capitalist politician?

This question is confusing only because of the two different senses in which we use the word *capitalism*. In the first sense, capitalism is a political economic philosophy—during the Cold War, it was understood as the alternative to Communism. In this way, when people say "capitalism," they mostly mean a free market, in which individuals spend, invest, and save their money mostly independent of government intrusion.

But capitalism is also the name for a certain sort of economic arrangement—one featuring institutions to facilitate the rapid and smooth flow of capital around the economy. The opposite of this would be an economy with no stock market, limited banking, and little in the way of what is now called investment.

The confusion about capitalism arises, in part, because the United States has both the freest market and the most vibrant financial system in the world. But the two ideas are separable.

A *noncapitalist* economy without a stock exchange could exist in a perfectly free market. A robust financial system could exist as a segment of a highly regulated and controlled economy. The latter is precisely Hamiltonian *capitalism*. Hamilton aimed to create a class of businessmen and investors who were loyal to and dependent on the federal government—an elite guardian class for the new Constitution. This did not involve low taxes and deregulation. On the contrary, it required an activist federal government.

Historian Charles A. Beard contends that the fathers of the Constitution, of which Hamilton was foremost, were motivated primarily by economic considerations. Beard wrote, "the men who favored the Constitution were affiliated with certain types of property and economic interests, and that the men who opposed it were affiliated with other types."[6]

Hamilton's first political crisis, years before the Whiskey Rebellion, was the problem of national debt and the bonds that had financed the Revolution. Rebels had bought millions of dollars in bonds to support the Revolution, but, fearing the new government would never make good on the loans, most original owners had sold the bonds to speculators, often at a deep discount. Hamilton, as treasury secretary had to advise Congress: Should the government repay the patriots who had financed the Revolution or the clever speculators who had gone bargain hunting amid the early crises of the nation and now held the bonds? Hamilton's allegiances here became crucial.

Hamilton, Beard makes clear, aligned himself with the financiers, the bankers, and the big businessman rather than the workers, the farmers, or the small shop owners. Hamilton, writes Beard, "knew that the Constitution was designed to accomplish certain definite objects, affecting in its operation certain definite groups of property rights in society. . . . [H]e achieved the task of completing their consolidation and attaching them to the federal government."[7]

First were the men who either owned government debt or private debt. Beard writes:

> He saw, in the first place, that the most easily consolidated and timorous group was composed of the creditors, the financiers, bankers, and money lenders. He perceived that they were concentrated in the towns and thus were easily drawn together. He saw that by identifying their interests with those of the new government, the latter would be secure; they would not desert the ship in which they were all afloat. . . . It is charged against him that he did not buy up government paper in behalf of the public at the most favorable terms; but to have done so would have diminished the profits of the very financiers whose good will was necessary to the continuance of the government.[8]

Second were the men in the business of making and selling goods:

> The second group of interests which Hamilton saw ready for organization were the merchants and manufacturers who wished protective tariffs. . . . Whether this was for the good of the whole people need not be argued here. Hamilton's relations were with the immediate beneficiaries. They were the men who were to throw their weight on the side of the new government.[9]

Finally were the land speculators:

> The third interest which Hamilton consolidated was composed of the land speculators and promoters and embraced all the leading men of the time—Washington, Franklin, Robert Morris, James Wilson, William Blount, and other men of eminence. This dealing in land was intimately connected with public securities, for a large portion of the lands were bought with land warrants purchased from the soldiers, and with other stocks bought on the open market at low prices. Hamilton saw clearly the connection of this interest with the new government, and his public land policies were directed especially to obtaining the support of this type of operators.[10]

Hamilton needed these men to help him "create an unshakable foundation for federal power in America."[11] Hamilton did not randomly choose these partners in his power project. Their enrichment did not serve simply as a payoff in exchange for their support of the economy—if Hamilton had been looking only for allies, he might have found it easier to buy off the poor farmers and laborers with a system of wealth redistribution. No, an elite of wealthy, landed men was central to Hamilton's vision of the new democracy.

Hamilton was an elitist, and he knew that the well-to-do would form the best allies of a powerful central government.

Meanwhile, the regular person found his champion in Thomas Jefferson, who was the foremost advocate of a free market without government interference (even if he did not live up to this standard in the White House). Historian Beard describes Hamilton's perspective on this divide thus:

> Thousands of small farmers and debtors and laboring mechanics were opposed to [Hamilton's] policies, but they did not have the organization or consciousness of identity of interests which was necessary to give them weight in the councils of the new government. They were partly disenfranchised under existing laws, and they had no leaders worthy of mention. The road to power and glory did not yet lie in championing their cause. It required the astute leadership of Jefferson, and the creation of a federal machine under his direction, to consolidate the heterogeneous petty interests against the Federalist group.[12]

Hamilton was the defender of those who already had land and already had wealth. He wanted these men to stay landed and wealthy and knew that laissez-faire would not do the trick. In order to keep the tops at the top, Hamilton proposed taxes, regulation, and central banking—big government. Hamilton was the most acute economic mind of his day, and he knew that an unfettered free market would turn the economy over and over, casting down the mighty and raising up the lowly—a condition of disorder Hamilton thought just as pernicious as unbridled democracy leading to a tumultuous political order.

Alexander Hamilton, the first American champion of big business and big government, has won. Today, people chortle at Jefferson's quaint dream of an agrarian America. Hamilton's vision in which a strong federal government actively supports a system of lending, borrowing, and investing has proved prophetic.

Hamilton also saw with perfect clarity the fact that has been missed by many politicians, journalists, businessmen, and businesswomen throughout this country's history: The wealthy and well positioned profit most from government intervention in the economy. As the federal government has progressively become larger over the decades, every significant introduction of government regulation, taxation, and spending has been to the benefit of some big business.

Henry Clay, Abraham Lincoln, and the railroad barons would all make fine examples, but, rather than review ground historians and writers have covered abundantly elsewhere, let us look at the twentieth century and start with perhaps the most misunderstood era of government intervention, the Progressive Period. Then let us work through the New Deal, the Great Society, and up to present-day compassionate conservatism.

Federal regulation of meatpacking was the desire of the largest meat packers. U.S. Steel turned to Teddy Roosevelt for salvation from laissez-faire. Woodrow Wilson seized control of the U.S. economy to the elation of big business. Herbert Hoover laid the groundwork for the New Deal, with the support of Henry Ford and Pierre DuPont. Franklin D. Roosevelt's New Deal found its greatest champions among top business leaders. Big business guided the drafting of the Marshall Plan. Dwight Eisenhower deflated conservative hopes of cutting government, thus elating corporate America. Lyndon Johnson, the icon of big government, was the favorite of big business. The story continues today.

Triumph of Conservatism

[T]he meat would be shoveled into carts, and the man who did the shoveling would not trouble to lift out a rat even when he saw one—there were things that went into the sausage in comparison with which a poisoned rat was a tidbit. There was no place for the men to wash their hands before they ate their dinner, and so they made a practice of washing them in the water that was to be ladled into the sausage. There were the butt-ends of smoked meat, and the scraps of corned beef, and all the odds and ends of the waste of the plants, that would be dumped into old barrels in the cellar and left there. Under the system of rigid economy which the packers enforced, there were some jobs that it only paid to do once in a long time, and among these was the cleaning out of the waste barrels. Every spring they did it; and in the barrels would be dirt and rust and old nails and stale water—and cartload after cartload of it would be taken up and dumped into the hoppers with fresh meat, and sent out to the public's breakfast.[13]

So Upton Sinclair wrote in *The Jungle,* perhaps the most famous work of the "muckraking" reporting that thrived in the early part of the twentieth century. When *The Jungle* hit bookstores on February 26, 1906, Sinclair's fellow socialist and writer Jack London praised it highly. The *Chicago Tribune,* however, reamed it in a 178-word review:

> Upton Sinclair seems to have been willing to accept as truth nearly every charge that has ever been made against the packers. . . . The book is strongly written in spots, but as a whole is crudely constructed and that it has as its object merely the propaganda of socialism is made clear by the last half dozen chapters, which consist of speeches at socialistic meetings.[14]

The *New York Times* gave Sinclair a few more column inches, but still no high praise. Speaking broadly of the muckrakers, the *Times* wrote:

> These young gentlemen who have so bravely come forward to assist in upsetting the established social order as a preparation for the Socialistic millennium on earth are all interesting.

But the review concluded:

> We lay aside *The Jungle* with a conviction that it is not, after all, a great and epoch-making work. We are afraid Mr. Sinclair has not been divinely appointed to be a deliverer of Labor lying prostrate. . . . Mr. Upton Sinclair does not remind the reader of John Knox or of Martin Luther, or of the leaders in the Abolition movement. He has not written a second *Uncle Tom's Cabin*.[15]

President Roosevelt, then, may have surprised the *Times* reviewer less than four months later when he signed a bill creating a robust new federal system of inspecting meatpacking plants.

Today's history books credit Sinclair with the reforms in meatpacking. Sinclair, however, deflects the praise. "The Federal inspection of meat was, historically, established at the packers' request," he wrote in a 1906 magazine article. "It is maintained and paid for by the people of the United States for the benefit of the packers."[16]

Gabriel Kolko, historian of the era, concurs. "The reality of the matter, of course, is that the big packers were warm friends of regulation, especially when it primarily affected their innumerable small competitors."[17] Sure enough, Thomas E. Wilson, speaking for the same big packers Sinclair had targeted, testified to a congressional committee that summer, "We are now and have always been in favor of the extension of the inspection, also to the adoption of the sanitary regulations that will insure the very best possible conditions."[18]

Small packers, it turned out, would feel the regulatory burden more than large packers would. Whereas the local independent butcher may have built up a trusting clientele through generations of personal friendship and close relationships, the big packers could now get a taxpayer-funded stamp of approval, telling the world their meat was just fine. As California Senator George Perkins wrote in a letter to J.P. Morgan, federal inspection of meat "will certainly be of very great advantage when the thing once gets into operation and they are able to use it all over the world, as it will practically give them a government certificate on their goods."[19]

To cast it in the analogy of Baptists and Bootleggers, the muckrakers such as Sinclair were the "Baptists," holding up altruistic moral reasons for government control, and the big meat packers, railroads, and steel companies were the "Bootleggers," trying to get rich from government restrictions on their business. Roosevelt was allied to the "bootleggers," the big meat packers in this case. To get federal regulation, he found Sinclair a handy temporary ally. Roosevelt had little good to say about Sinclair and his ilk, and it was Teddy who invented the term *muckraker*—as an insult. It was also Teddy who wrote in a personal letter: "in any movement it is impossible to avoid having some people go with you temporarily whose reasons are different from yours and may be very bad indeed." Roosevelt, though, was not talking about his pro-regulation alliance with the big packers. "Thus in the beef packing business I found that Sinclair was of real use. I have an utter contempt for him. He is hysterical, unbalanced, and untruthful. Three-fourths of the things he said were absolute falsehoods."[20]

Sinclair's era, from the turn of the century until the beginning of World War I, is called the Progressive Period. Theodore Roosevelt stands as the hero of this episode in American history, and his "trust-busting" as the central action of the plot. The history books teach that Teddy empowered the federal government and the White House in a crusade to curb the big business excesses of the "Gilded Age."

A close study of Roosevelt's legacy and that of Progressive legislation and regulation, however, yields a far different understanding and shows that the experience with meat—big business calling in big government for protection—was a theme. Roosevelt expanded Washington's power often with the aim and the effect of helping the fattest of the fat cats, according to historian Gabriel Kolko.

Kolko makes this case in *The Triumph of Conservatism* (by "conservatism" Kolko meant "preservation of the status quo"):

> There were any number of options involving government and economics abstractly available to national political leaders during the period 1900–1916, and in virtually every case they chose those solutions to problems advocated by the representatives of concerned business and financial interests.

If the Progressives followed business's commands, did that mean they were secretly deregulating the economy and freeing business to do as it wished? No, Kolko meant quite the opposite: The Progressives served big business by heightening federal regulation. "Such proposals," he wrote, "were usually motivated by the needs of interested businesses, and political intervention into the economy was frequently merely a response to the demands of particular businessmen."[21]

Dramatic mergers and consolidations marked the end of the nineteenth century, thanks to more efficient capital markets that allowed folks with money to invest it in the most promising businesses. From these combinations emerged the giant trusts that are depicted in the history books as villains, whose monopolistic designs the Progressives had to bring to heel. In truth, the trusts' *inability* to obtain stable monopolies led to the Progressive Era.

Kolko writes that "it was not the existence of monopoly that caused the federal government to intervene in the economy, but the lack of it."[22] As a case in point, he tells the story of one of the most famous "trusts" in American folklore: U.S. Steel.

In the 1880s and 1890s, rapid steel mergers created the mammoth U.S. Steel, out of what had been 138 steel companies. In the early years of the new century, however, U.S. Steel saw its profits falling, and stability in the steel industry was still elusive. U.S. Steel's insecurity brought about a momentous meeting.

On November 21, 1907, in New York's posh Waldorf-Astoria, 49 chiefs of the leading steel companies met for dinner.[23] The host was U.S. Steel Chairman Judge Elbert Gary. The gathering, the first of the "Gary Dinners," hoped to yield "gentlemen's agreements" against cutting steel prices. At the second meeting, a few weeks later, "every manufacturer present gave the opinion that no necessity or reason exists for the reduction of prices at the present time," Gary reported.

The big guys were meeting openly—with Teddy Roosevelt's Justice Department officials present, in fact—to set prices.

But it did not work. "By May, 1908," Kolko writes, "breaks again began appearing in the united steel front." Some manufacturers were undercutting the agreement by dropping prices. "After June, 1908, the Gary agreement was nominal rather than real. Smaller steel companies began cutting prices and distressed U.S. Steel managers clamored for steps to meet the competition. . . . In 1908 the prices of most important steel products fell sharply."

U.S. Steel lost market share during this time, which Kolko blames on "its technological conservatism and its lack of flexible leadership."[24] In fact, according to Kolko, "U.S. Steel never had any particular technological advantage, as was often true of the largest firm in other industries."

In this way, the free market acts as an equalizer. While economies of scale allow corporate giants more flexible financing and can drive down costs, massive size usually also creates inertia and inflexibility. U.S. Steel saw itself as a vulnerable giant threatened by the boisterous free market, and Gary's failed efforts at rationalizing the industry left only one line of defense. "Having failed in the realm of economics," Kolko writes, "the efforts of the United States Steel group were to be shifted to politics."[25]

Sure enough, on February 15, 1909, steel magnate Andrew Carnegie wrote a letter to the *New York Times* favoring "government control" of the steel industry.[26] Two years later, Gary echoed this sentiment before a congressional committee: "I believe we must come to enforced publicity and governmental control . . . even as to prices." The Democrats running the committee rejected Gary's ideas as "semisocialistic."[27] Such semisocialistic policy prescriptions by big business often were the seeds of what would become Progressive policy. This was true across the economy.

When it came to railroad regulation by the Interstate Commerce Commission, "the railroads themselves had been the leading advocates of extended federal regulation after 1887."[28] The editors of the *Wall Street Journal* wondered at this development, and editorialized on December 28, 1904:

> Nothing is more noteworthy than the fact that President Roosevelt's recommendation in favor of government regulation of railroad rates and [Corporation] Commissioner [James A.] Garfield's recommendation in favor of federal control of interstate companies have met with so much favor among managers of railroad and industrial companies.[29]

Once again, big business favored government curbs on business, and once again, the media was surprised.

Regarding the insurance industry, Kolko writes, "Herbert Knox Smith [Garfield's successor as Corporation Commissioner] visited Hartford in early 1905, and discovered that most presidents of the major companies favored federal regulation." Their smaller brethren, Kolko wrote, did not share this enthusiasm for federal involvement. "But the opposition, led by Senator Morgan Bulkely, president of Aetna Life Insurance, strongly feared that their New York competitors would dominate a federal bureau by weight of money and influence, and exploit the advantage."[30] Kolko further reports that "small Midwest and Western insurance companies regarded the movement for federal regulation as a menace, and organized to fight back."[31] In this case, the smaller businesses won.

Was federal meat inspection good for the country? It raised the cost of meat (which particularly hurt the poor), resulted in higher taxes, and harmed the smaller meat packers. It also did little to alleviate the conditions the workers faced, in Upton Sinclair's view. Federal regulation of the railroads was a supreme folly in the opinion of many historians and economists, requiring railroads to serve routes with few customers and hire more workers than needed, and the railroads lost a billion dollars a year in the 1970s. The aim of these federal laws, Kolko argued, was not "progressive," but "conservative": preservation of those businesses currently in power.

This preponderance of evidence drove Kolko, no knee-jerk opponent of government intervention, to conclude: "The dominant fact of American political life at the beginning of [the twentieth] century was that big business led the struggle for the federal regulation of the economy." With World War I around the corner, this "dominant fact" was not about to change.

Wilson Approaches "Omniscience"

In northwest Washington, DC, on the south side of Massachusetts Avenue between 10th and 11th Streets, stands a unique building defined by a large glass atrium the inhabitants call the Wintergarden—it is the headquarters of the libertarian Cato Institute. Across the street sits a monument to American Federation of Labor founder Samuel Gompers, once a Marxist, and today revered as the founder of the American labor movement. Given the disparate political leanings of libertarians compared to today's labor unions, this juxtaposition is amusing.

The men who gathered at the Department of War on December 6, 1916, however, struck a more startling contrast. Samuel Gompers (in the flesh) sat at the table with President Woodrow Wilson, Secretary of War

Newton Baker, Secretary of the Navy Josephus Daniels, Agriculture Secretary David F. Houston, Commerce Secretary William C. Redfield, and Labor Secretary William B. Wilson.[32]

Joining Gompers and these Democratic politicians were: Daniel Willard, president of the Baltimore and Ohio Railroad; Howard Coffin, president of Hudson Motor Corporation; Wall Street financier Bernard Baruch; Julius Rosenwald, president of Sears-Roebuck; and a few others including a scientist and a doctor. This extraordinary gathering was the first meeting of the Council of National Defense (CND), formed by Congress and President Woodrow Wilson, as a means for organizing "the whole industrial mechanism . . . in the most effective way."[33]

The CND coordinated the manufacture of munitions and other war necessities, but it did a lot more. The businessmen at this 1916 meeting had dreams for the CND that went far beyond America's imminent involvement in the Great War, both in breadth and in duration. "It is our hope," Coffin had written in a letter to the DuPonts days before the meeting, "that we may lay the foundation for that closely knit structure, industrial, civil, and military, which every thinking American has come to realize is vital to the future life of this country, in peace and in commerce, no less than in possible war."[34]

This march toward rationalizing industry found a priceless opportunity in the unprecedented global and national crisis that was World War I. In looking for a partner to prepare the nation for war, President Woodrow Wilson had naturally turned to major corporations, which he had always admired, calling them in 1910, "indispensable to modern business enterprise."[35]

The CND, after beginning the project of government control over industry, handed much of its responsibility to the new War Industries Board (WIB) by July of 1917. This coalition of industry and government leaders increasingly took control of all aspects of the economy. War Industries Board member and historian Grosvenor Clarkson stated that the WIB strived for "concentration of commerce, industry, and all the powers of government." Clarkson exults that "the War Industries Board extended its antennae into the innermost recesses of industry. . . . Never was there such an approach to omniscience in the business affairs of a continent."[36]

Just as with the CND, "big business leaders permeated the WIB structure."[37] Business's aims were much higher than government contracts, and certainly they did not lobby for laissez-faire. As Clarkson puts it: "Business willed its own domination, forged its bonds, and policed its own subjection."[38] Business, in effect, shouted to Washington, "Regulate me!" Business called on government to control workers' hours and wages as well as the details of production.

The industry giants, such as those at Secretary Baker's table in 1916, saw in government regulation freedom from the competitive pressures that a free market brings. Clarkson wrote:

> It is little wonder that the men who dealt with the industries of a nation . . . meditated with a sort of intellectual contempt on the huge hit-and-miss confusion of peacetime industry, with its perpetual cycle of surfeit and dearth and its internal attempt at adjustment after the event. From their meditations arose dreams of an ordered economic world. . . . They beheld the whole trade of the world carefully computed and registered in Washington.[39]

The "confusion" Clarkson spoke about was nothing else than the power that individual consumers, acting according to their own tastes, have over a free economy. The "ordered economic world" business wanted was, frankly, socialism.

But not everyone in the business world was pleased with the government management of the economy that the WIB brought about. For example, price controls set by the government became boons for big business but banes for small business. Clarkson admits as much:

> It cannot be denied that the horizontal-price plan applied on the plane of high cost production was a tremendous invigorator of big business and hard on small business. The large and efficient producers made larger profits than normally and many of the smaller concerns fell below their customary returns.[40]

Setting maximum prices was an idea that originated among the biggest businesses. Historian and libertarian economist Murray Rothbard writes that "it was big steelmakers—U.S. Steel, Bethlehem, Republic, etc.—who, early in the war, had first urged government price-fixing, and they had to prod a sometimes confused government to adopt what eventually became the government's program."[41]

Rothbard adds, "The smaller steel manufacturers, on the other hand, often with higher costs, and who had not been as prosperous before the war, opposed price-fixing because they wished to take full advantage of the short-run profit bonanza brought about by the war."[42]

Aside from price controls, the WIB made possible something that had always been an unattainable dream for business giants: cartels. Even before antitrust legislation, cartels usually failed because individual businesses had too much incentive to break their promises and undercut the rest of the industry, as the early twentieth century plight of U.S. Steel and the Gary Agreements demonstrated. But once the cartelizers had government behind them, it became truly possible for industry leaders to take control of the economy.

Harry Wheeler, president of the U.S. Chamber of Commerce, wrote in 1917 that World War I gave "business the foundation for the kind of cooperative effort that alone can make the United States economically efficient."[43]

Historian William Leuchtenburg wrote, "Perhaps the outstanding characteristic of the war organization of industry was that it showed how to achieve massive government intervention without making any permanent alteration in the power of the corporations."[44] As Kolko's treatment of "conservatism" suggests, the "massive government intervention," actually *solidified* the "the power of the corporations."

Efficiency and *stability* were the buzzwords of the day—they were the concepts that brought big business and big government together. The central-planning mind-set abhorred redundancy, and monopolies and oligopolies reduced duplication. Big companies, with their economies of scale, had a clear advantage in efficiency (if "efficiency" is understood in a narrow sense). As Gabriel Kolko's history of the Progressive Era made clear, the instability of the free market is a daunting thing to whoever sits atop industry.

Harmony in Hooverville

All in the Family ran from 1971 to 1979, and the writers found that bigoted and close-minded Archie Bunker became the favorite of most viewers. The opening credits combined Archie's and Edith's conservatism and loving relationship by showing them singing "Those Were the Days" in a duet at the piano. The two pined for the time before the New Deal, calling for "a man like Herbert Hoover," and a time before the "welfare state" when "everybody pulled his weight."

Just as Archie was off target in his racial attitudes, he was off target in his American history. The lyrics imply that Franklin Roosevelt and the New Deal upended the tradition of laissez-faire, which Herbert Hoover had guarded. Since Alexander Hamilton, there has been little "tradition of laissez-faire," and those who have tried to defend such have been defeated. Examining Hoover's record shows him to be one of a kind with FDR and

Wilson and other politicians who have been singularly focused on keeping government in power above and beyond all else.

Indeed, during Warren G. Harding's brief presidency, in the summer of 1922, the construction industry got a new trade association in the American Construction Council (ACC). The ACC's chairman was Commerce Secretary Herbert Clark Hoover and its president was former Assistant Secretary of the Navy, Franklin D. Roosevelt. At their first meeting, in June of 1922, Hoover pledged support of the government in standardizing and cartelizing the industry and increasing manufacturing contracts.[45]

As the secretary of commerce, Hoover won high praise from business leaders. Julius Barnes, former head of the U.S. Chamber of Commerce, wrote for a trade journal an article titled, "Herbert Hoover's Priceless Work in Washington." Barnes praised Hoover's work fostering "teamplay of government with the leaders of character in the various industries."[46]

Hoover's record was not one of leaving big business alone but of making government an active member of the team. As commerce secretary, he helped form cartels in many U.S. industries, including coffee and rubber. In the name of conservation, Hoover "worked in collaboration with a growing majority of the oil industry in behalf of restrictions on oil production."[47]

In the White House (where history books portray him as a callous and clueless practitioner of laissez-faire), Hoover reacted to the onset of the Great Depression by pressuring big business to lead the way on a wage freeze, preventing the drop in pay that earlier depressions had brought about. Henry Ford, Pierre DuPont, Julius Rosenwald, General Motors President Alfred Sloan, Standard Oil President Walter Teagle, and General Electric President Owen D. Young all embraced the policy of keeping wages high as the economy went south.

Hoover praised their cooperation as an "advance in the whole conception of the relationship of business to public welfare . . . a far cry from the arbitrary and dog-eat-dog attitude of . . . the business world of some thirty or forty years ago."[48]

Like the wartime maximum prices of the Wilson era, the high minimum wages of the Hoover days were disproportionately painful to smaller businesses, which dealt with smaller profit margins, and may have relied on personal loyalty and friendship to retain employees at lower wages in a downturn.

Hoover, it appears, got the ball rolling for the New Deal with his Reconstruction Finance Corporation (RFC). The RFC extended government loans to banks and railroads. The RFC's chairman was Eugene Meyer Jr., former Chairman of the Federal Reserve. Meyer's brother-in-law was George Blumenthal, an officer of J.P. Morgan & Co., which had heavy railroad holdings.[49]

Far from "everybody pull[ing] his weight," the Herbert Hoover economy was one of corporate welfare and pro-big business regulation aimed at curbing "destructive competition,"[50] by which Hoover meant the free market.

Hoover's postmaster general, Walter Folger Brown, was, like Teddy Roosevelt, a Progressive Republican. Like Hoover and Teddy, Brown believed in big business and big government. W. David Lewis, in his preeminent history, *Airline Executives and Federal Regulation,* wrote this of Brown:

> Brown belonged to the Progressive, or "Bull Moose," wing of the Republican Party. He subscribed to the views of Theodore Roosevelt. . . . More than any other person, Brown plotted the future course of American commercial aviation. . . . One of his primary aims was to put airmail operations in the hands of large, well-financed corporations and weed out small operators who lacked the means to carry out his ambitious plans.[51]

In all industries, Hoover never went as far as some of the corporate leaders of his day wanted. General Electric President Gerard Swope, for one, clamored for a continued march toward government control of the economy. Swope dreamed of a day when:

> the industry [would] no longer operate in independent units, but as a whole, according to rules laid out by a trade association of which every unit employing over fifty men is a member—the whole supervised by some Federal agency like the Federal Trade Commission.[52]

Hoover balked at such an idea, and, as he hesitated, the New Dealers trampled over him and into the White House.

Meet the New Deal, Same as the Old Deal

The 1936 election, Franklin D. Roosevelt's first reelection, is now understood as a referendum on the New Deal. The *Chicago Daily Tribune* was early in declaring it such, with a May 6, 1935, cover story:

The struggle is going to be a momentous one; its outcome will determine whether we are going to continue along the course of collectivism charted by the New Deal or are to revert to the individualistic economy obtaining before Roosevelt.

The third paragraph read:

The belligerent attitude of the Chamber of Commerce of the United States in its convention last week indicates that organized business intends to make a last desperate stand against the New Deal in the hope of halting its monetary manipulations and experimentation in state socialism. Led by the President, the New Dealers have accepted the challenge, confident the people will repudiate organized business and give the Roosevelt program a new lease on life.[53]

This depiction—Roosevelt saving the people from big business—is a standard one. Any *Tribune* reader who bought into this understanding of Depression-era politics, however, would have been surprised to learn about the gathering in the West Wing of the White House three days earlier.[54]

Henry I. Harriman, retiring president of the U.S. Chamber of Commerce obtained an audience with President Roosevelt, and made clear that he supported FDR's plans for a radical new program to be called Social Security and favored expansion and extension of the National Recovery Administration, the centerpiece of the New Deal. H. P. Kendall, chairman of the Business Advisory Council, declared "we are here to uphold the President's hand in the fight against the depression."

Twenty-three businessmen in total constituted that May 3 delegation to the West Wing. Every attendee enthusiastically and unequivocally supported Social Security and an extension of the National Recovery Administration. George H. Mead of Mead Paper Corporation, James H. Rand of the Rand Corporation, E. T. Stannard of Kennecott Copper Corporation, R. R. Deupree of Procter & Gamble, F. B. Davis of U.S. Rubber, Winthrop W. Aldrich of Chase Manhattan, Sidney Weinberg of Goldman Sachs, and others joined with Kendall and Harriman in endorsing FDR's "collectivism."

It is true that the members of Harriman's U.S. Chamber of Commerce had recently voted to reject continuation of the New Deal, but a truer picture than the one the *Tribune* painted would have shown the business community split on FDR's "state socialism." Regarding the anti-Roosevelt business leaders, New Deal historian Paul Conkin writes:

The enemies of the New Deal were wrong. They should have been friends. . . . [T]he meager benefits of Social Security were insignificant in comparison to the building system of security for large, established businesses. . . . Because of tax policies, even relief expenditures were disguised subsidies to corporations.[55]

Indeed, Roosevelt's callers on May 3, 1935, could have certainly seen some self-interest in promoting Social Security. New Deal historian G. William Domhoff writes, "from the point of view of the power elite [Social Security] was a restabilization of the system. It put a floor under consumer demand, raised people's expectations for the future and directed political energies back into conventional channels."[56]

Domhoff points to political and economic advantages business could find in this particular expansion of government. The political angle ("direct[ing] political energies back into conventional channels") often motivates business to support some big government program even when there is no direct financial gain from that particular expansion of government. In the 1930s, many industry chiefs supported the New Deal as a way to deflate the agitation toward a broader socialist revolution.

But businesses had reasons beyond the political to support bigger government. On competition grounds alone, Social Security was a boon to big business. Domhoff writes that, "the tax burden, to the degree that it was a burden, was greater on small employers."[57]

Big business fingerprints can be found on all the pieces of the New Deal. General Electric's Gerard Swope's ideas at the end of the Hoover era eventually came to fruition in the National Industrial Recovery Act. The National Industrial Recovery Act created the National Recovery Administration, which, like Wilson's WIB, helped cartelize industry and organize make-work government contracts.

In the September 1934 *Harper's* magazine, John T. Flynn sounded a rare note of skepticism about the true beneficiaries of the National Recovery Administration. "Whose child is the NRA?" his headline asked. Flynn concluded the law was nearly "entirely the influence and ideal of big businessmen."[58] Conkin's description of the National Recovery Administration bolsters Flynn's assertion: "The early New Deal seemed to have more treats for business than for any other group. As first implemented, the NRA was a wonderful gift its paternal blessings upon unencumbered business self-regulation."[59]

Franklin D. Roosevelt implemented the same sort of government controls on the economy during World War II that Wilson had put in place during World War I, complete with rationing and price controls. Big business profited from the controlled economy in much the same ways that it had under Wilson.

Marshall Plan and Onward

President Harry Truman wanted his secretary of state's June 6 speech to Harvard alumni to be a quiet one about the rebuilding of Europe. He didn't get his wish. The *New York Times* and the *Washington Post* both reported the story on the front pages. Within a day, the whole world knew about the "Marshall Plan."

But very few knew that a clique of mostly business leaders, called "The President's Committee on Foreign Aide" drafted the idea. William Averill Harriman, former vice president and chairman of Union Pacific Railroad, former director of Illinois Central Railroad, and secretary of commerce, ran the committee. Nine other businessmen joined him, along with "six college administrators . . . two labor leaders . . . the president of the Brookings Institute . . . and an out of work Midwestern liberal senator," reports historian Kim McQuaid.[60]

"Throughout, business members—particularly Harriman—set the agenda and the tone for the group's work," McQuaid writes. "Without the corporate politicians, Truman's effort would have failed. Men like Clayton and Harriman arrayed foreign aid in procapitalist, anti-communist attire."

"Admiring letters went out from corporate offices to massage the egos of conservative congressional power brokers," writes McQuaid. "CEOs of large, technology-intensive, and export-oriented firms like General Electric testified before committees and lobbied legislators."

Soon, Congress passed the unprecedented foreign aid bill, sending $22.75 billion in grants to Europe over the next seven years. American businesses had succeeded in getting U.S. taxpayers to finance the redevelopment of a new market for big business.

Perhaps the most striking fact about the cozy relationship between big business and big government is the monotony with which the issue repeats itself throughout history.

Many conservatives held out hope that the 1952 election would bring an end to the New Deal and the managed economy. Dwight Eisenhower's defeat of Robert Taft in the Republican primary was a setback, but the laissez-faire dreams persisted. Eisenhower, however, amid his warnings about a "Military-Industrial Complex" mostly left the New Deal alone (the Supreme Court had struck down the National Recovery Administration as unconstitutional) in order to build a vast network of interstate highways. Today, highway contracts remain a key medium for transferring taxpayer money to big business (in 2001, the Cato Institute calculated that the Department of Transportation handed out $10.3 billion in corporate welfare).[61] The Cold War brought more military spending, but fewer beneficiaries of the war budget. "By the end of Ike's presidency," McQuaid writes, "only twenty companies received half of the total dollar value of all prime military contracts."[62]

Lyndon Johnson's legacy is the Great Society, a vast expansion of the welfare state and regulations to protect workers and struggling Americans. LBJ, indeed, is nearly synonymous with big government. When LBJ faced small-government conservative Barry Goldwater, it is unsurprising that big business flocked to Johnson's side. Members of the Business Council gave LBJ $140,000 in the 1964 election, while giving Goldwater only $90,000.[63] "As Election Day, 1964 approached," McQuaid writes, "Johnson addressed hundreds of businessmen a night at White House dinners." The coalition of big government liberals and big business won, giving LBJ a full term.

On Sunday night, August 15, 1971, millions of Americans skipped an episode of "Bonanza!" to watch President Richard Nixon lay out his New Economic Policy. Nixon had come into politics as a staunch conservative and a believer in laissez-faire, or *non-interventionism* as it was called by the early 1970s. His New Economic Policy (a phrase borrowed, bizarrely, from Vladimir Lenin), however, showed Nixon to be a changed man.

The federal government would prohibit any increase in wages or prices for 90 days. The tax code would be adjusted to direct business spending, and rents would be frozen, too. Nixon created a "wage and price council" which, past the 90 days, would dictate to businesses when and how much businesses could increase wages, salaries, and prices.

The next day, W. P. Gullander, president of the National Association of Manufacturers, declared, "the bold move taken by the President to strengthen the American economy deserves the support and cooperation of all groups." The reaction was typical among big businesspeople. The *New York Times* reported on August 17, 1971, "Business leaders applauded yesterday, with varying degrees of enthusiasm, the sweeping proposals announced by President Nixon Sunday night."[64]

Perhaps no president in history did as little to increase government as Gerald Ford, who, in the wake of Watergate and facing solid Democratic majorities, could not have passed even a birthday wish to his mother. When Ford proposed tax cuts and spending curbs in 1975, the headlines showed him where business stood. "Kauffman opposes Ford's tax-cut plan," ran a *New York Times* headline about Salomon Brothers' chief economist.[65] "Ford's tax-cut proposal leaves executives cold,"[66] and "Business leaders only luke-warm to program,"[67] other headlines declared.

President Jimmy Carter, the famous champion of the ordinary American, extended a record subsidy deal to Rupert Murdoch, and three days later won an endorsement from the *New York Post,* which Murdoch owned. Carter also created the Department of Energy, which, in 2001, according to the Cato Institute, handed out over $5 billion in corporate welfare.[68]

Ronald Reagan famously proclaimed that "government is not the solution to our problem; government is the problem." However, his administration provided a nine-figure bailout to ethanol makers in the form of free corn, which was paid for by taxpayers. Reagan also pushed a tax increase that had the support of a major portion of the American business community.

His successor, George Herbert Walker Bush, "triumphantly"[69] signed a new Clean Air Act in 1990, which exempted ethanol to the pleasure of agribusiness giant Archer Daniels Midland, and turned into "a bonanza" for some businesses.

Bill Clinton's "Third Way" intersected nicely with both big business and big government, including his U.S. Chamber of Commerce-approved tax hikes, support for Enron-endorsed Kyoto, subsidy for GE moving its work to Mexico, biotech industry-endorsed regulation of genetically engineered foods, and more gifts to large ethanol makers.

George W. Bush, in the name of "compassionate conservatism," has handed big business big favors in the form of a prescription drug benefit from Medicare, an energy bill full of brand new special tax credits and subsidies to energy companies, and a record loan guarantee to facilitate business with known nuclear proliferators in China. A report by the directors of the Health Reform Program at Boston University's School of Public Health, found, "An estimated 61.1 percent of the Medicare dollars that will be spent to buy more prescriptions will remain in the hands of drug makers as added profits. This windfall means an estimated $139 billion dollars in increased profits over eight years for the world's most profitable industry."[70]

The history of big business is one of cooperation with big government. Most noteworthy expansions of government power are to the liking of, and at the request of, big business.

PART II

CORPORATE WELFARE

The term *corporate welfare* is used frequently in Washington and in the media, but most people who hear it (and many who use it) probably don't know exactly what it is.

Corporate welfare sounds sinister enough, evoking images of the government handing out welfare checks to fat-cat CEOs who then drive off in their Bentleys with the working man's hard-earned money in their pockets. While Jack Welch and Ken Lay never quite got in line outside the White House on the first of the month to pick up their welfare check, federal, state, and local governments do operate hundreds of programs aimed at benefiting businesses.

In short, corporate welfare is government action that directly enriches specific businesses rather than the nation as a whole. All corporate welfare has this much in common: It hurts taxpayers who pay the bills for government's generosity to big business; it hurts consumers by distorting the economy and making it run less efficiently; and it harms smaller businesses that don't have the same access to politicians that the big businesses do. Additionally, corporate welfare fosters the culture of corruption in Washington. With handouts around every corner, is it any wonder businesspeople and lobbyists swarm Capitol Hill bearing gifts?

What Does It Look Like?

Corporate welfare takes many forms. Some of it involves direct gifts to corporations. Farm subsidies, many of which go to *Fortune* 500 companies, are
the clearest example. Government contracts fall into this category if they do
not address a real need. Often, the government lends money at discounted
rates or guarantees loans to corporations—sometimes, as in the case of sugar
subsidies, the government forgives those loans if the corporations have a bad
year (bailouts usually take the form of subsidized or guaranteed loans). Federal, state, and local governments often carve out specific tax breaks targeted
at one company or industry, while leaving taxes higher on everyone else
(those left out could justly shout: "If you could afford to cut taxes a lot for
one business, why not cut them a little on all of us?").

Why Do They Do It?

In some cases, corporate welfare does seem like a payback to campaign
donors. The generosity of the Fanjul sugar family toward politicians is so immense, and the rationale for the program so tenuous, it is hard *not* to conclude that politicians are rewarding their patrons. In most cases of corporate
welfare, though, there are less insidious explanations.

When government takes family homes and businesses through eminent
domain and hands the land to developers, politicians likely believe that they
are helping all their constituents. Replacing a run-down wire factory with a
retail mall seems like an improvement, and politicians often see no reason
they shouldn't do it, even if they need to use brutal government power to
do so. Good intentions at least partly underlie export subsidies: Lawmakers
believe that if they can bring foreign money into the United States, they are
enriching the country and creating jobs—enriching big exporters is not
their primary aim.

Behind these noble intentions is the mind-set of the central planner.
Often describing their view as the "Third Way," many politicians call for a
closer business-government partnership. Some characterize this model as
one where business rows the ship of the economy while government steers.
Many politicians understand that business and its profit motive are far better
at doing things efficiently than bureaucrats will be. But they still want government to call the shots. Through corporate welfare, they hope to enrich

businesses that do what they want. This approach sounds appealing, but it has many problems.

Why Is It Bad?

Corporate welfare hurts taxpayers. If we eliminated all corporate welfare today, Congress could simultaneously pass a 10-year, $1 trillion tax cut (at least), allowing all Americans to keep more of their money. Corporate welfare also turns big business into a lobbyist for higher taxes, making tax cuts that much harder.

Corporate welfare hurts competitors. Small businesses do not have the same sort of access as big businesses to appropriators or government officials who cut checks. If your competition is subsidized, you begin at a disadvantage. If the government is guaranteeing loans, it takes up lending capital that some other business might have used.

Corporate welfare hurts consumers. In a free market, consumers are the ones in charge. If a business wants to make money, it needs to offer something consumers will buy at a price that they are willing to pay. Once government starts doing the buying or selling, or driving up or down the prices, the consumer loses his influence. While corporate welfare shifts money from taxpayers to businesses, it shifts power from consumers to the government.

Robbing consumers of their power makes the economy less efficient. Corporate welfare creates incentives for businesses to do things for which there may be no consumer demand, but only politician demand. Considered from the view of the whole society's prosperity, money spent on things people don't want is wasted money. If the taxpayers kept their own money, they would instead spend it on things they *do* want.

Corporate welfare corrupts the political process. Attempts to limit the influence of big money in politics or to curb the power of lobbyists will fail as long as Congress keeps up the practice of handing out billions of dollars every year. Corporate welfare draws businesspeople and lobbyists to Capitol Hill like rotting food draws rats and insects to a trash heap.

Finally, there is the moral problem with corporate welfare. The Export-Import Bank, sugar loans, bailouts, and all these other programs are Robin Hood in reverse: They take money from the poor and give it to the rich. More precisely, they take from the working person and give to the corporations.

Even if you believe the government has the right to redistribute wealth, it is hard to argue that it is just to redistribute it *upward*.

This Part

The number and variety of handouts to big business is so vast that a comprehensive accounting of American corporate welfare would resemble in size the mammoth *Code of Federal Regulations,* which dwarfs the *Oxford English Dictionary,* and take up 25 feet of shelf space. Instead, I tell the stories of a few representative companies and programs to give you a taste of what is behind the trillions in tax dollars diverted to select companies and industries.

In the following chapters, you meet the Fanjuls, the richest sugar farmers in America, and you see how taxpayers helped make them so rich. We shine a light on the U.S. government agency that exists almost solely to subsidize Boeing, a $50 billion-a-year company. And you see how a few developers have cashed in at the expense of many small businesses, thanks to eminent domain.

4

Robin Hood in Reverse

Corporate Welfare in America

Nobody knows precisely how rich the Fanjul family is. We know they own over 400,000 acres of sugar cane farms in Florida and the Dominican Republic. We know they own Casa de Campo, one of the most beautiful and luxurious resorts in the Caribbean, with 14 swimming pools and world-class golf courses. But nobody has hard numbers.

Whatever the magnitude of their wealth, we *do* know its sources includes the unwitting American taxpayers and consumers. We also have reason to believe the family's wealth comes at the expense of south Florida's environment.

Entrepreneurs have been looking for ways to get rich off the swamps of south Florida for over a century. The Fanjul family, like its fellow sugar giant, U.S. Sugar, has figured out what it takes to prosper in such a rugged environment: piles and piles of corporate welfare.

It all started in 1881 when Hamilton Disston, the heir to a millionaire saw manufacturer, had a bold investment idea. He would buy four million acres of south Florida swamp, and turn it into a cornucopia of cattle, fruit, and sugar.[1]

The land would be cheap—25 cents an acre—because the State of Florida needed to raise cash to pay back loans from investors, and the land was undesirable. It was mostly saw grass, alligators, and muck beneath inches of stagnant water. The land, known as the Everglades, was a useless swamp. But Disston had a plan: He would drain the swamp.

Disston's Atlantic and Gulf Coast Canal and Land Sales Company planned to reclaim the Everglades for agriculture by dredging the lakes at the head of the Kissimmee River, making them deep reservoirs to suck the water out of the surrounding muck. He also built a series of canals connecting Lake Okeechobee to the Caloosahatchee River. He had further plans to drain the wet southern shore of Lake Okeechobee south to the Shark River Slough.

The draining would expose the dark black soil that Disston hoped would turn his investment into rich farmland, which could be sold at a nice profit. As often happens when man takes on nature, unexpected complications threw the plan off course. Disston ran out of money and had to abandon his plan.

If Ham Disston and his millions couldn't conquer the Everglades, the State of Florida could—or so thought Napoleon Bonaparte Broward, the Progressive governor of Florida.

Governor Broward, a former gunrunner for Cuban revolutionaries, commenced digging in the Everglades' New River on July 4, 1906. His aim was much the same as Disston's—to make the land arable. The Broward administration, however, encountered the same problematic lack of funds. Broward's solution was to sell some of the state's land.[2]

In his last week in office, Broward sold a half-million acres of the Everglades to an investor at $2 per acre and dedicated most of the proceeds to digging five new canals. Draining the land proved more difficult than the state had thought, but in some small areas, the state made progress. However, using the former swamp after it was drained posed even greater obstacles. The muck soil, which was exceedingly rich with diverse organic compounds, lacked some crucial inorganic minerals, most notably copper. After a scandal regarding faulty studies by overoptimistic government engineers, the State of Florida, like Disston, raised a white flag in the Everglades.

It would take the resources, dedication, and legal authority of the U.S. government to tame the Everglades. Beginning with the Hoover Dike on Lake Okeechobee in 1928, and accelerating dramatically after the Army Corps of Engineers stepped in, in 1948, following disastrous hurricanes, the federal government was progressively able to conquer the apparently intractable swamp.

Today, the consequence of this federal involvement can be seen in the invasion of nonnative species to the Everglades, and in dramatic degradation of the soil. The complex irrigation and drainage system carries nutrient-rich water into the Everglades, where these nutrients are not native. This introduces foreign plants, including an infestation of cattails, and erodes the native soil. The disappearance of the Everglades' unique habitats is striking.

While nature lovers might cringe at what the federal government has done there, the "reclaimed" Everglades are a land of plenty for the Fanjuls—America's richest sugar farmers.

The Fanjuls are one example of how a partnership of business and government can develop—and how much it can cost taxpayers and consumers. The family is very generous and politically well connected.

Their wealth comes from their sugar business, a business that relies on protectionist trade policies, low-interest loans from the government, and government-made-and-maintained drainage and infrastructure. In the past, the American sugar industry has also relied on government assistance in finding cheap labor.

The sugar industry may provide the best example of corporate welfare, but it is hardly the only case where government policy serves to enrich big business more than the free market ever would. Wal-Mart, for example, benefits from more than $1 billion in government favors. Many federal programs exist solely to hand taxpayer money to businesses. None of this is so troubling until you realize where this money is coming from—you.

Corporate welfare is the transfer of wealth from taxpayers to huge corporations. A sizable portion of government spending is for corporate welfare programs, of which there are dozens. The mind-set underlying corporate welfare is that of a central planner, who puts more trust in the wisdom of politicians and favored industry giants than in consumers and investors. The politicians and the big businesses win out, while the customers, entrepreneurs, and especially taxpayers all lose.

First Family of Corporate Welfare

Among the more unfortunate legacies of Bill Clinton's impeachment scandal is the sordid Starr Report—the findings of independent counsel Kenneth Starr. The Report immediately hit web sites, often with a warning about the sexually explicit content.

In two infamous episodes in the president's "inappropriate relationship" with Monica Lewinsky, the couple "inappropriately related" while Clinton spoke on the phone to members of Congress.[3] Once, however, President Clinton asked the intern to leave the Oval Office so that he could take a call.

The caller was no mere U. S. Representative. It was Alfonso Fanjul, the Florida sugar farmer, who prompted President Clinton to send Monica away.[4] Such is the clout of the Fanjuls. The Center for Responsive Politics published a paper on the Fanjuls called "Sugar's First Family," which reported:

> With their wealth conservatively estimated at several hundred million dollars . . . the Fanjuls can afford to spread around lots of political money. And they do. Family members, corporate executives, the corporations themselves, and the Florida Sugar Cane League PAC have contributed $2.6 million to political candidates and committees since 1979.[5]

Those numbers were from 1994. Since then, the Fanjuls have given another million.

For his part, Alfie Fanjul probably deserved President Clinton's full attention. Alfie cochaired Clinton's Florida campaign in 1992, and cosponsored a fund-raiser in "Little Havana" Miami, pulling in six-figure donations for Clinton.[6]

While Alfie is a loyal Democratic donor, his brothers Alexander and Andres Fanjul mix their contributions between the parties. Jose, "Pepe," is the big Republican donor. Pepe Fanjul, together with his wife and children, gave $100,000 in the 2000, 2002, and 2004 election cycles—almost all to GOP candidates. Pepe was national vice chairman of finance for Bob Dole's 1996 run for the White House, and he hosted a $1,000-per-person fund-raiser for Dole at his Palm Beach mansion.

The cynic could contend that the Fanjuls, however, are only paying back the government officials who have so handsomely enriched their family. The business the Fanjuls run depends crucially on corporate welfare in the form of government largess. The family, through its company Flo-Sun, Inc., and many related companies such as Florida Crystals, controls about one-third of Florida's sugar production. The Fanjuls, together with their elder in the sugar industry, U.S. Sugar, own a majority of the cane fields in south Florida. These massive corporations might not exist—indeed there might be no sugar cane industry in Florida at all—were it not for corporate welfare.

Very literally, the government has laid the foundation for their sugar business. Without the intensive and expensive federal drainage of the Everglades, it would be impossible to plant sugar—the land would be too wet, and covered with saw grass and mustard trees.

After building the canals and dikes and dredging the lakes, the taxpayers continue to pay for the maintenance of the whole system that keeps the Fanjuls' land dry at the expense of the ecosystem. According to an estimate from the past decade, taxpayers pay about $52 million a year for the Army Corps of Engineers to control water flow for Everglades agriculture—mostly sugar.[7]

Enter the next government program from which the Fanjul's benefit: the U.S. Department of Agriculture (USDA). The USDA loans all sugar growers 18 cents for every pound of cane sugar they grow, and beet sugar farmers get about 23 cents a pound. In recent years, these loans have averaged more than $8 billion annually, with the Fanjuls receiving an estimated $65 million.[8]

The growers set the sugar aside as collateral. That means that if they can't or don't want to pay back the loans, made at lower rates than the market would dictate, the government takes their sugar, and forgives the debt. In other words, if you grow a pound of cane sugar, you know that the very worst you can do is sell it to the government for 18 cents—more than twice the going world price for sugar many years.

In 1999, for example, U.S. taxpayers were left on the hook for $105 million after Florida sugar cane farmers were unable to unload 590 million pounds of sugar for more than 18 cents a pound.[9] During most of that year, the average world price of raw sugar was 6.55 cents per pound.[10]

But this is all chump change compared to the real sugar ripoff, which costs Americans $1.9 billion per year—all of which lines the pockets of sugar farmers, including the Fanjuls. This transfer of wealth happens because the Fanjuls and other American sugar growers charge (and American consumers have little choice but to pay) more than twice the world price for sugar.

How do sugar makers get away with charging that much for sugar? They make sure the government keeps the world's sugar out of the United States. The U.S. government allows each country's sugar growers to sell only a certain amount of sugar into the United States. These quotas artificially limit the supply of sugar Americans can buy. This drives up not only the price of a bag of sugar but also of candy bars, soda, and any other food that contains sugar. From 1998 until 2004, American consumers have paid an average of about $1.8 billion more for food annually because of these import quotas.[11] The General Accounting Office (GAO) also estimated that almost half of that money goes to large sugar growers, such as the Fanjuls.

Even when the sugar growers pay back their loans to Uncle Sam, which is a vast majority of the time, there is still a cost to the taxpayer. The

low-interest loans take money that could be circulating through more productive sectors of the market, or providing for those in need, and redirects
it to the pipeline between the USDA and subsidized sugar growers.

Besides the consumer and the taxpayer, the cost is borne by food manufacturers such as candy makers—and their workers. In Holland, Michigan,
600 workers at a Life Savers plant lost their jobs when the company moved
north to Canada to avoid the artificially high sugar prices in the United
States. Brach's moved from Chicago, Illinois, to Mexico in 2003 for the same
reason.

As with most corporate welfare, the subsidy is hardly a hand up to the
little grower. Both the federal loans and artificially high prices profit sugar
farmers proportional to how many pounds of sugar they can make. A pre-
1994 federal study found that "just 17 of the nation's 1,700 cane farms get
almost 60 percent of federal sugar benefits."[12]

Furthermore, sugar growers' brethren, corn growers, like this deal, too.
The artificially high price of sugar has created the market for high fructose
corn syrup, which American food and drink makers use where the rest of
the world uses sugar. Corn growers also get subsidies, tariff protection, and
special tax breaks.

The sugar must be stored somewhere before it can be sold. Washington
was not about to let the Fanjuls and their ilk foot the bill for that. The 2002
farm bill created the Sugar Storage Facility Loan Program under which the
government lends tax dollars to sugar farmers so that they can build or up-
grade their storage facilities.

While the benefits for U.S. Sugar may end there, the Fanjuls get one
more gift from Washington. The United States grants the highest sugar import quota to the Dominican Republic—where the Fanjul family is the
largest private exporter of sugar, selling about 100,000 tons of raw sugar to
the United States.[13]

In the quest to reclaim the Everglades, the federal effort was the only
one that succeeded, leaving environmental destruction. But the private,
state, and federal efforts all pointed toward transforming this unique habitat
into a corporate cash cow.

Disston's investment was straightforwardly capitalist: He laid down
money with the hope of getting rich. Broward's effort was more opaque. As
McCally writes:

> Florida's Progressive politicians believed that the railroads had too
> much power, and they sought to protect the people from abuse by

these largest of American corporations. In Florida this meant, at least ostensibly, keeping the Everglades out of corporate hands, so that the people could share in the prosperity projected to follow the conversion of these wetlands from worthless marsh to productive farmland. In reality, these Progressive politicians were untroubled at the prospect of selling large blocks of the people's land to speculators at bargain prices so that funding would be available to complete the drainage program.[14]

In this way, Broward's attitude and actions toward business reflected Teddy Roosevelt's modus operandi of hostility toward some fat cats and generosity toward others.

Similarly, the federal aid to the huge sugar farmers—draining the land, providing low-interest loans, keeping out competition, ensuring cheap labor, promising high prices, and more—has harmed America in ways unrestrained capitalism never could have. The federal government drives up the price of sugar, transfers taxpayer money to sugar companies, devastates the Everglades, and drives jobs out of the country.

If not for corporate welfare, there might be no cane sugar grown in the United States. This would be a good thing. Without influential families and businesses like the Fanjuls to protect, Washington would drop its barriers to the world's sugar. The world sugar price might rise slightly when the United States started buying more foreign sugar, but Americans, who typically pay 50 percent to 100 percent more than the world price, would undoubtedly save on both their grocery bills and their tax bills. The Everglades might recover, and candy makers might move back to the United States. But that's all wishful thinking.

Sadly, the story of sugar—an industry that thrives not on the American ideal of free enterprise but on the sap of corporate welfare—is more the rule than the exception with big business.

Welfare for Wal-Mart

Some people love to hate Wal-Mart. They hate Wal-Mart because it doesn't hire union workers. They hate Wal-Mart because it drives Mom n' Pop out of business. They hate Wal-Mart because, for many Americans, faceless corporate uniformity is unsavory.

But millions of Americans love Wal-Mart—for the same reasons. Wal-Mart offers everything Mom n' Pop can offer, and Wal-Mart sells it for less.

Those lower prices are possible, in large part, because of Wal-Mart's clever and intricate business model.

In many towns, the folks who hate Wal-Mart try to get their elected officials to use the might of government to keep out the retail giant. In Maryland, in 2006, the legislature passed, over the veto of the governor, a bill that would require Wal-Mart, and only Wal-Mart, to provide costly health benefits for its employers—a mandate not made on any other businesses. Other states are considering similar bills. Many legislative assaults on Wal-Mart are not defenses of Mom n' Pop but gifts to the labor unions. Rather than first running to the government for special favors, defenders of Mom n' Pop would do well to start by trying to cut off the billion-dollar spigot of government aid that Wal-Mart receives.

The story of Wal-Mart corporate welfare is an illuminating one. It shows the many forms in which corporate welfare comes. It also helps explain *why* governments would give their citizens' money to huge companies. It's not all in exchange for campaign contributions or other personal favors. Often, the officials handing these welfare checks to the likes of Wal-Mart believe that it is in the common good.

They say in Florida that the farther north you go, the more Southern you get. The town of Macclenny is a case in point. Macclenny is the county seat of Baker County, named after James McNair Baker, one of Florida's two senators in the Confederate government.

Sidney J. Catts, the prohibitionist governor from 1917 to 1921, appeared on the steps of the historic county courthouse one day and famously told the folks of Baker County that they had three friends in the whole world: Jesus Christ, Sears-Roebuck, and Sidney J. Catts.[15]

Catts is gone, and so is the Sears catalog. But Macclenny has a new friend: Wal-Mart. In 2001, Wal-Mart began work on a 35-acre distribution center in Macclenny, with the promise of 600 jobs. Previously known as a bedroom community of Jacksonville, Macclenny hadn't had any major private enterprise since it was the moonshine capital of Florida during Catts's prohibition laws.

What brought Wal-Mart to Macclenny was not its rich history but its tax laws. In Baker County's early days, the law required a base tax of 50 cents on every white male over 21 years old and under 50, "except paupers, idiotic and insane persons."[16] These days, the laws are different, but they seem to exempt, "mega-retailers with revenues over $250 billion."

The first thing Baker County did was to give Wal-Mart the land, on the outskirts of Macclenny, where the distribution center would go. That was worth an estimated $1.54 million. The city also waived more than $170,000 in fees it normally would have charged.[17]

But there was a problem: There was no way to get out to the land. So, the state's Economic Development Transportation Fund handed over $1.76 million to pave West Enterprise Boulevard, which runs out to Wal-Mart's new property.

To get plumbing in the new center, Baker County installed $1.9 million in water infrastructure. A federal Community Development Block Grant and a Rural Infrastructure Grant paid for some of this, and the taxpayers of Macclenny and Baker County picked up the rest.

A nonprofit organization called WorkSource helped Wal-Mart staff the distribution center. WorkSource is funded by federal tax dollars. The State of Florida contributed $360,000 to that effort in Quick Response Training funds, and another $25,300 for recruiting and screening applicants. Tallahassee also granted a special tax refund of $2.9 million to Wal-Mart as a member of a Qualified Target Industry.

Finally, the new low-income housing being built in Macclenny (to the displeasure of the long-time residents) will be subsidized by the federal government. This makes it easier for Wal-Mart to pay lower wages.

This means that the people of Macclenny, Baker County, Florida, and the United States are paying for nearly $9 million of what Wal-Mart should be paying for. A less well-connected business would have had to (1) buy its own property; (2) pay for the recruiting, screening, and training of its employees; (3) pay all its taxes and fees; and (4) pay its employees a wage that would allow them to afford rent in the community.

In a free market, you could also argue that Wal-Mart should pay for the roads and sewers that are being built strictly or primarily for its benefit. In the world of corporate welfare, however, the taxpayer covers all those costs.

Macclenny is hardly the only town to bend over backward to attract a Wal-Mart. Good Jobs First, one of those groups that hates Wal-Mart, put out a study that found 244 Wal-Mart stores and distribution centers had received government favors, which they valued at $1 billion for Wal-Mart or the developers involved.

Trying to track down dozens of subsidies from thousands of sources to over 3,000 stores does not allow for airtight methodology, and so the Good Jobs First study should be seen as a rough, low-end estimate. But the study sheds light on how these corporate giants do business.

The blame, however, lies not with Wal-Mart, but with the folks so eager to please the retailer. Politicians desperately want to leave a legacy. In

Macclenny, nobody forgets State Senator Edwin Fraser, who brought Northeast Florida State Hospital to the town in the 1950s. Today's Macclenny and Baker County politicians wanted to leave a similarly impressive mark of revitalization and employment. So, they lured in Wal-Mart.

But as the $1 billion figure shows, Wal-Mart has many communities that are willing to pay them to come to town. If you are Wal-Mart, you have cities and states offering you handouts at every turn. "They expect it," one local official in Delaware told Good Jobs First.

(In the effort to lure businesses to town, politicians get creative. Community Development Block Grants (CDBG) are a favorite tool of corporate welfare. CDBG is a federal program, which passes money from Washington to local governments for developing poor towns and communities.

Not only does this money often go straight to corporations but it also tends to go to America's wealthiest communities. In 2002, Westchester County, New York, one of the wealthiest counties in America, received over $7 million in CDBG funds. Greenwich, Connecticut, with over three times the national average per capita income, received nearly $1.2 million in CDBG funds.[18])

Local politicians are willing to waive the tax bills of these corporations in the hope that in the end, the new business will fill the coffers with even more cash. Building the special roads and parking lots has simply become standard practice. When offered these sweet deals, how could Wal-Mart say no? To be fair, it's not as if Wal-Mart is the only party to benefit. Six hundred people will find jobs, which will generate other businesses. In some cases, the net costs to taxpayers of subsidizing the housing, building the sewers and parking lots, and so on might be offset by new wealth the distribution center brings to the community. West Enterprise Boulevard might have other uses, and other businesses might set up shop along it. Macclenny's politicians might also point out that if Macclenny didn't bribe Wal-Mart to come, some other town would get all those jobs.

None of this changes the fact that politicians are giving your tax dollars to Wal-Mart and giving Wal-Mart a pass on the taxes that you have to pay. Wal-Mart is an exceptionally well-run business, which is why it is able to sell its goods for so cheap. Why does it need a handout?

Wal-Mart is far from alone. Sports teams are notorious for their outrageous demands of local governments. All of the big-box stores do the same thing. Many of the folks who hate Wal-Mart point to its ascendance as a deleterious effect of the free market. For the taxpayers of Macclenny, however, Wal-Mart's arrival was anything but free.

Overseas Private Investment Corporation: Public Risk for Private Profit

As Richard Nixon was changing welfare for America's poor to cut out the middleman (government agencies), he was changing welfare for the world's poor to *bring in* a middleman (American corporations). Initially advertised as a foreign policy tool—aiding the third world as an aspect of Cold War policy—the Overseas Private Investment Corporation (OPIC) is a federal agency whose mission is not easy to pin down.

The "Corporation," today, typically ascribes to itself three goals: (1) to help poor countries develop, (2) to help U.S. businesses gain a foothold in certain countries, and (3) to advance the national interest of the United States. It aims to accomplish this all by insuring American companies' overseas investments and finances them with loans and loan guarantees. OPIC is also very proud that it does this "at no net cost to taxpayers."[19]

Although OPIC claims that its financing advances U.S. foreign policy, this would be hard to examine without the knowledge and perspective of U.S. intelligence agencies. The claim that OPIC helps the U.S. economy is a dubious one on its face. As with most corporate welfare, OPIC takes money from taxpayers, gives it to corporations, and then claims it is "creating jobs."

In 2000, OPIC provided insurance worth $50 million to the Ritz-Carlton corporation. Istanbul needed its own Ritz-Carlton, and the U.S. taxpayers (unknowingly) saw to it that Istanbul got the hotel. If anything went wrong with the project, OPIC was there to bail out the corporation.[20]

If the U.S. taxpayers fear they were investing in a lemon, they would do well to look at a Turkish web site description of the Ritz-Carlton Istanbul:

> [T]he luxurious 244-room hotel is part of a multifunctional complex that includes upscale condominiums, exquisite boutiques and modern offices. . . . The hotel offers wireless Internet access in public areas as well as a Technology Butler service. The . . . Award-winning Laveda Spa indulges and pampers guests with a variety of therapy alternatives as well as an authentic Turkish Hamam, indoor pool, steam bath, sauna and gym. In the summer months, the Laveda Open Air Spa offers a chance to escape the daily stress of the city. Enjoy its Jacuzzis, bijoux pool and Thalasso therapies while overlooking the legendary and magical waters of the Bosphorus.[21]

Lest you think that OPIC was playing favorites, the agency provided a $61.1 million guarantee for Hyatt International Corporation in Brazil in 1999. In 2001, OPIC also financed Unocal's oil exploration in Indonesia to the tune of $350 million.[22]

According to the Cato Institute, Citibank is the top beneficiary of OPIC financing. The top 10 list also includes Enron, Unocal, Bank of America, and Intergen (a joint venture of Bechtel and Shell).[23]

After OPIC got involved in a power-plant project in India in the late 1990s and early 2000s, things got messy. The foreign client, a local government in India, refused to pay the bills. One of the American investors, Enron, collapsed. The Bank of America, Bechtel, and General Electric all lost money. Overseas Private Investment Corporation bailed them out on the taxpayer dime.[24] Then, OPIC sued India's government and got most of the money back.

OPIC's scheme is known as "public risk for private profit." That means the taxpayer bears the risk for Ritz-Carlton's potential profit. An analogy on an individual level highlights how this deviates radically from the American entrepreneurial tradition.

If you wanted to invest in a penny technology stock offered by a start-up company, you know that your money would be put at risk with the possibility of a high reward—you play, you lose; you play, you win. If you had access to OPIC financing, you could borrow the money to invest and have it guaranteed by the U.S. taxpayer. If your stock made it big, congratulations—you are rich. If your stock crashes, don't worry—the American people will cover the loss. Who wouldn't take advantage of this offer from OPIC? It's hard to fault the Ritz or the Hyatt for taking advantage of the program when a business would almost be stupid not to do so.

But might this form of corporate welfare nonetheless benefit America as a whole? Nobel laureate in economics Milton Friedman doesn't think so. "I cannot see any redeeming aspect in the existence of OPIC," Friedman wrote in 1996 to the chairman of the Budget Committee of the U.S. House of Representatives. "It is special interest legislation of the worst kind, legislation that makes the problem it is intended to deal with worse rather than better. . . . OPIC has no business existing."[25] In 2003, the Cato Institute reaffirmed Friedman's point, "OPIC lowers U.S. economic output by transferring resources from productive uses to politically favored ones."[26]

Most people agree that there are times when the most economically productive uses of money ought to be sacrificed. Building weapons to defend the United States or spending money to help the poor are both sacrifices most Americans are willing to make. It is a different matter, however, when we are being asked to sacrifice for the sake of a Ritz-Carlton on the Bosphorus Straits.

The Overseas Private Investment Corporation has many cohorts in the business of subsidizing exports:[27]

- The Agriculture Department's Commodity Credit Corporation spent $315 million in fiscal year 2001 on its *Export Loans Program* (ELP). At a time when poor nations are struggling to develop their own economies, the U.S. government is subsidizing farmers with this special export subsidy agency for farmers, loaning money to foreign buyers so that they will buy American crops. Taxpayers spent $4 million on this in 2005.[28]
- The USDA also runs the *Export Enhancement Program* (EEP), which is a more direct subsidy than the ELP. Under this program, farmers can sell their crops overseas at a discount, and the EEP (i.e., the taxpayer) pays the difference. Thankfully, the Bush administration is aiming to scrap this program.
- Similar to the ELP, *Public Law 480* created programs within the USDA that promote agricultural exports through loans to buyers and by subsidizing the freight carriers of the subsidized crops. This cost taxpayers an estimated $1.45 billion in 2005.[29]
- In case foreign shoppers do not know that all this subsidized American food is in their markets, the USDA runs the *Market Access Program,* using taxpayer money to advertise overseas, showcasing the products of major U.S. food makers as well as American food in general. On all its food export promotion subsidies, the USDA estimated that it spent $123.4 million in 2002, compared to the actual exporters, who spent $208.0 million on promotion.[30]
- The Department of Commerce's *International Trade Administration* (ITA) does the work of a consultant and an advertiser for U.S. exporters. Instead of doing it at the expense of the exporters, ITA gets its paycheck—$398.1 million in 2005—from U.S. taxpayers.
- The Pentagon, through *Defense Export Loan Guarantees,* underwrites arms sales from major U.S. corporations to foreign governments. Again, the taxpayers bear the risk, and the corporations reap the profits—$15 billion a year, according to *National Defense* magazine.[31] You can bet these weapons exporters are not Mom n' Pop businesses.

- Similar in mission but much larger in scale is the *Foreign Military Financing Program,* which issues grants and loans to subsidize military sales to foreign governments. U.S. taxpayers finance most overseas arms sales by U.S. corporations. This behemoth will redistribute $4.8 billion in 2006, from the taxpayer to the likes of McDonnell Douglas and Raytheon.[32]
- The *Agency for International Development* (AID) is the crux of U.S. foreign aid. Its primary effect is to transfer money from American taxpayers to American companies. Agency for International Development admits, "The principle beneficiary of America's foreign assistance programs has always been the United States. Close to 80 percent of the U.S. Agency for International Development's contracts and grants go directly to American firms." These American firms got to slobber over AID's $8.55 billion budget in 2005.[33]

Lighting the Night Strip for Gamblers

From 30 miles away on Interstate 15, drivers can see the eerie glow on the mountaintops that surround Las Vegas. The bright lights of the strip—illuminating the mini-New York skyline, the Egyptian pyramid, the Eiffel Tower, and the countless other casinos and attractions—are legendary. The opulence and the excitement are unparalleled.

It wasn't cheap to build the strip. Trillions of dollars of investment made it what it is today. But trillions of dollars in gambling, eating, drinking, and entertainment attracted the initial investors: In short, the strip was built by your gambling losses.

But the lights burn bright, in part, because of your tax dollars. The Western Area Power Administration (WAPA) is a federal agency that sells power to utilities throughout much of the American West, including Las Vegas. It does so at lower prices than the free market would charge, with the taxpayers picking up the difference. Western Area Power Administration is one of four regional federal power administrations, which make up the Power Marketing Administration (PMA), part of the Department of Energy.

WAPA, for example, sells utilities the power generated by federal dams in the West, including the Hoover Dam. The federal government sets the price of the power, not at the going market rate, but at the rate necessary to recover some of the government's costs of the production and distribution of the power.

The Department of Energy brags that the PMA operates at no net cost to the taxpayer, but that claim ignores many costs. For one thing, WAPA employees, like all federal employees, receive a civil service pension from the taxpayer. The PMA does not count these pension payments or postretirement health care expenses as a cost when calculating the cost of its power. In 1996, the GAO estimated that these PMA retirement costs added up to $436 million.[34]

The GAO also said that taxpayers, rather than PMA customers, would pay for some federal power programs or irrigation facilities that died before completion. Taxpayers also have paid for the environmental mitigation costs incurred by the PMA and its power suppliers. This came to about $134 million by the end of 1995.[35]

Finally, as with so many corporate welfare programs, the PMA benefits from favorable financing—interest rates far below market rate. Like the other subsidies, this saving is passed on to the utilities, and then the electricity users, such as the casinos on Las Vegas's strip.

Families and customers certainly benefit in the form of lower monthly bills and hotel tabs, but those savings simply reflect the subsidy they are paying for. In other words, for every dime a family's monthly electricity bill is lowered by the PMA, their taxes are at least a dime higher. This means there is no net gain to the average taxpayer and electricity user.

The only ones who gain are those who use more electricity than they pay in taxes, which brings us back to the strip. Subsidizing electricity for everyone discourages conservation by hiding the true costs of energy use.

Reverse Robin Hood

In a 2001 Policy Analysis, Stephen Slivinski at the Cato Institute estimated that "federal subsidies to private businesses cost taxpayers $87 billion per year."[36] Chris Edwards at Cato put that figure at $90 billion in June of 2004.[37]

But those numbers are only a small slice of the pie. To begin with, Cato's $90 billion figure only includes the direct federal outlays of money and not the indirect subsidies, such as Army Corps of Engineers' work to keep fields drained. State governments can be as bad or worse at transferring wealth from taxpayers to corporations. Then, local governments add their dollars to the mix.

Cato's experts also don't count special targeted tax breaks—which should be considered corporate welfare. Lower taxes, in general, mean more freedom and less government. Although Democratic politicians called

George W. Bush's lowering of tax rates a "tax giveaway," there is no giveaway involved. Cutting the 15 percent tax rate on individual income by one-third and the 39.6 percent rate by about one-tenth, as Bush did in 2001, was not giving anything to anyone; it was letting workers keep more of their money.

But *targeted* tax breaks are a different story. While also not an outlay (the government usually doesn't cut a check to the beneficiary of a targeted tax cut) it *is* special treatment. A broad-based rate reduction helps everyone who pays income taxes, regardless of who they are or what they do. When a town grants Wal-Mart or a baseball stadium a special exemption from property tax—a tax the other businesses in town have to pay—that's special treatment. When the government uses the tax code to pick winners and losers, it is corporate welfare.

The actual cost of corporate welfare, when you take into account direct outlays to corporations, government financing of corporate activity, special tax breaks for corporations, government building infrastructure, or advertising for corporations is probably immeasurable. We know it is well over $100 billion per year. As some in Washington might say: A hundred billion here, a hundred billion there, and pretty soon you're talking real money. This real money is coming from the taxpayers and going to America's largest corporations—allegedly the heroes of the capitalist system.

The rationale for most corporate welfare is that it combines the creative power of private business with the broad vision of government. Government officials want to direct the robust marketplace toward perceived public needs, and they will use the tools at their disposal—tax dollars, control of the borders, and police power—to do so.

The justification for corporate welfare lies in the mind-set of central planning. The unpredictable free market is unreliable, and so it must be controlled, the central planners conclude, in order to increase efficiency and ensure the public good. But corporate welfare always takes the form of transferring wealth from taxpayers to big business.

Corporate welfare is often compared to a reverse Robin Hood who robs from the poor and gives to the rich—in some cases, the very rich.

Welfare for Single Mothers Reformed— Welfare for Big Corporations Flows

Often touted as the greatest accomplishment of both the eight years of the Clinton presidency and the 10-plus years of Republican control of Congress, welfare reform removed bad incentives from federal law and saved tax-payers millions by overhauling the system of welfare for poor individuals.

But welfare reform didn't include corporate welfare: Despite Republican promises to limit government and Democratic rhetoric against big business, the web of welfare for corporations is bigger than ever.

There are a few glimmers of hope. Deliberations over the Central American Free Trade Agreement (CAFTA) suggest the Bush administration is considering increasing the quota of sugar imports from our southern neighbors (and quotas are already increased for 2006 due to U.S. crop damage from hurricanes). In the meantime, sugar prices in the United States rose to 23 cents in the first weeks of 2005 while they were 12 cents in the rest of the world.

On the whole, corporate welfare is alive and well. Sugar subsidies, CDBG, infrastructure grants, and the other programs and special considerations only scratch the surface.

5

Boeing's Bank

The Export-Import Bank
of the United States

As Jimmy Carter sat in the White House on the morning of February 19, 1980, the world was in tumult, and his own fate was in doubt.

In Tehran, Iran, 66 Americans were still being held hostage after more than 100 days. In Afghanistan, the Soviet Union had amassed nearly 50,000 troops after having invaded the country a few weeks earlier. Oil prices were skyrocketing.

In New Hampshire, Senator Ted Kennedy was on the campaign trail, trying to oust his president in the Democratic primaries. George H. W. Bush and Ronald Reagan were preparing for their first debate, both men eager for the chance to take on Carter in the general election.

Not everything, however, was beyond the president's control. Two blocks from the White House, just on the other side of Lafayette Square, the owner of Australia's Ansett Airlines was meeting with one of Carter's friends, John Moore. Moore, an Atlanta attorney, was Carter's appointee to head a little-known federal agency with offices on Vermont Avenue.

The Aussie explained his circumstance to Moore. His competitor, TA Airlines of Australia, was buying brand new jets, and Ansett needed to do the same if it wanted to compete. Unlike TA, which bought Airbus planes manufactured by a European company, Ansett wanted Boeing's new product, the 767.

Why were President Carter and his administration involved in this purely commercial matter? Boeing and Ansett were free to conduct their business of buying and selling planes without U.S. government intervention. It may have been a big-dollar deal, inevitably involving high finance and intricate contracts, but trades like that go on in all corners of the business world every day. The difference was that the high finance in this deal included a loan of $657 million from U.S. taxpayers.[1]

John Moore headed the Export-Import Bank of the United States (Ex-Im). Its purpose is to loan taxpayer dollars to foreign companies, such as Ansett Airlines, so that they in turn would buy American goods, such as Boeing jets.

At the time, interest rates were about 16 percent, but the Aussie wanted a loan for just above 8 percent. The businessman ended the meeting by noting he was walking across Lafayette Square to have lunch with the president.

The businessman was Rupert Murdoch. The lunch between Murdoch and Carter bore fruit three days later when the *New York Post,* owned by Murdoch, became the first major paper in the country to endorse the re-election of President Carter. Murdoch's meeting with Moore bore fruit a week later when Ex-Im's board, in record time, approved a cut-rate loan to Murdoch's Ansett Airlines.

This was the sort of thing Ted Kennedy's campaign manager and brother-in-law Stephen Smith was referring to when he told a *National Journal* reporter earlier that week (just before the endorsement and before the proposed deal was public):

> We knew the powers of the incumbency were formidable but were surprised at the forcefulness with which they have used the resources at their command, including White House personnel, federal grants, patronage.[2]

That spring, the Senate Banking Committee investigated the deal as part of a broader inquiry on the purpose and efficacy of Ex-Im. After hearings, staff reports, and tough questions—such as why the normal process was circumvented, and why the loan approval was rushed—the Democratic Congress gave Ex-Im the medicine they decided it needed: more money. In

August 1980, Carter signed a bill increasing Ex-Im's lending limit to $5.1 billion from $3.75 billion.[3]

A Child of FDR

The flurry of articles that spring on the Ansett loan marked a rare moment in which Ex-Im popped into public awareness. It is far from a secretive agency, but neither business nor government has any interest in publicizing its existence. The unknowing dues payers are the taxpayers, and the beneficiaries are the few U.S. corporations that pocket most of the loan dollars.

The Export-Import Bank of the United States was born in Franklin D. Roosevelt's first term. It was only secondarily a New Deal tool, aimed at boosting American manufacturing during the Great Depression. Primarily, FDR created Ex-Im as a foreign policy tool.[4]

Specifically, Ex-Im enabled Roosevelt to circumvent Congress in providing aid to his ally, Josef Stalin in the Soviet Union. This was a difficult task in the political climate of that day. In their preeminent history of Ex-Im, William Becker and William McClenahan write:

> Since the Bolsheviks had seized power in Russia in 1917, the United States had refused to accept the legitimacy of the new Soviet regime. Throughout the 1920s, Presidents Harding, Coolidge, and Hoover conditioned recognition on the USSR agreeing to accepted standards of international conduct. That is, they wanted the Soviet government to end its support of revolutionary activities in other countries, return confiscated property, and accept the international financial obligations of its predecessor government.[5]

But Roosevelt sided with his foreign policy advisers and the leading business interests of the day and moved toward normalized relations with the USSR. By executive order on February 2, 1934, FDR created the Export-Import Bank. The Bank was initially capitalized by borrowing $10 million from the New Deal's Reconstruction Finance Corporation on top of smaller amounts from the Departments of State and Commerce.

A few weeks later, FDR created a second Ex-Im, specifically to facilitate trade with the brand new Batista government in Cuba. In June 1935, the two banks merged. Soon, they kicked into full gear.

Naturally, U.S. exporters welcomed Ex-Im. Aggravating the difficulties caused by the depression was a Federal Reserve policy that discouraged competitive lending by private banks. American banks were prohibited from discounting long-term loans, which kept U.S. exporters from offering attractive financing to their customers.

By the late 1930s, the Roosevelt administration had expanded the Ex-Im beyond its original goal of aiding Germany's rival, the USSR, and Ex-Im was soon aiding China, under siege by imperial Japan.

After the war, Congress wanted to be involved in Ex-Im, which existed only under FDR's order. In 1945, Congress passed the Export-Import Bank Act. The Act increased congressional control over the agency, and focused its mission. Since 1945, the purpose and activities of Ex-Im have contracted, expanded, zigged, and zagged. Today, though, Ex-Im is generally the same agency it was in 1945. Every few years, Congress must reauthorize the agency, or it expires. It was last reauthorized in 2002, and in 2005 Ex-Im held $1.2 billion in taxpayer money.[6] At the end of fiscal year 2005, thanks to Ex-Im loans, U.S. taxpayers were exposed to $63 billion of risk, between outstanding loans, loan guarantees, and insurance policies issues.[7]

The primary function of Ex-Im is to support American exports through financing. Ex-Im does this in a few ways, but primarily, it can (a) loan money to foreign governments or foreign companies, which in turn use the cash to buy products from American companies; or (b) guarantee loans made by private banks to foreign buyers of American goods. When Ex-Im lends money directly, the cash comes straight out of the Treasury Department and goes to the foreign buyer, though not for long. Usually, the money is immediately transferred to the U.S. exporter. Some deals take the form of a U.S. Treasury payment to a U.S. corporation, and all the foreign buyer gets from Ex-Im is some debt.

On a loan guarantee, Ex-Im sets aside a fraction of the loan, based on the perceived risk of default. The ratio is calculated differently for different buyers in different countries. A guarantee on a riskier loan requires more money to be set aside than a guarantee on a safer loan of the same dollar amount.

As Ex-Im went before Congress in 2001, asking for reauthorization, it made certain to tout the agency's support for small business. Ex-Im's Chief Financial Officer James Hess, told a congressional committee, "eighty-six percent of Ex-Im Bank's transactions directly benefited small businesses."[8]

This statistic, like many statistics, is true but misleading. Ian Vasquez of the Cato Institute cast the same data in a more telling light. He testified that if the transactions are weighted by their dollar amount, 86 percent of Ex-Im's loans and long-term guarantees in fiscal year 2000 directly benefited just 10 large companies.[9]

The top-10 list included General Electric (GE), Bechtel, and Halliburton, but number one on the list was Boeing, the recipient of $3.38 billion of Ex-Im financing, or 43.1 percent of the total from that year according to Vasquez. Boeing might have been disappointed with that paltry subsidy, after getting $6.13 billion the year before—that's 75 percent of all Ex-Im financing in fiscal year 1999. Out of the $63.5 billion in Ex-Im loans and long-term guarantees between 1998 and 2005, Boeing received $33 billion. That's more than 52 percent of all of Ex-Im's large subsidies.[10] How can anyone say with a straight face that Ex-Im does not exist primarily to subsidize one corporation?

Boeing versus Airbus

Boeing's defenders correctly point out that Boeing is not competing in a free-market arena. Its only competition in the industry of big passenger jets is Europe's Airbus. Whereas Boeing may be the largest recipient of American corporate welfare, Airbus is nearly a government agency. Beating Boeing and thus the United States is a point of pride for many European government officials. Former French Prime Minister Lionel Jospin said it plainly, "We will give Airbus the means to win the battle against Boeing."[11]

And they have tried. European governments have their own versions of Ex-Im, the government-controlled airports seem to discriminate in favor of airlines that buy Airbus, and the European Union extends "launch aid"—research and development loans that the government forgives if the research doesn't succeed—to Airbus projects. Airbus is subsidized in many ways at many levels. In fact, it is partly owned by government.

After Canada's *Financial Post* carried an article I wrote in 2005 about Boeing and Airbus under the title "Subsidy Queens," Boeing Vice President Thomas Downey wrote a letter to the editor. Downey praised me for calling out the subsidies European governments give to Boeing's rival Airbus, but he objected to my treatment of Boeing and its U.S. subsidies. Downey's letter began:

> Mr. Carney's op-ed piece does an admirable job of refuting the weary arguments used by Airbus and the European Union to defend their direct subsidies for developing new airplane models.

However, he misses the mark in suggesting that the loan guarantees the U.S. Export-Import Bank provides for the purchase of American products are "unquestionably a subsidy." These guarantees do indeed help foreign customers secure the private-sector loans they need to buy American goods, but they are not exclusive to Boeing or airplanes—nor are they prohibited by the World Trade Organization.[12]

In other words, Ex-Im financing is not really a subsidy because 48 percent of it goes to companies other than Boeing.

Since 2003, a trans-Atlantic trade skirmish has been heating up over these dueling subsidies. The scene is reminiscent of the gang fight in the musical *West Side Story*. The Jets and Sharks agree not to bring weapons to the scheduled rumble. The Jets among themselves acknowledge that weapons would be unfair, but they should bring some knives anyway just in case those dirty Sharks break the rules. In the Sharks' camp, there is similar dislike of knives, but, heck, you can't trust those Jets, so bringing weapons is the only safe thing to do.

Boeing officials and American politicians often say they would rather not have subsidies for Boeing, but as long as Airbus is subsidized, we have no choice. Europeans make the same arguments, just in French and German (although in Europe, it seems, more people are willing to defend the subsidies in their own right). It's a vicious circle. In *West Side Story*, gang members Riff and Bernardo die. In the trans-Atlantic story, all the taxpayers lose.

Boeing's Bank

Boeing also defends its subsidies by pointing to its unique market position. In 2001, Boeing spokeswoman Cheryl Russell pointed out to me that Boeing was the top U.S. exporter of manufactured goods.[13] If you grant the legitimacy of an export-subsidy corporate welfare program, it makes sense that the top exporter would get the most subsidies. But that doesn't quite do the trick in Boeing's case. Ex-Im's James Hess said that 2 percent of all U.S. exports get Ex-Im financing.[14] Russell told me 20 percent of all Boeing exports got Ex-Im financing. These numbers show Boeing is 10 times as likely as the average exporter to get Ex-Im subsidies.

Russell explained that Boeing needs subsidies more than other companies because of the magnitude of its exports. Jumbo jets cost lots of money. "Some of these sales," she told me, "will be the largest purchase that our overseas customers have ever made."

That is certainly true in the case of Air Nauru. Nauru is a tiny island in the South Pacific, only eight square miles, and 400 miles from its nearest neighbor. For a century, Nauru's chief commodity was guano—or bird droppings. The bird droppings contain phosphate, which is a very rich organic fertilizer. Nauruans were among the richest people in the world, thanks to their phosphate exports for 100 years.

But after decades of strip-mining, the phosphate is nearly gone now, and years of profligacy and bad investment have left the island in serious financial difficulty. Air Nauru, the government-owned airline, and the island's only real link with the outside world, found recently that it could no longer pay its debts to Ex-Im, for the Boeing 737-400 it owned—the *only* plane it owned.[15]

Just around Christmas 2005, the Export-Import Bank repossessed the jet after an Australian court ruled in Ex-Im's favor on Air Nauru's nonpayment. This left Nauru without an airline, for now. It also left Nauru's athletes—hoping to return from the 2005 Micronesia Games to spend the New Year with their families—stranded in Majuro on their way home from Saipan.[16] Finally, it left the U.S. taxpayers with a Boeing 737 they never asked for. Boeing and Boeing's private lenders, however, were just fine. After all, Ex-Im is all about protecting big businesses from nonpayment by nations speeding toward bankruptcy. In January of 2006, Ex-Im put the Boeing jet up for auction.

Maybe Air Nauru never could have afforded that 737 without Ex-Im help, but the same can hardly be said for Saudi Arabia. The Saudi people may not be wealthy—they rank 71st out of all 232 nations in per capita gross domestic product[17]—but the government sure is. Saudi Arabia is a monarchy, and the royal family runs the show. Unsurprisingly, the House of Saud is pretty well off. Prince Alwaleed Bin Talal Alsaud was the fifth-richest man in the world in 2005, worth $23.7 billion according to *Forbes*.[18]

In the 1990s, as oil prices turned downward, the House of Saud took a financial blow. Never ones for self-pity, the royal family took real efforts to pull themselves up by their bootstraps. The U.S. State Department writes: "Saudi Arabia was a key player in coordinating the successful 1999 campaign of OPEC and other oil-producing countries to raise the price of oil to its highest level since the Gulf War by managing production and supply of petroleum."[19] The Saudis were the chief price-fixers, driving the price of oil from less than $10 a barrel at the beginning of 1999 to more than $20 (and climbing) by year's end.[20]

That same year, as the House of Saud was driving up prices for American drivers (the average price for a gallon of gasoline rose from 94 cents to

$1.27 that year),[21] Ex-Im issued two loan guarantees to the Sauds' state-owned airline, subsidizing $1.9 billion in Boeing sales and locking in a lower-than-market rate for the Saudi government.[22]

Seeing how much they depend on government kindness, it makes sense that Boeing is well connected. In the typical election cycle, Boeing employees give about $1.5 million to federal candidates. Boeing's PAC adds on another $800,000 every two years. In the 2000, 2002, and 2004 cycles, the PAC gave a combined $2.4 million, about 58 percent to Republicans and 42 percent to Democrats. Individual contributions from Boeing employees break down along similar partisan lines.[23]

Although the Boeing cash may favor Republicans, the company has an in with the Democrats, too: Linda Hall Daschle is a lobbyist for Baker, Donelson, Bearman & Caldwell. She is well qualified for the job, being a former deputy administrator of the Federal Aviation Administration. Another fact that makes her valuable to prospective clients: her husband Tom used to be the majority leader of the U.S. Senate. One of Mrs. Daschle's clients, from 1998 until 2005 at least, is Boeing.[24]

On Boeing's behalf, Mrs. Daschle has lobbied Capitol Hill, the FAA (her old place of employment), and the Department of Transportation about Homeland Security appropriations, Department of Transportation appropriations, and post-9/11 security bills, according to Senate records. While her husband was a senator, Mrs. Daschle avoided lobbying the Senate to avoid the appearance of impropriety. Still, as conservative reporter David Freddoso noted: "The income Mrs. Daschle ultimately derives from her clients also enters the Daschle family budget, improving Sen. Daschle's finances as he considers actions that will affect these clients."[25]

In June of 2002, as Congress was considering reauthorizing Ex-Im, Freddoso asked Senator Daschle whether he might recuse himself on the question of Ex-Im, seeing as it exists primarily to fund his wife's client. Daschle dismissed that idea. "No. I feel very strongly about the Export-Import Bank," the Boeing lobbyist's husband and Senate majority leader said. "It's a very good bill. It's one I strongly support. I think it's good public policy. I would hope we could get broad bipartisan support for it."[26] Records show that Linda Daschle never lobbied Capitol Hill on Ex-Im reauthorization. But Ex-Im is hardly the only benefit that Washington gives the airline giant.

When the European Union complains about U.S. aid to Boeing (remember, the European Union subsidizes Airbus to the hilt), Europeans mostly point to Boeing's defense contracts. Boeing was the number two recipient of Pentagon contract cash from 1998 through 2003.[27] While Europeans might have a distorted idea of defense, they are right on this much: what Boeing develops for the air force or navy can have a commercial use, meaning the Pentagon contracts have spillover benefits for Boeing. Most Americans would deny this is corporate welfare. However, what if Boeing gets military contracts that don't best address real defense needs?

In 2002, the air force planned to lease 100 Boeing 767s for 10 years to serve as in-air fuel tankers. The Congressional Budget Office (CBO) estimated that the lease would cost taxpayers $37 billion. Buying the planes, the CBO said, would cost only $25 billion.[28] Why would the air force lease them, then? Senator John McCain, probably the top Senate watchdog of waste, said in 2002 that the lease "has nothing to do with national defense and everything to do with taking care of Boeing."[29]

McCain's suspicions were bolstered a few months later when one air force official involved in the deal took a job at Boeing.[30] Any doubt was erased in June of 2005, when the *Washington Post* quoted an e-mail from another air force official saying, "We all know that this is a bailout for Boeing"[31]

The corporate welfare comes from all angles. When Boeing announced it was moving its corporate headquarters out of Washington state in 2001, the company started asking which city would give the most handouts. Illinois and Chicago won by offering $63 million in favors. When Boeing found that its preferred location within the Windy City was occupied by another tenant, the government bought that tenant out for $1 million.[32]

Tulsa, Oklahoma, offered Boeing $350 million in welfare in 2003 if the company would build its new plane model there.[33] Washington state bested them by convening a special session of the legislature, called the "Boeing Session" by lawmakers and journalists, in which they pieced together a package of special benefits and more broad-based changes to business law.[34] The state estimated the aerospace industry would benefit to the tune of $3 billion over 20 years from the Boeing Session.

"My Taxes Are Paying to Ship My Job to Mexico"

Ex-Im's defenders—who are mostly limited to those who work for Ex-Im, profit from Ex-Im, or receive campaign contributions from either—say that there is a positive ripple effect for the U.S. economy. Ex-Im loans may transfer money from taxpayers to corporations, but they create jobs in the process. "Jobs through exports" is the slogan.

That slogan assumes Ex-Im has *created* the money it is lending. It hasn't. The agency has simply taken money from taxpayers—nurses in Phoenix, accountants in Chicago, and janitors in Boston—and then given it to Boeing. If the taxpayers still had their money, they would spend it or invest it; this spending and investing would also create jobs. However, nurses in Phoenix, accountants in Chicago, janitors in Boston probably would not spend their extra income buying airplanes from Boeing. While they might take more airplane trips if they had more disposable income, they might also spend the money on their children's education, renovate their homes, invest for retirement, or maybe even buy a boat—none of which is good for Boeing. Ex-Im doesn't create wealth or jobs, it just directs that wealth and those jobs toward jumbo jets. Why is it government's job to decide that jumbo jets are the best use of your money?

The *best* Ex-Im can do is move money around the economy, with no net gain because of the movement. The *worst* Ex-Im can do is to move jobs overseas. If you ask workers in Bloomington, Indiana, a better slogan for Ex-Im might be "Exporting jobs."

Tracy Pritchard stood in a mostly empty parking lot on the outskirts of Bloomington, Indiana. For the past 10 years, Tracy drove to this lot five days a week to go to work at the factory. Ten years ago, when Tracy started at the factory shortly after graduating high school, it was tough to find a parking spot at the plant with over 3,200 employees.

Those workers spent eight hours a day standing before a conveyer belt or some machine doing the same thing over and over again. Some workers would drive a bolt into a hole on a thousand different units—all day long. Some would inspect thousands of paint jobs on plastic casings, rarely finding a flaw.

They were making GE refrigerators. These weren't just any refrigerators—these were the Cadillacs of refrigerators: side-by-side refrigerator-freezer units, up to 30 cubic feet in volume and $2,400 in price. Alongside the humble lightbulb, these fridges were the flagship product of GE.

It was mind-numbing work to make them, but it paid well—$24 per hour. That adds up to nearly $50,000 per year, and it comes with benefits and the possibility for overtime. It wasn't a bad deal for a kid with no experience and no college. It was no wonder it was the biggest manufacturing employer in Bloomington.

Then the first round of layoffs came. By 1999, GE decided to terminate about half of the jobs. The layoffs would happen by seniority, and so Pritchard, fairly junior at the factory, got the axe. A few months later, they rehired him.

On March 31, 2005, Pritchard faced the axe again. General Electric was paring the factory workforce down to about 1,000, and the next day, April Fools Day, would be his last. This time, Pritchard saw little hope of being re-hired. Workers who had been at the plant for 17 years were being laid off, and so about 450 workers would be ahead of Tracy if an opening occurred.

Between GE, the State of Indiana, and the federal government, Pritchard had access to some benefits including schooling. He was consider-ing becoming an electrician. "I'm gonna stay outta factory work," he told me as he showed up for his second-to-last day on the job. "Not much future there."

He's right. That same day, just a bit down Curry Pike, a few contract workers at the Otis Elevator plant were hauling out the last of the manufac-turing equipment and tossing it in the dumpster. The last 19 manufacturing workers were being sent home that day, some of them, such as Bary Brown, having given 38 years to the plant.[35]

It's not that people have stopped riding elevators or keeping their food cold—no, GE refrigerators are selling just fine. It's just that GE has no reason to pay those high wages in Bloomington, Illinois, when workers in Celaya, Mexico, do the same work for about $3 per hour.

"Free trade and NAFTA are the worst things that have happened to the working man," Pritchard told me. He wasn't alone. Most of the laid-off workers blamed the 1993 North American Free Trade Agreement (NAFTA). To be sure, NAFTA played a role. By eliminating import duties on goods from Mexico, NAFTA made it more profitable for American companies to have their goods made in Mexico and then shipped back to the United States for sale.

Dennis Briscoe, who also lost his job at GE on April 1, 2005, didn't re-ally blame the company for sending his job south of the Rio Grande. "Hell, if I had my own business, I'd do the same thing."

While the lower wages—pure market forces—create a huge incentive to move jobs south, these workers don't know that the money that came out of their paycheck in federal income taxes is also to blame. Ex-Im has created an artificial incentive for the offshoring.

All of the largest GE side-by-sides are made in Celaya, Mexico, at a huge plant owned by Mabe, a GE joint venture. As GE was laying off Pritchard and about 1,500 others in 2000, they were building a plant in Celaya that would supply plastic and metal components for the refrigerators made in the Mabe plant. Some of the equipment for this smaller plant was coming from Califor-nia and Illinois, and so GE, as part of another joint venture, came calling on

Ex-Im. Ex-Im agreed to help finance the sale by providing a loan guarantee to cover the sale of this equipment.[36]

The deal went like this. GE and a Mexican company, Elamex, formed the joint venture Qualcore, which would supply Mabe with parts for the refrigerators being assembled there. To make plastic parts, Qualcore would use a procedure called "plastic injection molding." Qualcore decided to buy the equipment needed for plastic injection molding from two American companies.

Instead of paying straight out for the equipment, GE asked Wells Fargo for a loan, which is standard practice for a big business deal. Then, they asked Ex-Im to sweeten the deal for Wells Fargo by guaranteeing the loan. Once Ex-Im agreed, the deal was a no-brainer for Wells Fargo—if Qualcore failed to repay the loans, U.S. taxpayers would pay instead.

In other words, U.S. taxpayers, including the Bloomington workers, were subsidizing GE's plan to move refrigerator manufacturing to Mexico. If GE had tried to build its new plant in Indiana, it would not have been eligible for a U.S.-government-backed loan guarantee, and Wells Fargo might not have loaned them the money (or may have charged higher interest for the loan). Ex-Im has financed 56 GE sales since 1997—deals totaling $2.7 billion.[37]

The issue of "offshoring" or "outsourcing" (where U.S. manufacturers move their manufacturing overseas to take advantage of lower labor costs) was a prominent one in the 2004 elections. Labor unions found their voice in the brief, loud candidacy of Ohio Congressman Dennis Kucinich who vowed to repeal NAFTA and restore old tariffs—in short, using big government to (Kucinich argued) save jobs. Those who lamented the job losses in Bloomington, however, could have started—instead of demanding big government protection—by objecting to big government's *subsidizing* of the export of American jobs.

At the Bloomington office of the International Brotherhood of Electrical Workers Local 2249, Joe Adams, the local's vice president, lost his job at the plant on April 1. I didn't tell most of the laid-off workers about Ex-Im subsidy, but I told Joe. "Well, that's just great," he said, "my taxes are paying to ship my job to Mexico."

Supplying the Suppliers

Weapons of mass destruction are a very bad thing in the wrong hands. Most people would agree that Iran and Pakistan having nuclear weapons is not a good thing and that the people who help these countries develop nuclear weapons are deplorable. At least on that last score, the Ex-Im does not agree.

Ex-Im made news on February 18, 2005, when its board granted a preliminary commitment for a $5 billion package of loans and loan guarantees to the China National Nuclear Corporation (CNNC).[38] The deal, intended to help Westinghouse sell two nuclear reactors to China, would be the largest in Ex-Im history, according to Ex-Im officials. It was rare for Ex-Im to make its way into the news, but the foreign buyer had made headlines many times in the past.

The front page of the *Washington Times* on February 5, 1995, carried the headline, "China nuclear transfer exposed; Hill expected to urge sanctions." The article began, "The CIA has uncovered new evidence China has violated U.S. anti-proliferation laws by exporting nuclear weapons technology to Pakistan."

The article continued: "According to intelligence sources, the CIA recently notified the State Department that China sold 5,000 ring magnets to the A.Q. Khan Research Laboratory in Kahuta, Pakistan, last year."[39]

Ring magnets can run high-powered centrifuges used in enriching uranium. Enriching uranium transforms it from mostly harmless dust into radioactive material for nuclear power or an atomic bomb by filtering out the more stable uranium in favor of the U-235 that can more easily create an atomic reaction.

The CIA believes that the criminal Pakistani nuclear weapons scientist A.Q. Khan did not buy the ring magnets in 1994 for peaceful reasons. Khan's desire for a uranium centrifuge was well known among world governments: The Dutch convicted him in his absence in 1983 for stealing centrifuge designs from a Dutch lab (the conviction was later overturned on a technicality). Many Pakistanis revere Khan for bringing them the bomb—a point of pride for India's rivals. But Khan's services extend beyond his home country. He has admitted helping arm North Korea, Iran, and Libya with nuclear weapons technology.

Khan's supplier in 1994 was the China National Nuclear Corporation. U.S. intelligence officials frowned on the CNNC selling Khan the ring magnets. The Clinton administration responded by imposing sanctions on China. Once China made a commitment to stop its proliferation activities, though, Clinton lifted those sanctions.

Years later, a Congressional Research Service (CRS) Issue Brief reported, "the Clinton Administration's decision-making was apparently complicated by considerations of trade interests of U.S. corporations with business in China."[40]

Those corporations included Westinghouse, Bechtel, and, of course, Boeing. But Washington didn't stop at opening the door for these big businesses to deal with China—Washington also *subsidized* their dealings. Ex-Im loaned $383 million to the CNNC in late 1996 to facilitate a deal with Bechtel and Westinghouse building nuclear power plants in China.[41] (Bechtel is a well-connected company. Between corporate gifts and individual contributions from brothers Riley and Stephen Bechtel, the company has given well over $1 million to federal political campaigns. The contributions are nearly evenly split between the parties.)[42]

One of the three Ex-Im board members in 1996 was Maria Haley, who, according to the *New York Times,* "helped John Huang, the Riady family's senior American executive, get a job at the Commerce Department."[43] John Huang pleaded guilty in August 1999 to funneling more than $150,000 in illegal foreign contributions to President Clinton.[44]

But China did not keep its "commitment" to stop proliferating. Around the same time as the 1996 Ex-Im loan to the CNNC, the *Washington Times* disclosed a report from the CIA alleging that the China Nuclear Energy Industry Corporation (CNEIC; part of the CNNC) had also sold Pakistan special furnaces used for weaponizing plutonium and uranium.[45] In May of 1998, Pakistan tested a nuclear weapon for the first time.

Pakistan wasn't the only client of the CNNC. The *Washington Post* reported in April 1995 that CNEIC was planning to sell Iran equipment to weaponize uranium.[46]

President Bush has spent significant diplomatic capital trying to curb the spread of nuclear technologies. On February 11, 2004, at the National Defense University, President Bush addressed the issue sternly, calling on the international community to use all available "means to bring to justice those who traffic in deadly weapons, to shut down their labs, to seize their materials, to freeze their assets." He continued:

> We must act on every lead. We will find the middlemen, the suppliers and the buyers. Our message to proliferators must be consistent and it must be clear: We will find you, and we're not going to rest until you are stopped.[47]

Despite this rhetoric, Bush's message was not consistent and clear, when one year later, in February 2005, his administration offered a $5 billion subsidy to the CNNC, certainly one of the "suppliers" he was talking about. This loan deal (completely separate from the 1996 loan) was an attempt to

get the CNNC to choose Westinghouse over French and Russian companies all bidding for the right to build China's newest nuclear power plant.
The $5 billion dollars could be some combination, yet to be determined, of
loans and loan guarantees. Of course, France and Russia are subsidizing their
bidders, too. (As of April 2006, China has not yet chosen from among
its suitors.)

When Bush leaned on Russia in early 2005 to stop aiding Iran's nuclear
program, it's little surprise that he didn't get very far. It is also questionable
whether Westinghouse Electric is really an "American company." The reac-
tors, it is presumed, would be built in Monroeville, Pennsylvania. But Westinghouse Electric is owned by Toshiba, a Japanese company. At the time of
the subsidy offer in early 2005, Westinghouse Electric was owned by British
Nuclear Fuels, Ltd., which, in turn, was owned by the British government.
In other words, the U.S. taxpayers would bear the risk on this deal if it goes
through, while the British government would have reaped the profit. Now,
U.S taxpayers will bear the risk for the profit of a Japanese company.

The Moral Problem

In all the deals outlined, the money passes through the U.S. Treasury, Ex-Im,
and the hands of the foreign buyer. However, the U.S. taxpayer stands at the
giving end, and companies like Boeing stands at the receiving end. Ex-Im
like all of corporate welfare is simply a transfer of wealth from the American
people to the largest corporations.

The moral problems of a reverse Robin Hood are clear to see: Why
does Boeing, which profited $1.9 billion in 2004, deserve the money of the
average American worker, who earns about $36,000 per year?

But the need for a subsidy demonstrates that Boeing airplanes may not
be as important as some argue. If Americans or anyone else wanted Boeing
jets badly enough, they would choose to pay, through higher ticket prices,
more money to have those jets. If we removed subsidies for Boeing, maybe
Americans would willingly pay the higher ticket prices. In that case, the
subsidies are unnecessary transfers of wealth from those who don't fly to
those who do. However, if people wouldn't pay the higher prices for more
planes, this suggests Boeing is making something people don't really want.

Americans find shoes very important, which is why they pay good
money for them. Nobody in the government is agitating to subsidize the
crucial shoe industry. Subsidies are more defensible for goods used largely by

the poor. There may not be market demand for such goods, but people who are too poor to pay the price might really need them. Public transit such as city buses fit this bill in many urban areas. Airplanes do not. Middle-class to rich Americans fly the most. Boeing's defenders are left, in the end, with the patriotic argument. Without subsidies, Boeing might go out of business, and all large passenger jets would be made in Europe by Boeing's rival Airbus. There is a national interest in preserving a U.S. passenger plane industry, they argue. One could respond, though, as long as some company in the world is making good, safe jets, why should it matter whether they are a U.S. company or not? Do we care if the Italians, French, or Chinese make shoes as long as they are available at a price we are willing to pay?

Perhaps the most compelling argument for the preservation of a U.S. jet-maker hinges on the fear of a future war: We need to preserve Boeing in case a war demands the sort of jets and technologies that they produce. We can't afford to depend on Europe though in the past we've managed to gear up when military equipment has been necessary. Never has Ex-Im claimed that this is the reason for its existence. Over the years, it has been touted as a tool of foreign policy (promoting trade with allies), a tool of economic development (helping the United States out of a recession), a tool to support U.S. jobs (by spurring exports), and a counter to foreign subsidies (such as European support for Airbus). It ought to be left to the Pentagon budget to ensure that the United States is well protected, not an export credit agency.

Whatever the benefits of Ex-Im, it is hard to see that they are worth all the costs. Ex-Im diverts money from more efficient sectors to politically favored sectors, dragging down the economy. The agency makes our taxes higher and our deficits greater. It often implicates the U.S. taxpayer in unsavory deals, such as the Chinese nuclear program and GE's exporting of jobs. It creates an opportunity for corruption as the Jimmy Carter-Rupert Murdoch example demonstrates. For what gain?

Ex-Im, created to help Josef Stalin, now helps big business, at your expense.

If after being laid off by GE you went into business on your own, you're still helping GE—through your tax dollars thanks to Ex-Im. If you are worried about nuclear proliferation, you share some of the blame yourself—Ex-Im used your money to subsidize one of the world's worst proliferators. But if you're Boeing, with $50 billion in revenues annually, Ex-Im is your friend.

6

Eminent Domain for Corporate Gain

The "Public Purpose" of Big Business

A government big enough to give you everything you need is big
enough to take away everything you have.

—Ronald Reagan

Wilsonilliam Minnich stood in the shell of a building in Harlem and
looked up. He saw the sky. There was no roof. The building
had no electricity. A dreary, decaying wire factory next door
was on its last legs. The East River, just yards away, ran toxic with filth and
sewage. It was 1981, and all around him in this dark corner of a tumultuous
Manhattan, crime and drugs ran rampant.[1]

He was sold. Minnich bought the property, renovated it, and moved his
woodworking business there from the East 72nd Street space he had been
renting. This was the same business his father, Valentine, had started when he
got off the boat from Germany in 1923, and William had been working
there since he was seven years old. The Minnichs did pretty well, on occasion building and codesigning furniture with Frank Lloyd Wright, some of
which landed in the Metropolitan Museum of Art. The elder Minnich was

also commissioned for pieces for the 1939 World's Fair, and his father's shop made a wooden reindeer that appeared in *Miracle on 34th Street*.

Now, they owned a slice of Manhattan. It was a piece of land nobody else wanted, but it was theirs. William now ran the shop with his nephew Bill, the third generation. They had changed the nature of the business from custom installations, like the one in *Miracle on 34th Street*, to original custom furniture that could be shipped. In the new building, they even installed a loading dock to expedite getting their flood of orders out the door.

William is a warm man, and he's not afraid to sound hokey. His family's story—from Ellis Island to owning his own business—is the American dream, he'll tell you. They hadn't gotten where they were by being lazy. William says he worked about 80 hours per week.

And so it wasn't unusual that William was in his office on a March Sunday in 1998. He is a tall and broad man, very visibly of German descent. His features are softened so much by age that even with no beard, he is reminiscent of Santa Claus, with a shock of white hair atop his head. As Minnich sipped his coffee and ate his breakfast that Sunday morning, he turned to page 33 of the *New York Times* where he saw the headline: "Retail center is proposed in East Harlem." The subheadline promised "revival." The mayor, Rudy Giuliani, and governor, George Pataki, were going to announce a major new shopping center development. The article bubbled with the promise of "2000 jobs," and "East Harlem's rebirth."[2] But when Minnich flipped to page 35, a little map of the neighborhood caught his eye. The shaded area marked "Site of proposed East River Plaza" looked a little funny to him. Oddly, it included his shop.

The fifteenth paragraph of the article explained: "Other difficulties could arise because the site will provide only about 75 percent of the land sought by the developer. State officials plan to use the state's power to condemn property to acquire adjacent lots for the project."

In other words, the city was going to take away his property and tear down his shop in order to build this shopping mall—"the anchor of the economic renaissance in Harlem," in the governor's words.

What historians call the "Harlem Renaissance" had its roots where most revolutionary movements do: in the confluence of talented and ambitious individuals. Pataki and Giuliani's new Harlem Renaissance had its birth in the confluence of big business and big government.

The Blumenfeld Development Corporation, developers from Long Island, were as smitten in 1994 with that sliver of East Harlem as William Minnich was in 1981, and city and state governments were eager to help the developers get it while, it must be observed, no one helped Minnich get the property in 1981. Top government officials decided to use their power of eminent domain to condemn Minnich's shop, take it from him with compensation, and sell it to Blumenfeld. The Blumenfelds (generous contributors to the crucial New York politicos) would, with some taxpayer subsidies, turn the lots into retail outlets, which would generate more tax revenue and create more jobs, thus serving the public interest and justifying the taking.

The Minnichs and their employees? Well, they didn't quite fit into the plan. Minnich was not the only small businessman to have his thriving business condemned by the City and handed over to bigger businesses. New York is certainly not the only place it happens, either. Increasingly, local governments are seizing the land of small property owners, land that they believe would be better used by big business. In 2005, the U.S. Supreme Court said it was all fine.

The process is called *eminent domain,* and it is enshrined in the Constitution. Federal, state, and local governments can condemn properties and force the owners to sell to the government. The idea behind this power is that the government will occasionally need to acquire private property for public use such as a military fortification, road, school, park, fire station, or the like.

The Constitution, in the 5th and 14th Amendments, specifies that governments can use eminent domain only (1) "for public use," (2) with "just compensation," and (3) with "due process of law." This was a key issue at our founding because it was a major grievance of the colonists. The British abuse of property rights in the colonies was one of the factors that spurred the revolution.

Throughout America's history, there have always been eminent domain takings. Property owners in most of these cases complain that their compensation was unjust and the process was unlawful. In many cases, the "public use" turns out to be "big business use."

Take the story of Bill Brody,[3] a hardware store owner who bought run-down buildings in Port Chester, New York, blocks from a tiny tributary of the Long Island Sound. After renovating the buildings and renting them out to businesses, he expected to retire on the income from his investment.

The Village of Port Chester had a different idea. As part of their community redevelopment, Port Chester decided to condemn his buildings and sell them to a developer who would level them for a grocery store parking lot.

Using eminent domain, governments have turned a small car dealer's lots over to a larger dealer (BMW), and transformed an entire community into General Motors factories.

Eminent domain for corporate gain introduces a new angle to the vehement arguments over whether big chain stores drive small Mom-n'-Pop operations out of business. In many cases, the ruthless free market is not what kills the small businesses. For Minnich, Brody, and thousands of others, Mom n' Pop would have done just fine if the government hadn't intervened in favor of big corporations.

The culprit here is the mind-set of central planning that entices politicians, bureaucrats, and big business. A sharp departure from the American tradition of pioneering and rugged individualism, the central planners believe that a better life is best brought about by those in power.

They Paved Paradise

Eyeing the same stretch of East Harlem that had attracted Minnich 15 years earlier, Blumenfeld Development first contacted the Empire State Development Corporation (ESDC), a New York state government agency, in 1995, according to *Fortune* magazine.[4] That area provided just about the only slice of land large enough to have the sort of large stores and shopping centers you find in nearly every suburb. For a developer like Blumenfeld, it also promised some government goodies.

In 1996, a federal law made this bank of the East River an "empowerment zone," entitling any developer to tax breaks and low-interest loans, but not helping Minnich or the other businesses that were already established there. And so Blumenfeld made his move.

Working with ESDC, Blumenfeld developed a plan centered on an abandoned wire factory on FDR drive. Blumenfeld bought the factory from the city in 1996 for a bargain, $3.1 million. That factory, however, wouldn't be enough land for Blumenfeld's plan.

Meanwhile, Minnich had no idea what was afoot. Not City Hall, nor Albany, nor Blumenfeld informed him. Minnich was busy running his business, but a situation in Ossining, New York, one town away from his home in Mahopac, caught his eye.

Flavor Sciences, Inc., a family-owned flavor and perfume plant, was being forced to sell as part of that Hudson River town's waterfront redevelopment. Minnich read about this in the local paper and took a keen interest.

The Minnich family had some experience with eminent domain proceedings already; Minic (as his father named the company to preserve some privacy) had been forced, in the 1940s, by eminent domain to sell its first Manhattan property, a shop in a slaughterhouse district that then became part of the United Nations.

With some history on the topic, and a firm belief in the Constitution, honest entrepreneurship, and in property rights, Minnich went to a public meeting on the Ossining redevelopment plan and continued to follow it closely. But even with this previous experience, he didn't quite know how to react when he learned from the *New York Times* that the government planned to take his land, which he did not want to sell.

That Sunday morning in March 1998, Minnich called his wife and his nephew Bill, who was a co-owner of the business. The next day, he called the ESDC. They told him he needed to talk to the developer. Minnich then launched a full-court press. He wrote every member of the city council, objecting that his land was being stolen. He tried to get Al Sharpton and Johnny Cochran involved. He petitioned local Congressman Charles Rangel. It was all to no avail.

In August 1998, ESDC proposed the official plan for the East River Project to the City Council. "The principle objective of the Project," the plan said, "is to eliminate the blight and physical decay that prevails the Project area. . . . Despite its excellent location, the Project Area has seen no successful private investment or development activity for more than sixty years."

Minnich disagreed. He had poured $250,000 into fixing up his building: He had installed the electricity, a roof, and a loading dock. He had put down wood flooring, fire-resistant walls, and concrete supports beneath the equipment. For the next few months, Minnich found that everyone acted as though he didn't exist.

Particularly upsetting to Minnich was his treatment by the *New York Times*. One April 1999 article noted only that, "The proposed East River Plaza has drawn some opposition from local residents who are concerned that it would bring too much traffic to the neighborhood."[5] The complaint that the development would use property that didn't belong to the developer—and that a developer would profit hugely by getting the government to intervene to take another's private property—was completely ignored.

When the *Times* reporter covering the project came to see Minnich's shop, she told Minnich he was not a real cabinetmaker because she did not see any cabinets being made. *Cabinetmaker* is a term for fine woodworkers who make furniture, and Minnich said any good reporter would have learned that.

In June 1999, Minnich says he saw posters around the neighborhood for a public meeting regarding the development project. He and his nephew walked over to Thomas Jefferson High School to have their say at what they thought was a meeting about the environmental impact of the project.

At the dais of the meeting were not just ESDC officials, but the developers themselves. The big businessmen, it was clear, were now running the show, and effectively wielding the power of condemnation. The developers and officials took no questions—in fact, the officials didn't speak at all.

While the Minnichs thought this meeting was only a preliminary discussion at an early stage of the proposed project, the ESDC went behind closed doors afterward and reached their final decision. They published a document a few weeks later called "Determinations and Findings" in which they concluded Minic should be condemned.

As Minnich increased the pace of his campaign, retaining at least three lawyers, he didn't realize his time was running out. On October 21, 1999, 30 days after the findings were published, Minnich lost his right under state law to appeal the condemnation. Six days later, the City Council, all of whom had received his letter and ignored his pleas, approved the developer's plan.

The government was going to take his property, and now they told him there was nothing he could do about it. The land he had bought with his savings, repaired with his sweat, and invested with his future, now belonged to the State of New York, which was going to turn it into a shopping center parking lot. Minnich decided to keep fighting.

"I didn't think I had a chance in hell," he says now. He just wanted to "make it as costly to those guys as possible."

In the next month, Minnich and his new group, Business and Residents Alliance (BARA) went to court. The New York State Supreme Court dismissed the suit because he had not protested within the 30-day window dictated by law, even though he believed he had not been given notice.

With the courts, the city, the state, and the developers aligned against him, Minnich tried turning to the public. He wrote letters to every paper he could. "I had no idea how to fight this," the woodworker said. "I just knew you gotta bug people." Minnich was aided in the bugging with lawsuits filed by Atlantic Legal Foundation and the Institute for Justice, two nonprofit public-interest law firms.

"Incidental Benefit to Certain Private Individuals"

After a few press reports took the Minnich's side, the officials and developers were forced to defend their course of action. David Blumenfeld told one television reporter, "It's an unfortunate situation, but I feel the benefit to the community as a whole outweighs Mr. Minnich's desire not to sell."[6]

Randy Daniels, of ESDC put it his way: "You've got to look at the greater good. No one is saying Mr. Minnich or anyone else will be put out of business. What we're simply saying is that they're being asked to help accommodate the community's larger need."[7] Minnich might not characterize the seizure of his property as "being asked" anything.

The shopping center in an otherwise neglected neighborhood would provide revitalization by bringing in money, jobs, and a place to buy affordable goods. Minnich's shop created a few jobs, but few other benefits for the community. A lawyer for Blumenfeld, Jesse Masyr, made his critique more pointed: "Anyone against this project is sticking a knife into the heart of East Harlem."[8]

Whether Blumenfeld, profiting hugely from the deal, is a credible source on the matter is one question. The other is how much power the government ought to have in determining exactly *what* best benefits the community.

Joe Petillo, a lawyer for ESDC, told the webzine *Gotham Gazette* at the time, "The fact that there might be some incidental benefit to certain private individuals or private businesses, doesn't undermine the overriding public purpose that we would be seeking to accomplish."[9]

Petillo had good reason to be defensive. His agency had been raising eyebrows for years, and those "certain private individuals" might include his political patrons.

In 1996, Democratic State Senator Franz Leichter released a report titled, "Give a Little, Get a Lot: Pataki's Economic Development Agency Resembles Political Slush Fund." Leichter reported:

> In the first year and a half of the Pataki Administration, the State agency charged with improving New York's economic development has more closely resembled a political slush fund for Governor Pataki than an engine for job growth. Since Pataki took office, more than 25 firms that made campaign contributions to Pataki, U.S. Senator Al D'Amato and other State Republican political committee have received grants and loans from the Empire State Development Corporation.[10]

In fact, Charles Gargano rose to the presidency of the ESDC from being Pataki's chief fund-raiser in the 1994 campaign, and he continued to be an active fund-raiser while condemning property and handing out grants. In 1995, he chaired the state GOP's fund-raising dinner.

The report showed many businesses contributed to the top local politicos and then got ESDC contracts or loans. Blumenfeld was no exception. Since 1989, according to city campaign finance records, the Blumenfelds gave at least $7,000 to Mayor Ed Koch, $3,000 to perpetual candidate Mark Green, $2,200 to Giuliani, $1,250 to Al D'Amato, and tens of thousands more to other politicians of both parties.[11]

Public records suggest these were good investments: The city and state didn't stop at condemning property for the East River Project. They also subsidized the shopping center, doling out special tax breaks and cut-rate loans to the Blumenfelds.

The Blumenfelds' biggest beneficiary may be New York Senator Chuck Schumer, who has netted over $10,000 from the Blumenfelds in the past decade. The senior senator from New York, Schumer is one of the Democrats' best fund-raisers. For 2006, he is the chairman of the Democratic Senate Campaign Committee, which is responsible for helping Democrats get elected to Congress's upper chamber.

Since his election to the Senate in 1998, Schumer has raised more money from Wall Street ($3.3 million) and from real estate businesses ($1.8 million) than any other lawmaker in either party. He's gotten millions more from other industries. Schumer's voting record and claims indicate that he is very liberal—a fact that does not keep him from doing the bidding of developers and big business.

In 2001, Schumer and former Treasury Secretary Robert Rubin formed the "Group of 35" business, political, and labor leaders in New York City. This included Kevin Corbett, chief operating officer of the ESDC.

"Dedicated to identifying opportunities for commercial development both inside and outside of Manhattan in order to accommodate the increasing space demands of New York City's growing industries," the group's final report sought to remove "barriers to new office development."[12]

One such barrier was "Difficulty in Completing Site Assemblage." In plain language, sometimes somebody else owns the land you want. The report stated:

> The assemblage of sites with the appropriate size and configuration for office development can be difficult, especially if it requires the purchase of numerous parcels held by various owners. When assembling

sites, private developers face the risks of both holdout owners and tenants. The public sector can assemble through the use of condemnation, a process that can be expensive and time consuming but is often more predictable than assemblage by the private sector.

The report recommended the City "make greater use of public condemnation for assemblage."

Schumer's paper was praised as great cooperation between business and government. A *New York Times* editorial called a "welcome suggestion" the proposal that the "city employ its zoning, taxing and condemnation powers to speed office construction."[13]

The *Times* failed to mention in its editorial that the New York Times Company was pursuing a new office building in Times Square, and needed the city to use eminent domain because they wanted a building whose owner didn't want to sell.

Sidney Orbach owned a 16-story office building on 42nd Street, which ESDC condemned on the *Times*' behalf. While under threat of demolition, he received an offer from the *Times*, which he says was about one-fifth the value of the building. With millions in special tax subsidies, the *Times* has now finished (under budget) construction of their headquarters on what used to be Orbach's land. As of January 2006, Orbach still didn't have his money.[14]

"Public Use" and "Public Purpose"

Back in Harlem, the Minnichs eventually threw in the towel, took the check, and gave up the family business. Albany's actions were driving their legal bills sky-high and a continued fight would drive their bills to over half a million dollars. Realistically, the Minnich's odds of winning didn't look good if only because the state had the financial resources to fight longer than Minnich. Further, the courts have regularly sided with governments over landowners during the past half-century.

The stage for takings such as the East River Plaza was set back in 1954. Congress in 1945 passed the "District of Columbia Redevelopment Act" calling on the federal government to remove the slums and blight of DC "by employing all means necessary and appropriate."

Using this law, federal officials condemned hazardous slums, with no plan to transform them into schools, roads, or other such public uses. The Constitution, however, allows for eminent domain only for "public use." A

property owner in DC sued to keep his land, saying there was no justification for the eminent domain taking.

Although the government planned to sell this land to a private interest,
the Supreme Court, in the 1954 decision *Berman v. Parker,* found that the taking served a "public purpose" by getting rid of the ghettos. This subtle shift in
language from "public *use*" to "public *purpose*" opened the door wide for governments wishing to change the landscape of their cities. The court said that
governments were at liberty to define what was or wasn't a public purpose.[15]

This approach to eminent domain reared its head most notably in
1981, in a small suburb of Detroit. A neighborhood there (called Poletown,
because the population was primarily Polish immigrants), sat inconve-
niently where General Motors (GM) wanted to build a new plant. Detroit
officials thought this new plant would be the centerpiece of urban renewal
in a struggling city. Some of the residents sold, but others held out. The
local Catholic pastor led a resistance movement that was soon taken up by
GM scourge, Ralph Nader. With Nader came national media attention and
a big court case.

The Michigan Supreme Court ruled that Detroit was within its rights
to take all of the property in rundown Poletown by eminent domain and
then sell it to GM because it would serve a public purpose. In this context,
other states followed suit, expanding public purpose to mean increased tax
revenues, more jobs, and the promise of renewal. In such an environment,
no property, no matter how well maintained or productive, is safe as long
as some other use could generate more profit per square foot.

The issue of eminent domain came into the spotlight in June 2005
when the U.S. Supreme Court had a chance to overturn *Berman,* but instead
the Court affirmed the right of towns, cities, and counties to use eminent
domain in these ways. The *Kelo v. New London*[16] ruling was upsetting to most
property owners, but it particularly disturbed many liberal bloggers and
writers who tend to hate corporations and try to protect the little guy. These
writers were disturbed because the pro-big business opinion (allowing private homes to be taken by a developer for a corporate business park) was
written by the court's leading liberal, John Paul Stevens. On *Kelo,* all four of
the liberal justices ruled in favor of eminent domain for corporate gain,
while all three conservatives ruled against allowing the takings (and the
moderates split).

"You just own your house on suffrage," says Institute for Justice Senior
Attorney Dana Berliner. "It's yours until some big business wants it."[17] In
1776, this circumstance helped spur a rebellion and a war.

"Then We're Gonna Take Them"

Berliner's remark also describes the story of Bill Brody. Brody operates a hardware store and lumber shop in the Bronx, not far from the Westchester County border. Brody is not tall, and his serious face and New York accent convey what he is all about: getting the job done well and efficiently.

He has run the shop for 25 years, as both a manager and a craftsman. Sitting behind the little desk at the front of his shop, he says, "I can fix anything." It's not bragging. It's simply telling it like it is. In recent years, Brody the businessman and craftsman has been forced to become a lawyer, too. Big developers and eager local government have handed him a problem he may not be able to repair.

A few yards from Brody's shop runs U.S. Route 1. If you take a right on that road (called Boston Road at that point), you could follow it all the way down to Key West. If you go left, it takes you up through the varied towns of Westchester. Through the suburban enclave of Pelham, Route 1 forms the town's biggest intersection, called Four Corners, featuring two small shopping plazas, two parks, an office building, the Presbyterian church, and the town's best pizza place. The road crosses into New Rochelle, where it becomes Main Street, which once housed two movie theaters, but now seems to be mostly nail salons until you reach New Roc City, a shopping mall with a multiplex and an arcade—*the* place to be for local adolescents. Through Larchmont and Mamaroneck, Route 1 civilizes a bit, featuring old family restaurants and Irish Pubs, later hugging the shore of the Long Island Sound, fronting parks and country clubs. The road becomes downright bucolic as it passes through Rye, home of Playland amusement park and the solid public schools the Brody children attend. Just before crossing into famously posh Greenwich, Connecticut, and eventually on to Maine, Route 1 turns north, and runs alongside the small Byram River in the Village of Port Chester.

On this stretch of road, ragged by comparison to Rye and Mamaroneck, Brody bought the ugliest buildings on the block in 1996. Using his construction and repair dexterity, he fixed them up. "I spent four years of my life in those buildings," he says today, holding back a grimace. Brody rented them out to 10 businesses—businesses he felt elevated the street, which was the commercial center for the largely Hispanic immigrant community that lived around the area.

"That place was more or less gonna be my retirement." Brody uses the past tense because, in 2003, the Village of Port Chester sent in bulldozers and leveled the buildings—in the name of redevelopment. In 1999, the neighborhood was definitely on the way up. A man from G&S Investors approached Brody and told him they wanted to buy the buildings. "I'm not gonna sell," Brody told him.

"Then we're gonna take them," Brody remembers the developer saying. Bill Copella, a tenant of Brody who ran the laundromat ("the best, cleanest, cheapest laundromat in the neighborhood," Brody would boast) had heard chatter about the Village taking buildings through eminent domain as part of the Marina Redevelopment Project. Brody wanted to get to the bottom of the gossip and chatter, but when he called the Village government, they told him he would have to talk to the developers—the same experience Minnich had in New York City.

Brody soon figured out what was to become of his land. The property next to his was going to be a Stop n' Shop. The developers needed his land so that Stop n' Shop's patrons would have somewhere to park. "If a Stop n' Shop is a public use, then so were the businesses I already had in my shop," Brody objects.

The buildings, he says, were not blighted by any definition of the word. They were fully renovated, including a handicapped-accessible elevator. But they didn't fit the vision Port Chester officials had for the banks of the Byram. As with Minnich, the Village saw a public purpose here. The Stop n' Shop and the development as a whole would generate more jobs and more profit per square foot than would Brody's buildings. That would mean more tax revenue for the Village.

When the Village told him in April 2000 that they were going to take his property, he tried to file an appeal. However, under New York's Eminent Domain Procedure Law (EDPL), his deadline had long passed. He was legally prohibited from appealing the decision to condemn his property.

Brody has gone to federal court, arguing that the EDPL violates the 14th Amendment's due process requirements. But the Village has evicted all of the tenants and the developers demolished the buildings. Brody has won in court, and New York has changed its procedures, but Brody's buildings are gone.

"I Just Wanna Run My Business"

Sitting in his Bronx store, Brody tries to watch what he says because he still has cases pending. Our conversation was interrupted by Brody telling one angry customer to buzz off and later helping one of his workers sand down a wooden radiator cover. At one point in our talk, though, he blurts out, "if you look at the EDPL statute section 304, the law clearly says . . ."

This is a startling way for a carpenter to talk, but this is what his ordeal has done. Once a craftsman first and a businessman second, Brody is now a lawyer above all. "Who really wants to do this?" Brody asks, referring to his fight against the Village. "I just wanna be left alone. I just wanna run my business. I'm not one of those *green* people, going around to save the planet." This is what the partnership of big business and big government does—it degrades the virtues of the entrepreneur in favor of the lawyer and the lobbyist. Brody lost his retirement investment, and his hardware business has suffered because of the time he has invested in the case.

Of course, the developers were forced to hire lawyers and wrangle with politicians, too, but this is where their advantage lies. Litigating, lobbying, and politicking is a central part of the business of big developers. They have an infrastructure built in for doing this, and they have experience and expertise in those areas. If some area of law or politics arises where the big developers don't have an expert already on the payroll, they have the cash to hire one on the spot. Brody and Minnich never had staff lawyers, nor did they spend their careers building political connections or legal expertise. Instead, they spent their careers developing skills, customers, and employees.

The ESDC has a web site run out of Albany about the opportunities for businesses in New York state. One of the icons on the home page declares "NY [HEARTS] SMALL BIZ." If you follow that link, the ESDC has a "Business Readiness Plan," which includes a quiz to see if you're ready to start your business. The questions include, "Do you know what your business structure will be?" and, "If you will be hiring employees, do you know your Employer Obligations?"[18]

If it were to be complete, it would need to ask some other questions:

- "Do you read the legal notices in the *New York Times,* the *Daily News,* the *New York Post,* and all of the local papers every day?"
- "Do you have a staff lawyer who is familiar with Eminent Domain Procedure Law?"
- "Have you fostered good relationships with powerful local politicians of both parties, including generous campaign contributions?"
- "Are you ready to spend hundreds of thousands of dollars in legal fees and lose your property anyway?"

If They Can Take It There, They Can Take It Anywhere

Eminent domain for private gain may be most broken in New York, but the problem extends throughout the United States. The Institute for Justice, lawyers to both Brody and Minnich, compiles a list of what they consider eminent domain abuses. It's a long list.[19]

Three examples show how unsavory these takings and givings can be. In the late 1990s, Merriam, Kansas, had a BMW dealership right next to a used car dealership. The BMW dealer wanted to expand. William Gross, who owned the neighboring lot, did not want to sell. The town condemned Gross's lot, took it by eminent domain, and sold it to BMW because the luxury cars would sell for more, bringing in more tax revenue.

Las Vegas, Nevada, widow Carol Pappas lived off the rental income from a commercial building her late husband had left her. The Las Vegas Redevelopment Agency condemned her property in order to sell it to gambling interests who wanted to build a garage for the casinos.

DaimlerChrysler wanted to expand its operations in Toledo, Ohio, in 1999, but it ran out of room. Unwilling to lose the factory, city officials *made room*—by condemning 83 homes.

There are thousands of cases like these, with a similar theme: Big business uses big government to accomplish what it never could in a free market. The Institute for Justice counted over 10,000 filed or threatened condemnations for the benefit of private parties between 1998 and the end of 2002.

Dubious Benefits

Government claims that the new, bigger businesses broaden the tax base which allows for increased public services. Localities are not wrong to see big shopping centers in this light. The Port Chester development, for instance, will increase the number of dollars exchanged on Port Chester's Main Street, and thus fatten the government's coffers, which will allow for more spending on schools and public services. The jobs lost in the businesses eliminated in this case will be fewer than the new jobs the new stores will bring. Perhaps most important to local residents, in these less-than-tony neighborhoods of Port Chester and Harlem, is that being able to shop in the same high-quality, large-selection stores as the residents of Greenwich and Rye is a good thing.

Considered on a larger level, however, the reasoning is deeply flawed. On the moral level, taking people's property is stealing. Paying them for it does not change the fact that they did not want to give it up in the first place. Paying them for it in a "forced" sale almost guarantees that the price will not be fair. Imagine having to sell your house to one buyer who tells you what the price will be irrespective of other property values around you.

On a pragmatic level, this use of eminent domain also poses short- and long-term risks. Typically, after a developer or sports team gets land through eminent domain, localities give those same businesses special tax breaks as part of the whole central-planning project. Those tax breaks often erase the supposed tax benefits the new bigger business was supposed to provide. For example, sports stadiums, often the beneficiaries of eminent domain, tend to be net losers. In 2004, a Major League Baseball team came to Washington, DC, and Mayor Anthony Williams fell over himself trying to accommodate the Nationals. He promised a new stadium that was to be built with tax hikes and eminent domain. At the time, the Cato Institute released a study that reported:

> In stark contrast to the benefits claimed by most economic impact studies commissioned by teams or stadium advocates, the academic research overwhelmingly concludes that the presence of professional sports teams has no measurable positive impact on economic growth as measured by the level of real income in cities over a 35-year period. Our own research suggests that professional sports may actually be a drain on local economies rather than an engine of economic growth.[20]

Dozens of cities have taken land to give it to sports teams promising economic recovery but instead getting stagnation, if the Cato Institute is correct.

Frequent use of eminent domain creates its own long-term problems. It creates a disincentive for anyone to buy land. Just as someone would need a serious discount to buy a house in a flood plain, wherever the government can easily take your land away, property values will be dragged downward. In places such as Harlem, this effect is obscured by the overall rise in property value, but that rise might be stronger or more enduring if small property investors felt they could be as safe as the big companies in their right to keep their land.

Even renters face an additional risk, as Bill Copella and Bill Brody's other tenants found out. Who would invest in developing a loyal client base if he knew he might be forced by the government to move at any point?

As proof of this, after the Minnichs lost their woodworking shop, they gave up trying to do business in New York. Looking around, they noticed New Hampshire and bought a carwash there. William Minnich says they chose the "Live Free or Die" state because it had the best record of respecting private property and not using eminent domain.

Public opinion is fairly uniform that eminent domain for corporate gain is bad in principle, but folks sometimes have difficulty identifying the villain. It's easy to demonize Home Depot but perhaps not fair. First, the party doing the actual taking is the government, typically on behalf of a developer. Second, the party lobbying for the taking is usually the developer. Home Depot clearly profits from the taking, but should it be expected to pass on the offer of land obtained legally?

If a Home Depot or any other retail business declines the cut-rate property obtained by eminent domain, the developer will simply turn to its competitors. If you are Home Depot, do you bite on the great offer or say no on principle and lose the business?

Institute for Justice's Berliner sees reason for landowners to hope. The Michigan Supreme Court overturned its Poletown decision in 2004 (though far too late for the neighborhood's residents, of course).

Brody has won his lawsuit challenging New York's *process* of eminent domain, but real reform would mean limiting the state's right to condemn property and the meaning of public use. While the Supreme Court has refused to intervene, local and state legislatures are stepping in to limit the government's takings powers. In dozens of states and in Congress, lawmakers have proposed and passed laws doing just that.

Although eminent domain for private gain brings together government, developers, and big business on the same side, it often galvanizes neighborhoods and the media on the other. Public pressure in New Rochelle, New York, recently sunk that city's plan to replace a residential neighborhood with an Ikea.

While the *Kelo* ruling has eliminated federal courts as a possible avenue of relief, the public outcry following the ruling has already spurred elected officials to push laws limiting eminent domain for private gain.

PART III

REGULATE ME!

B ig business is often the chief lobbyist for, and the primary beneficiary of, government regulation. The media typically do not notice
this, while big corporate executives and bureaucrats obscure their
partnership, leaving the taxpayer, the consumer, the worker, and the entrepreneur in the dark about how big government and big business are ripping
them off through regulation.

The United States has the freest economy in the world, but still, the
U.S. marketplace has some restraints. The *Code of Federal Regulation* takes up
25 feet of shelf space according to Susan Dudley of the Mercatus Center,
containing hundreds of thousands of rules, restrictions, and requirements on
what people and businesses can, can't, or must do.

Politicians and bureaucrats often portray these regulations as tools for
restraining business in order to protect workers, consumers, the environment, or fair competition. Taking their word for it, the media tend to depict
any debate about regulation as a battle pitting the government against big
business, with big business asking to be left alone.

The truth is quite different. George Stigler, who won the Nobel Prize
for economics in 1982, laid out the true story clearly and convincingly in a
1971 essay. "Regulation," wrote Stigler, "is acquired by the industry and is
designed and operated primarily for its benefit."[1]

At the same time, many of these regulations do not address legitimate needs of the people, or they address them ineffectively. That means that many government regulations act like corporate welfare: They enrich big business at the expense of consumers, competitors, and taxpayers.

How Does Regulation Hurt Me?

Every proposed regulation has its detractors and its supporters, as do all existing regulations. This much is true: Every regulation imposes a new cost. Whether that cost outweighs the benefit is usually the matter for debate.

Regulations take up the resources of businesses. This will almost always result in business raising prices, decreasing services, cutting jobs, or—if a company finds it cannot do any of those things—going out of business. Sometimes, we think these costs are worth the gains. Rules requiring fire escape routes from workplaces certainly add to the costs of businesses, but if it saves lives, most people would think it is worth it. But rules requiring florists to take costly courses and get licensed before arranging a bouquet impose high costs for no real benefit—except to the existing florists who get to keep their competition away and their prices high.

How Does Regulation Help
Big Business?

If regulation is costly, why would big business favor it? Precisely *because* it is costly.

Regulation adds to the basic cost of doing business, thus heightening barriers to entry and reducing the number of competitors. Thinning out the competition allows surviving firms to charge higher prices to customers and demand lower prices from suppliers. Overall, regulation adds to overhead and is a net boon to those who can afford it—big business.

Put another way, regulation can stultify the market. If you're already at the top, stultification is better than the robust dynamism of the free market. According to Nobel Laureate economist Milton Friedman:

> The great virtue of free enterprise is that it forces existing businesses to meet the test of the market continuously, to produce products that meet consumer demands at lowest cost, or else be driven from the

market. It is a profit-*and-loss* system. Naturally existing businesses prefer to keep out competitors in other ways. That is why the business community, despite its rhetoric, has so often been a major enemy of truly free enterprise.[2]

There is an additional systemic reason why regulation will help big business. Congress passes the laws that order new regulations, and executive branch agencies actually construct the regulations. The politicians and government lawyers who write these rules rarely do so without input. Often the rule makers ask for advice and information from labor unions, consumer groups, environmental groups, and industry itself. Among industry, the *stakeholders* (beltway parlance to describe affected parties) who have the most input are those who can hire the most effective and most connected lobbyists. You can guess that isn't Mom n' Pop.

As a result, the details of the regulation are often carefully crafted to benefit, or at least not hurt, big business. If something does not hurt you, or hurts you a little while seriously hindering your competition, it is a boon, on balance.

Another reason big business often cries "regulate me!" is the goodwill factor. If a politician or a bureaucrat wants to play a role in some industry, and some executive says, "get lost," he runs the risk of offending this powerful person. That's bad diplomacy. Bureaucrats, by their nature, do not like to be told to mind their own business. Supporting the idea of regulation but lobbying for particular details is usually better politics.

Finally, there is the principal-agent problem. In a business, who is doing the actual lobbying for or against a regulation? It is typically the company's government relations person. His or her job is to work with regulators and help the company find its way through the maze of regulation. To the extent government gets out of his or her company's hair, the government relations executive becomes less important.

Big Business Loves Taxes, Too

Taxes are similar to regulation—both impose costs on economically productive activity with the promise of furthering some other social good. There's another similarity: Big business often supports higher taxes.

This belies the common line that tax cuts help the rich—if big business is included in "the rich." When this dynamic of pro-tax businesses becomes known, it strains the friendship between businesses and their supposed patrons in the Republican Party. Big business can have all sorts of reasons for favoring taxes, ranging from obvious self-interest to long-term strategy to cunning economic calculations.

For many big businesses, their prime customer—or only customer—is the government. If you live off of porkbarrel spending or government contracts, you need fat government coffers.

For others, higher taxes offer the same benefits as stricter regulation. High taxes hurt small business more than they hurt industry giants. A complex tax code is a barrier to entry and provides opportunities for the wealthier and more connected corporations.

This Part

Some regulations you were told would help you, really just help big business. Many regulations you've never heard of and never could have imagined are making your life more expensive today while helping big business stay big by keeping out their competition. This section shows you just how regulation can rip you off for the benefit of big business.

In these chapters, we recall the twisted tale of airline regulation, wherein politicians and airline chiefs conspired for decades to make sure nobody would ever have to cut prices or innovate. We also meet some small businessmen, such as a gardener in Tucson, whom the government has kept from making a living in a misguided attempt to protect consumers or perhaps in an underhanded scheme to protect big business. We see why the war against tobacco is less an effort to make America healthy than it is a racket for trial lawyers and Philip Morris. Finally, we see just why the likes of Warren Buffett, the Chamber of Commerce, and Kaiser Permanente work desperately to keep your taxes high.

7

Regulators and Robber Barons

How Government Regulation Protects the Big Guys and Rips Off the Little Guys

Pistol in hand, his open shirt flapping in the wind, Ed Daly was trying to get his plane off the ground. At the foot of the stairwell of his Boeing 747, the amateur-boxer-turned-airline-executive beat back the soldiers trying to board his plane—the last flight out of Da Nang, a South Vietnamese city about to fall to the Vietcong.

Daly finally climbed aboard, raised the ramp, and shut the doors, with an unruly throng of Vietnamese soldiers still on the tarmac. He gave the order, and pilot Ken Healy got ready to take off. Someone had turned off the runway lights. Machine-gun fire rang out below. One solider fired his pistol just past the cockpit window. The runway was littered with trucks and other vehicles driven by the frantic soldiers and refugees who wanted to board this last plane to safety. The control tower radioed in to Healy and Daly, "Don't take off! Don't take off!"

Healy, taking a cue from his boss's bravado, sent one last message to the tower: "Just watch me." With a wing flap damaged by a grenade, Healy, Daly, and over 300 South Vietnamese refugees took off in the dark. Healy could not lift the landing gears—seven of the refugees had packed into the wheel wells. He also couldn't climb above 10,500 feet—dozens of Vietnamese were crammed in the cargo holds, which could not be pressurized.

Daly and Healy brought these refugees to safety in Saigon, where they would eventually be taken out of a country that American soldiers had already abandoned. Daly's flight marked the end of the U.S. effort to save refugees from Da Nang, which was reportedly about to be sacked by the Vietcong. His flight was also unauthorized—Washington had called off the refugee airlift the day before.

A few days later, Daly led "Operation Babylift," flying Vietnamese orphans from Saigon's Tan Son Nhut airport, darkened and also under threat of Vietcong attack, to Oakland, California, from which point they would be placed with American families and many set on the road to normal lives. This flight, too, was unauthorized. "I've been told for 25 years I've been in this business that things can't be done. But I'm a believer," Daly said.[1]

Back home, the newspapers and networks sang Daly's praise. "The Bravest Man in South Vietnam," blared one headline. The attention served Daly's other purpose well—fighting the U.S. government.

The Da Nang flight was on Saturday, March 29, 1975. The Tan Son Nhut flight took off against orders on Wednesday, April 2. On Friday, in Washington, DC, Ed Daly's lawyers made a visit to the Civil Aeronautics Board (CAB). Their visit had nothing to do with orphans or refugees. In fact, their request was not a new one at all.

Daly owned World Airways, which flew cargo and charter flights. In the 1960s, Daly hatched a plan to start regular passenger flights from coast to coast for less than $100—cheaper than riding the Greyhound bus. But the federal airline regulations of those days forbade any airline, even one used and trusted by the federal government (the Pentagon contracted World to fly cargo to Vietnam during the war), from flying a passenger route without CAB approval. As a result, not a single new airline had entered the passenger flight business since 1955.

Daly tried to break that streak in 1967, filing a petition to fly cheap coast-to-coast flights. He would cram the passengers into narrower seats with no-frills box lunches instead of the luxurious in-flight meals typical of the time. Customers, he told the government, would sacrifice space and food quality for low prices.

But the CAB did not jump at the idea. In fact, Daly never even got a hearing with the CAB for his 1967 proposal. After five years, the CAB threw out his application. The cause for dismissal: The request was now "stale."[2]

On April 4, 1975, days after his infamous flights out of Vietnam, Daly got the attention of the CAB. He filed a nearly identical request with the CAB—he still wanted to fly people coast-to-coast for $89 one way, or $194 roundtrip, counting taxes and charges. The going rate at the time was $388 roundtrip.[3] A CAB staffer told the *Chicago Tribune*, "In today's climate there is nothing about Edward J. Daly that's going to get stale."[4]

Despite the adulation in the press, Daly had his critics. The U.S. embassy in Saigon was clearly not pleased with him. His detractors called his rescue flights foolhardy and even said his rescue missions were a publicity stunt aimed at improving the odds of his CAB petition. Even those who admired his actions granted that there was some truth to this last accusation.

The critique of Daly should have served as an indictment of federal airline regulation: If a man spent a week flying in and out of Vietnamese airports, dodging bullets and grenades, and defying the orders of airport officials, with the Vietcong closing in, as a lobbying ploy, the government had too tight a grip on the airline industry.

Because no airline could fly a route unless the CAB granted approval, passengers often only had one or two options for most routes. Just as the CAB declared who flew where, the agency also set the price of the flight. The CAB determined the price of a ticket by estimating the cost of the flight and predicting the number of passengers, and then allowed for a profit of 12 percent. When some airlines tried to offer discount fares, the CAB said no.

One aviation expert in the days after Daly's flights told the *Chicago Tribune* about the industry, "you can't blow your nose without approval from Washington."[5] In short, the government had total control over what the airlines could do and what they could charge for it. The big airlines loved it.

Daly's flights came at the beginning of an era in Washington when some staffers in Congress and in the executive branch were beginning to take seriously the idea of deregulating the airways, but the big airlines fought to preserve the strict regulation. Before telling the end of Daly's tale, it is worthwhile to discuss more of the historical background of federal regulation of the air.

"A Naive and Dangerous Idea": Consumer Choice

Deregulatory fever was sweeping through all aspects of air travel in the 1970s, including charter flights, which the government also controlled. In

1974, Congress considered deregulating the industry. One witness before Congress was vehement against deregulation. Paul Ignatius, president of the Air Transport Association, whose members included all the major airlines, testified that allowing more laissez-faire in charter flights would be "the beginning of the end of the nation's air transportation system as we know it today."[6]

No one should be surprised that Ignatius would like burdensome regulations on a competing industry, but some might wonder why the big passenger airlines also wanted to keep *themselves* regulated. And boy, were they *regulated*.

Even if an airline could acquire the requisite airport slots, planes, pilots, staff, safety standards, and customers, it could not fly a new route unless the CAB decided that allowing the new entry was "required by public convenience and necessity," according to law. If someone else was already flying that route, it would be hard to argue that redundancy was necessary. Many of the routes in the 1970s were the same as they had been for decades, since Herbert Hoover and his Postmaster General Walter Folger Brown parceled them out in 1930. The idea back then was that the post office would pay private companies to fly its mail. The airlines would also pack passengers onto their mail flights. Author W. David Lewis, in his history of the airline industry makes it clear that Brown, a Progressive like Teddy Roosevelt, believed that bigger was better:

> One of [Brown's] primary aims was to put airmail operations in the hands of large, well-financed corporations and weed out small operators who lacked the means to carry out his ambitious plans. Summoning representatives of leading airmail carriers to Washington, he forced them to submit to mergers establishing three large transcontinental systems. . . . Small businessmen were not invited to the meetings, and they had to sell out to the big companies.[7]

United, American, TWA, Eastern, and later Delta controlled the market for long-range domestic flights. Competing directly with these five giants was, in effect, illegal. Because the CAB also set the prices, the profits were small—in fact, the smallest of any industry in the 1960s and 1970s. A 1977 study by the General Accounting Office (GAO) would find that between 1969 and 1974, regulation added nearly $2 billion every year to the airlines' operating costs.[8] Although costs were high and profits small, the profits were steady—for anyone lucky enough to have CAB permission to fly. The five big domestic airlines in 1975—American, Delta, Eastern, TWA, and United—controlled nearly 70 percent of the industry.[9]

Sure, the regulation protected big business, but maybe it was ultimately to the benefit of consumers? It doesn't seem so. The GAO found that prices were higher, costing consumers about $1.8 billion per year in higher ticket prices. When the U.S. Senate looked at the cost of regulation, it determined that customers paid as much as $3.5 billion extra per year.[10] For these higher prices, customers received frills they would not have paid for in a free market: more stewardesses, prettier stewardesses, piano bars, and planes that were 50 percent empty. In effect, you had no choice but to fly first class. There is no evidence that flights were safer before deregulation than they are now.

As the industry began to grow, the companies soon learned that the most important asset to have was good relationship with the federal government. Lewis's excellent history of early airline executives demonstrates this pattern clearly. Who did well? Lewis writes: "The pathway to success . . . was exemplified by the burgeoning career of C. R. Smith, president of American Airlines."[11] Smith had cut his teeth on government, working with FDR's Works Progress Administration, becoming operational chief of the Air Transport Council. He "had close ties with a galaxy of powerful government leaders, including Jesse Jones, Sam Rayburn, and Lyndon B. Johnson." Later, Smith became Johnson's secretary of commerce.

Who did poorly? Eastern Airlines' Eddie Rickenbacker, for one, he wanted nothing to do with government. Lewis writes:

> Rickenbacker was a throwback to an earlier era of unbridled free enterprise. His fierce entrepreneurial spirit and dedication to the work ethic made him a living symbol of the American Dream, but his passionate individualism, grounded in traditions of self-help that had once been dominant in a nation that he loved as a bastion of human liberty, put him at odds with the New Deal and everything it stood for.[12]

In 1975, with the New Deal a generation in the past, the CAB considered loosening restrictions on the industry. Columnist George Will described the industry response:

> Most American corporations divide their energies between denouncing regulation in general and lobbying like furies against a dread specter of deregulation plans that affect them. Recently, for example, the three largest domestic airlines—United, American, TWA—joined in denouncing a CAB plan for permitting a smidgen of flexibility— which might mean competition—in route structures and pricing.[13]

President Gerald Ford that same year threatened the big airlines' pleasantly rigid oligopoly by proposing a bill to abolish CAB price controls and route controls, thus allowing airlines to do largely what they please.

The biggest airlines counterattacked even before Ford introduced a bill. Delta's Senior Vice President for Finance Robert Oppenlander, speaking at Harvard Business School's transportation club, objected that Ford's plans, "could lead to the possible destruction and at the very least a severe disruption of the air transportation system in this country."[14]

Five states away that day, United Chairman Edward Carlson also foresaw disaster if Washington deregulated. In front of a conference of the Federal Aviation Administration in Chicago, he predicted that "profits would vanish and financial problems would follow." He added, "in general we believe that our regulators are doing a creditable job."[15]

The *Washington Post* the next day reported, "Both Oppenlander and Carlson defended the present CAB-regulated air transport system, claiming it is efficient, safe, inexpensive compared to other goods and services."[16]

American Airlines joined its fellow industry leaders. The November 21, 1975, *Chicago Tribune* carried a story under the surprised headline, "What's this? Airline chief wants continued control." American Airlines President Al Casey opposed Ford's deregulation, saying it would send many airlines into bankruptcy.[17] On another occasion, Casey predicted deregulation would cause "grave and irreparable damage" to the industry.[18]

Harding Lawrence, the president of Braniff International, another leading airline of the day warned, "there would be chaos."[19] In June 1976, TWA Chairman Charles Tillinghast testified to the Aviation subcommittee of the Senate Commerce Committee and chastised CAB (TWA was suffering) but opposed the sort of broad-based deregulation that Ford and Kennedy were discussing. At the same hearing, Richard Maurer, Delta's senior vice president, called for some added fare flexibility, but said: "The existing Federal Aviation Act of 1958 is a good flexible law which has served the nation well, continues to do so, and needs little alteration." Bolder deregulation, he argued, would ruin the industry.[20] These airline titans certainly did not ask to be unchained.

Ford's bill never passed, but the idea of deregulation did not die. Perhaps hoping to dissuade President-elect Jimmy Carter from following in Ford's free-market footsteps, in November 1976, American Airlines' Al Casey wrote a small Op-Ed for the *New York Times*. It began: "A naïve and dangerous idea is abroad in the land—the notion that a major change in airline regulation can somehow yield, as if by magic, better service and lower fares for everyone."[21]

In February 1977, Senator Ted Kennedy introduced a deregulation bill much like Ford's bill. Days later, the airline industry again spoke up. The *New*

York Times reported: "William E. Jackman, assistant vice president of the Air Transportation Association, said . . . that the carriers fear disruption of services if airlines were allowed to enter or leave various markets at will."[22] The *Times* article quoted Jackman: "We know there is change in the air. We welcome some right to be flexible in fares, and we want the regulatory process made quicker and more efficient, but the freedom to change routes would jeopardize less lucrative markets and harm the airport operators."

One of the biggest carriers of the time was Eastern Airlines. In March 1977, Eastern President Frank Borman told a Senate subcommittee that deregulation bills "threatened the very basic core of our system." Granting airlines the liberty to set prices as they wish "ultimately could destroy our air transportation network," Borman claimed. He conceded that some reforms could be made to airline regulations, but he demanded that new rules preserve CAB limitations on new entries into routes and firm limits on ticket pricing.[23]

Borman's dire prediction—that air travel would disappear if the government did not protect it with regulations—is a common objection of industry chiefs when deregulation or subsidy cuts are proposed. Behind Borman's claim was the implicit suggestion that price wars and competitions would drive profits so low that *every* airline would go out of business—an impossible argument on its face. History has shown Borman's warnings to be overblown. Instead, the poorly run airlines, such as Eastern in 1991, have gone out of business, leaving the more efficient ones that are better at giving the consumers what they want. With Borman's doomsday warning, all five of the biggest domestic airlines—American, Delta, Eastern, TWA, and United—had come out against deregulation.

Not every airline executive wanted to keep the regulations in place, though. Pan Am and USAir were the most notable proponents of deregulation. Pan Am flew only internationally, and it wanted to break into the domestic market—an expansion that regulation prevented. USAir was the upstart airline of the day, only recently having changed its name from Allegheny to USAir, trying to show it was a national carrier. Continental, also not one of the big five, wanted to fly to Hawaii, and so favored deregulation. Southwest, which had avoided federal regulation by flying only within the borders of Texas, was happy about the proposition of expanding beyond the Lone Star State.

In 1978, Congress passed, and President Carter signed, a bill dramatically rolling back the regulation of the airlines. Since then, some of the big airlines' fears have come true: Eastern and TWA have gone out of business, and United and Delta are in bankruptcy in early 2006 (though one could

argue that these bankruptcies are more a restructuring of poor management decisions than a result of bad business conditions or deregulation).
Southwest has thrived, and many little airlines have entered the market, including Independence Air for a brief stint and JetBlue. USAir had some
good years before running into trouble. American adapted and prospered
in the liberalized air. Pan Am bet wrong, it appears, and withered away in
the competitive deregulated market. In short, since deregulation, airfares
have decreased, routes have increased, safety has stayed the same (or improved), and excepting security issues that have led to travel headaches,
consumers are better served by the industry in 2006 than they were in
1976.

And Ed Daly, the gun-toting cargo cowboy, was finally able to enter the
passenger-flight business, taking customers from coast-to-coast for less than
a bus ticket, setting off legendary price wars to the thrill of customers.

Paper Tigers

At the Madison Hotel on 15th and M in downtown Washington, DC, a
Transportation Department lawyer sat down with two cargo shippers the
night before the lawyer was scheduled to testify to Congress. The lawyer,
John Barnum, wanted to go before a House subcommittee the next day and
tell Congress to loosen its tight regulations on cargo flights, which were just
as regulated as passenger flights.

His bosses said he could only take such a bold stance if he got approval
from these two men, Joe Healy and Wayne Hoffman. Healy was the president of the Flying Tigers, at the time the largest cargo air carrier in the
country. Hoffman was the Tigers' Chairman and CEO.[24]

Healy and Hoffman said no. The hearings and Barnum's request were
the fruit of a public relations campaign by a start-up cargo shipper named
Fred Smith. Smith, like Daly, had flown in Vietnam—but Smith as a pilot
for the Marines. His company, Federal Express (FedEx), did things differently than other shippers. Everything that FedEx carried would go
through the central facility in Memphis, Tennessee. If you were shipping
something from New York to Miami, it would go through Memphis. If
you were shipping something from Buffalo to Boston, it would go through
Memphis.

Of course, this novel model created some inefficiencies, with many
packages covering the same ground twice, but it eliminated many other in-

efficiencies. Consider this hypothetical model: If a business always flew everything from the city of pickup directly to the city of delivery, and it had customers in 100 cities, it would have 9,900 routes (planes flying out of 100 cities, each to 99 other cities). Smith's hub system would have only 200 routes (100 flying into Memphis, and 100 flying out of Memphis). This meant that *every* package coming out of New York, whether it was headed to L.A., Miami, Boston, or Newark, would be on the same plane to Memphis—creating a squeeze on FedEx's cargo space.

Smith's model cut costs dramatically and enabled him to lower prices. This drew customers away from the older cargo carriers. Consequently, FedEx soon had too much cargo going into and out of some of the major markets—the cargo could not fit on one plane.

The CAB would not let him fly a bigger plane though—the regulations dictated the size of the planes, too. Smith, then, had to fly two planes wing-to-wing between Memphis and his biggest markets. Smith launched a publicity campaign, pleading for looser rules that would allow him to fly a bigger plane. It worked, and Smith was able to gain Congress's attention enough to get a hearing.

Barnum, then, was not surprised when Healy and Hoffman, the bosses of the cargo industry's leading shipper, gave him the red light. They wanted the strict regulations of their industry kept in place.

Regulation certainly imposed costs on the Flying Tigers, and deregulation would provide some benefits to the company. FedEx, however, would benefit far more from looser rules. The rules imposed a smaller burden on those shippers who followed a more traditional business model with less-packed planes on more routes. But the rules stifled upstart Smith's innovation—which was good news for the reigning kings of the mountain, Healy and Hoffman.

So, for a time, the strict regulations stayed in place. This perseverance of big government was good for big business (Flying Tigers, in this case), and bad for the smaller, up-and-coming business (FedEx). The regulation was also bad for consumers, who would have benefited from lower prices if Smith had been able to cut his costs by flying one plane. Such is often the case in the world of business regulation—to the extent government has control of industry, big business gains while consumers and competitors suffer.

Eventually, Congress would deregulate cargo flights, and the little cargo shipper, FedEx, became the big cargo shipper, in the end swallowing the Flying Tigers. Soon enough, though, as tends to happen in a free market, new competitors arose in the liberalized market, including Airborne Express, DHL, and UPS.

Frankenfood's Monster: More Regulation

Bill Clinton hardly slept for those last few days. During that week in mid-January 2001, the outgoing president refused to go gently into the role of private citizen. By never resting, Clinton hoped to make the final hours of his presidency "feel like four years."[25]

His goal, he said, was to leave a lasting legacy that President-elect George W. Bush could not easily undo. In this, Clinton succeeded. A *Newsweek* article a month later explained: "He created eight new national monuments, nominated nine federal judges, packed federal commissions with political allies—and, in a final flurry of executive orders and rules, wrote hundreds of new federal regulations filling nearly 4,000 pages."[26]

Most famously, in the waning hours of his reign, Bill Clinton issued a pardon to Marc Rich, a fugitive financier, who fled the country in the 1985 while facing a slew of federal criminal charges including tax evasion, fraud, and trading with the enemy. Rich's wife Denise had raised more than $1 million for the Clintons.

Rich was not the only big businessman to receive an 11th-hour favor from Clinton. Biotech giant Monsanto also got a last-second gift—in the form of a proposed regulation.

The January 18, 2001, *Federal Register* included a proposed rule from the Food and Drug Administration (FDA) that would impose new restrictions on any company that sells genetically modified foods. The rule would require that companies submit information about their genetically modified food 120 days before releasing the food onto the market.[27]

While a drug company may not introduce a new drug into the U.S. market without prior approval from the FDA, a food company or farmer can sell food unless the FDA finds it dangerous. In other words, drugs are assumed unsafe until proven safe, while food is presumed safe until proven dangerous. Clinton's 11th-hour rule would put genetically modified foods somewhere between drugs and nongenetically modified food. A company would not need FDA *approval* before selling a genetically modified food product, but it would need to give the FDA 120 days to review the proposed product and possibly ban it.

For every new food product a company wanted to sell, this rule would impose an estimated 209 more hours of drudgework. That's more than five weeks of labor. The FDA estimated the rule could cost genetically modified food makers as much as $67,444 per year. Also, the rule would make it more likely that the FDA could reject a proposed food product before it ever reached the market.

Monsanto loved the rule. As the nation's largest producer of genetically modified food, Monsanto is notorious among anti-genetically-modified-food activists, and its name is synonymous with big biotech. On May 2, 2001, Monsanto filed its comment with the FDA on the proposed mandate. "Monsanto supports the FDA's framework for regulating foods and feeds produced through biotechnology," wrote Sheila A. Schuette, Monsanto's director of regulatory affairs. "Monsanto supports the FDA's initiative to require a Premarket Biotechnology Notice (PBN) notice at least 120 days prior to the commercial distribution of a food or feed produced through biotechnology." The letter continued:

> Monsanto has always voluntarily consulted with the FDA before placing any new food or feed on the market. We believe that a mandatory regulatory system will further assure the American public that the FDA processes for regulating foods and feeds, including those derived from biotechnology, are both rigorous and appropriate.[28]

Schuette suggested a few revisions to the FDA's proposed rule, never asking the FDA to narrow the scope or lighten the burden of the rule.

Monsanto was hardly alone among big biotech firms. The next day, the FDA received a similar letter, this one from the Biotechnology Industry Organization (BIO). Biotechnology Industry Organization is one of the leading lobbyists on Capitol Hill, well funded by members such as Monsanto, Bayer, and Dow. Biotechnology Industry Organization's letter read like Monsanto's. "BIO strongly endorses a mandatory premarket notification process that will ensure review by the Food and Drug Administration . . . of all food and feed products produced using biotechnology." BIO stated its members "fully support a rigorous FDA review process."[29]

Again, this regulation would have imposed a new requirement on biotech companies—submitting a PBN to the FDA 120 days before releasing a new food product. On top of the estimated 209 hours per new product the regulation would impose on biotech companies,[30] the FDA estimated that the rule would cost companies tens of thousands of dollars per year.[31]

So, why would Monsanto and BIO support such a costly rule? Their motives, as usual in business, are complex, and somewhat opaque. The available information gives us some clues.

We can start with the public reason Monsanto and BIO gave for supporting the rule, which is also the argument the FDA itself gave: boosting public confidence in genetically modified foods.

"Jeannette Glew," wrote a reporter for the *Fort Myers News-Press* in April 2001, "an FDA environmental scientist, said the new rules were proposed to keep public confidence in the food supply."[32] Senator Dick Durbin, a Democratic member on the Agriculture Appropriations subcommittee, sounded the same theme in endorsing the rule. Durbin, in support of the rule, wrote:

> Biotechnology has enormous potential to improve our nation's food supply, and I am concerned about the adverse impacts if the American public were to lose confidence in the safety of foods produced through biotechnology. The Food and Drug Administration has taken a good first step in bolstering public confidence by issuing its January 18, 2001, proposed rule. . . . Public confidence will be well-served by changing the status of pre-market reviews from voluntary to mandatory.[33]

For Durbin, the primary benefit of this rule was clear. The senator mentioned public confidence in genetically modified foods three times in three sentences. It's no surprise that Monsanto and BIO would support regulation that would bolster public confidence in their product. Indeed, any company facing questionable public confidence in its products would love to have the government work actively to boost that confidence. Is it a legitimate role of a federal agency to build up confidence for specific products and services? Shouldn't that be the job of the people making and selling those products and services?

Most businesses need to do the hard work of boosting consumer confidence themselves. Some businesses offer introductory discounts to lure new customers, or hire trusted public figures to endorse their product. Small, local, family-owned businesses might spend generations building community confidence. Monsanto and BIO found a way to have the government do it for them.

The confidence argument also raises another question: Shouldn't FDA regulations be aimed at making food *safer*? But that wasn't the argument the FDA gave. Indeed, in the rule itself, the FDA wrote, "there does not appear to be any new scientific information that raises questions about the safety of bioengineered foods currently being marketed."[34] While it was drafting the regulation, the FDA judged that genetically modified foods were not different from nongenetically modified foods. This echoed the view of most of the scientific community. The National Academy of Sciences, the American Dietetic Association, the American Medical Association, and many other scientific groups have all agreed that genetically modified foods pose no new risk that traditionally bred foods do not. The Royal Society of London, the Brazilian Academy of Sciences, the Chinese Academy of Sciences, the Indian National Science Academy, and the Mexican Academy of Sciences concur.

Biotechnology Industry Organization, Monsanto, and the FDA, therefore, were all pushing a rule that addressed no real safety concerns but imposed heavy costs on food companies. For the cynical reader, those regulatory costs give another clue to big biotech's support of the rule. Requiring the 120-day PBN adds to the cost of introducing a new product. This acts as a barrier to entry, which favors the entrenched, well-capitalized firms, such as Monsanto, Pfizer, and Novartis. The details of the proposed rule itself contain even more signs that this regulation would hurt potential competitors more than the existing giants of the genetically modified food industry.

"FDA finds that this proposed rule would have a significant economic impact on a substantial number of small entities," the rule reads.[35] But this finding apparently didn't faze the FDA much, because the rule rejected the notion of special accommodations for small businesses.

Additionally, the rule would create a bias in favor of existing companies by making mandatory what the existing businesses were already doing. As the FDA put it, "FDA believes that, to date, all developers of bioengineered foods commercially marketed in the United States have consulted with the agency prior to marketing the food."[36]

If, as a company, you are already doing more than the government requires (and, in this case, more than sound science requires), it is in your interest to push the government to *require* what you are doing—thus creating a new barrier to entry.

The regulations would impose a greater burden on new companies than on existing companies in hours per product and dollars per product. The FDA's estimate of 190 hours to prepare a PBN was an estimate of the additional burden on companies that are already voluntarily consulting with the FDA. The FDA rule suggests that the new regulation would cost a new company about 255.5 hours of preparation,[37] or 34 percent more than it would cost an existing company.

Additionally, the rule proposed that any food derived from a plant line already submitted to the FDA be exempt from the required 120-day PBN. In other words, Monsanto's improvements on its existing products would not face any additional scrutiny under the new rule.[38]

While Monsanto and BIO lauded the rule, opponents of genetically modified food lambasted it. Greenpeace and many similar groups resist genetically modified organisms (GMO), arguing that they pose unknown dangers to consumers and farmers. These anti-GMO groups wanted stricter rules that would require safety testing before any genetically modified food could be allowed on the market—in other words, they want genetically modified foods to be treated like drugs. They also wanted mandatory labeling.

This provides an insight into another reason why big businesses sometimes support government regulation. Monsanto and BIO may have hoped that if the proposed 120-day notification were put into place, some of the wind would be taken out of the sails of the anti-GMO crowd calling for more drastic regulations that could possibly be harmful to the biotech companies.

While Monsanto and BIO filed their letters supporting the rules, thousands of private citizens and activists were mailing in postcards and letters calling for tougher rules. Many of these letters came from campaigns sponsored by Greenpeace, Whole Foods, and others, arguing that genetically modified foods were fundamentally different from "regular" food and thus posed unknown risks. The FDA rejected this argument.

On this subject, Monsanto and BIO have not gotten their wish. The 120-day rule, proposed in Clinton's final hours, has withered in the Bush administration. But big biotech has continued to battle for bigger government. Biotechnology Industry Organization and some of its members fought in 2002 for strict government oversight of a process called *biopharming* in which some plants are genetically modified so that they contain certain pharmaceuticals.[39]

The current federal involvement in genetically modified foods, through regulations and proposed regulations—by the FDA, the Environmental Protection Agency, and the United States Department of Agriculture—has already had the effect big business might desire: consolidation of the industry. Authors Henry Miller and Gregory Conko describe the effects of government involvement in genetically modified foods:

> When the late-stage development of new, gene-spliced crop varieties requires field trials, financial resources can be quickly consumed by pa-

perwork burdens and superfluous tests and analyses. The biggest casu-
alties have been research and development by small firms and university laboratories.[40]

Twelve major biotech corporations in 1994 have, through a series of
mergers, become six. Miller and Conko write, "Today, the six remaining
major agbiotech companies—BASF, Bayer, Dow, DuPont, Monsanto, and
Syngenta—have achieved virtual monopoly."[41]

On another front, Miller and Conko argue that big biotech's pro-
regulation stance has backfired. They argue that attempts to appease the anti-
GMO crowd will never work. No amount of regulation, short of banning
genetically modified foods altogether will satisfy this crowd, they argue.
Halfway measures simply grant legitimacy to the position that genetically
modified foods are scary and need to be regulated more than "normal" food.

Consumers and taxpayers, as always, feel the most acute cost. If Clinton's regulation had gone through, consumers would pay more for genetically modified foods, so that the FDA could study them, even though the
scientific community agrees they warrant no more study than non-GMO
food. The regulation would also keep universities or smaller food companies
from entering the market, preventing some food products from ever coming
to be. Of course, the regulation would make new work for the FDA, costing
the taxpayers.

Regulation in Your Water—And Hair, and Lawn, and Cable TV

Adam Vinatieri deserves a spot alongside Joe Montana, Bart Starr, and Vince
Lombardi as a Super Bowl legend. The kid who played soccer at Central
High School in Rapid City, South Dakota, was the hero in two of the most
exciting moments in Super Bowl history.

In January 2002, after a breakneck drive led by rookie quarterback, Tom
Brady put the underdog Patriots within striking distance of the goliath St.
Louis Rams. Vinatieri booted a 48-yard field goal as time expired to give the
Pats the win 20–17.

Two years later, this time playing the favorite, Vinatieri did it again,
kicking a game-winner at the buzzer to give the Patriots their second title
in three years. But Vinatieri does not even approach the fame of Montana or
Lombardi. Partly, this is due to the sad anonymity kickers endure in the

NFL. Mostly, it is because someone else stole the headlines at Super Bowl XXXVIII.

The morning after the Patriots' second thrilling title, more Americans were talking about Janet Jackson's right breast than Vinatieri's right foot. The "wardrobe malfunction," as her costar Justin Timberlake called it, stole the headlines, and ignited a firestorm. In Washington, DC, of course, the incident sparked proposed new laws and regulations.

Lawmakers called for stricter punishment of indecency, but some parent groups wanted more—they wanted a way to protect their children from seeing smut in the first place, not merely punishment for anyone who airs it.

Senator John McCain proposed one idea: require cable companies to offer channels *a la carte*. Consumers, then, would have more choices than merely basic, expanded, gold, or whatever. Customers could then choose which channels they wanted and pay for only those channels. A parent could order such premium channels as Discovery Channel, Food Network, or the History Channel, but keep out more objectionable stuff like HBO, MTV, and, presumably, whoever was carrying the Super Bowl that year. McCain would describe his idea as *allowing consumers* to buy channels *a la carte*. More accurately, he wanted to *force cable companies* to offer channels *a la carte*.

Cable companies had voluntarily tried this approach before, but found it unworkable. Four barriers stood in the way. First, *true a la carte* was prevented in some cases by federal rules ("must-carry") requiring cable providers to carry broadcast channels, such as the local ABC or NBC. Second, cable *programmers,* the middlemen between the stations and the cable providers, typically "bundled" stations together, meaning the cable providers usually couldn't buy channels *a la carte*. Third, the experiments with *a la carte* in the 1990s showed that the economics of *a la carte* just did not work. Finally, the technology required to control, in minute detail, which stations went into which houses would be prohibitively expensive.

For the most part, cable companies rejected McCain's proposal. The National Cable and Telecommunications Association officially came out against mandatory *a la carte,* filing a comment on August 13, 2004, arguing that such a regulation would raise prices for consumers and hurt cable companies. On that same day, however, one cable company offered a different viewpoint.

Cablevision, the leading cable company in the nation's biggest media market, New York, filed a comment with the Federal Communications Commission (FCC) supporting government efforts to make *a la carte* more available. While never explicitly calling for mandates on cable companies such as itself, Cablevision's filing never came out against the rule—a silence that easily can be taken as consent. The company called for one free-market reform: the abolition of must-carry rules. But then they asked the government to regulate their dealers, the programmers, by prohibiting the programmers from offering bundles—in other words, forcing an *a la carte* mandate on the middlemen.

But McCain wanted to apply the same mandate to Cablevision and its competitors, and Cablevision never objected. In December 2005, after FCC Chairman Kevin Martin, testified before McCain's committee, calling for an *a la carte* mandate, Cablevision Chairman Charles Dolan applauded. "Cablevision agrees with FCC Chairman Kevin Martin," Dolan said in a statement, "that the opportunity to purchase programming on an *a la carte* basis would be in the best interests of consumers. Like Chairman Martin, we do not believe in the long term that selling programming *a la carte* will be detrimental to either programmers or cable operators."[42]

Dolan was confident that, at least, *his* company would not be harmed by this mandate, as his August 13 filing suggested:

> Cablevision has been at the forefront of efforts to enhance consumer choice. It has conducted several a la carte experiments. It has invested heavily in the technology that allows subscribers to select (or not select) add-on services, such as digital tiers, foreign language programming, on-demand services, voice service, and broadband service.[43]

In other words, Cablevision is ahead of the rest of the industry in overcoming the fourth obstacle—the technological requirements of giving each customer only that for which he pays. Cablevision believes it could offer *a la carte* today if it wanted to, and nobody is telling them they can't. But if the government mandates *a la carte,* other companies will all be playing catch-up to Cablevision.

The debate over *a la carte* cable is ongoing in 2006, but there is an interesting footnote. As McCain pushed for mandatory *a la carte* rules and most cable companies resisted, he portrayed himself in his favorite role—as the reformer battling against big money. However, in early 2005, some reporters discovered that Cablevision had sent $200,000 to a think tank McCain ran in the same building as his campaign offices and his PAC.[44]

In 1999, Sylvia Swanson wrote a farewell letter as she prepared to retire as the president of the International Bottled Water Association (IBWA). In the letter, she listed her top accomplishment:

At IBWA, we've used these years well by focusing on three main areas. The first was to raise the "technical" bar for our industry by pushing for stricter regulation at federal, state, and industry levels. We've seen the Food and Drug Administration finally issue both binding standards of identity and quality standards for bottled water. We succeeded in attaching an amendment to the Safe Drinking Water Act that ensures our industry will never again fall behind municipal water systems with regard to regulations for quality standards. We continued to raise the bar on contaminant testing in our Model Code, and our certified plant operator exam.[45]

In other words, the people who bottle and sell water bragged not about raising the quality of their product but about raising the level of regulation on their product. Was this addressing any actual problem in drinking water safety? Not according to Swanson, who told ABC news that same year, "The Centers for Disease Control has never documented one single outbreak of anyone getting ill from drinking bottled water."[46] Again, the entrenched water bottlers were using government power to "raise the bar" for entry that potential competitors would face.

In the early 1970s, Michael Maynard invented a machine that would break eggs. A baker would place a bunch of eggs in the middle of his device and turn it on. The machine would spin rapidly, and centrifugal force would send the eggs flying against the outside of the center cylinder, cracking them. The cylinder was perforated, and so the centrifugal force would then send the yolks and the whites into the outer container, while trapping the shells in the inner cylinder.

Maynard's machine, called the Egg King, would reduce costs for bakers, drive down the price of egg-containing products, and thus drive up demand for eggs, increasing the price of eggs. The egg industry responded in the 1980s by driving Maynard into bankruptcy. The United Egg Producers argued that the machine, used improperly, could lead to salmonella. In other words, if a baker's egg dealer sold him or her a bad egg, the Egg King's ruthless efficiency could spread the contamination to the whole batch of eggs.

There were many solutions to this. Maynard included instructions on the machine to use only high-grade, sanitized eggs, and never to use the Egg King for products that would not be thoroughly cooked. As a second check, egg producers could make added efforts not to sell infected eggs. Instead, in the late 1980s, the producers turned to big government. They got a bill on the floor of the House of Representatives that would have outlawed the Egg King. They failed in Washington, DC, but succeeded in many state legislatures.[47]

Nearly everyone agrees that doctors should have medical licenses before they can practice medicine, and pilots, too, ought to be certified. But in Louisiana, florists can run afoul of the law if they practice floristry without a license.

The state requires any would-be florist to pass a licensing exam.[48] Who are the judges? They are currently practicing florists. The result: A majority of applicants fail. In short, the state has given current florists the power to keep potential competition out of the market. Only with the help of big government could the existing businesses maintain such an oligopoly. Such pro-incumbent-business regulations abound.

Allen Iverson and Donovan McNabb are the two superstars of Philadelphia sports. Iverson is the point-guard on the Philadelphia 76ers, while McNabb quarterbacks the Eagles. McNabb, newer to Philly than Iverson, has recently adopted Iverson's hairstyle—cornrows, or tightly wound braids across the scalp. As evidenced by McNabb's gold tooth and diamond earrings and Iverson's $2.4 million mansion, the two can afford to pay top dollar for their hairdos—which is a good thing, considering Pennsylvania state law that keeps prices high for hair braiding. Hair braiders must take a 1,250 hour training course in "cosmetology," before they can legally braid hair in Philadelphia or anywhere else in the state.[49] As a point of comparison, federal law requires pilots to log 40 hours of flight time before getting a license.

While the reason for the braiding regulation is hard to imagine, the harmful effects are clear. Hair braiding could be the ideal job for a black woman—either a mother re-entering the work force, or someone looking for a second job. In cities where the practice is fairly unregulated, such as Washington, DC, the field provides exactly this opportunity. In Philly, the state has made it much harder to pursue this line of work. Of course, keeping the number of hair braiders low drives up the price for consumers—which is good news only for those who had the time and the resources to get their license. Once again, government has created a cartel, not only in Pennsylvania, but also in seventeen other states that require hair braiders to obtain training and licenses.[50]

If you have weeds on your property in Arizona, you should probably study the state code before trying to remove them. Paying your neighbor's son to spray them with Weed-B-Gone, or any standard over-the-counter weed-killer, probably violates the law. It's illegal to do it yourself if you are a renter, but it's also illegal for your landlord to spray. Maybe you know a gardener whom you could hire to do it? You'd better check that he has 3,000 hours worth of experience spraying weeds, otherwise the Arizona Structural Pest Control Commission (SPCC) may come after you both.

Gary Rismiller found this out the hard way, when the SPCC hit him with a $500 fine when one of his workers was found spraying weed-killer on a client's lawn.[51] Only after his guy got busted on February 4, 2004, did Gary learn the law: Nobody in Arizona may spray weeds without an operators license. Rismiller thought he would go get licensed by passing the test the SPCC administered. But then Rismiller learned about the other requirement: he would need to document that he had spent 3,000 spraying weeds in the past 5 years. That would be more than 10 hours per week. In dry Arizona, though, weeds only really grow twice a year—after the December rainy season and the July monsoon season. There is no way anyone but a full-time weed-sprayer could accumulate those hours—especially not an all-purpose landscaper such as Rismiller.

Rismiller had to cease and desist spraying weeds, and so he hired a weed specialist—at a price. "Some of the prices that he shot at me," Rismiller told me in a phone interview, "I could do it for half that—even less." But Rismiller was in no position to negotiate. His other options were worse. He could just stop providing his customers with weed control, tell them they were on their own when it came to weeds, and risk losing them as customers. Or he could just start picking the weeds by hand—with huge costs in added labor and decreased morale. Finally, he could try to get licensed himself. But that would take suspending his business and going to work for some licensed spraying company until he racks up 3,000 hours, which, at 40 hours per week would take 18 months. "All my customers would leave me if I was gone for a year and a half," Rismiller says.

Rismiller's customers pay higher prices now than they used to. Rismiller estimates he is losing as much as $20,000 per year by having to contract out the weed spraying. But the regulation is good news for some folks. One day, Rismiller got a call from a major pest-control company, and the caller said he understood Rismiller was unlicensed to spray, but this corporation could handle it for him. "This guy opens up the phone book and calls all the landscapers, knowing that the law put them in this situation. He's gotta love it."

If you've ever looked out the window of a tall building in New York down onto the street, you might think that there are a million yellow cabs in Manhattan. In fact, there are precisely 12,787 taxis that operate legally in New York. If you've ever tried to hail a cab during rush hour, you might think that not even one is open. For this frustration, you can thank the Taxi and Limousine Commission (TLC), which actively and aggressively limits the number of cabs in New York.

No one, no matter how immaculate his driving record, or intricate his knowledge of the city streets, can drive a cab in the City without a medallion. You might be able to get your hands on one if you've got $200,000 sitting around (though one sold for more than $700,000 recently).[52] The TLC did not issue new medallions for 50 years before creating 900 new ones in 2004.

Of course, immigrants from poor countries—the profile of most cabbies in New York—can't afford six-figure medallions. Instead, they rent the medallions from the handful of big companies who own them. *New York* magazine reported in 2004 that "17 percent of medallions are owned by cab fleets; 54 percent are owned by leasing agents, who delegate management to fleets; and 29 percent are owned by independent drivers."[53]

However much the TLC's taxicab squeeze might inconvenience a tourist or resident of the Big Apple, it takes away the livelihood for many would-be-cabbies. An aspiring hack either faces a huge barrier-to-entry (access to at least $200,000 on the spot) or has to become, in effect, a sharecropper, leasing the right to drive a cab from a leasing agent or cab company. This makes it harder for a cabbie to make a living. If City Hall let all qualified and capable drivers enter the business, the price of a cab ride would surely drop, saving New Yorkers hundreds of dollars every year. The fat cats who own the medallions have too much pull in City Hall to allow that.

In Oklahoma and Tennessee, casket sellers have a similar cartel. In Florida, currently practicing athlete's agents comprise the athlete's agents licensing board, which decides who can or can't represent an athlete. All of these "pro-consumer" license requirements hurt not only would-be florists, casket salespersons, and agents but also consumers, who pay higher prices in the squeezed market.

But before closing this chapter, we need to return to the plight of Ed Daly of World Airways. After Congress killed the stifling regulations on commercial air travel, Daly entered the market in 1979.

A *New York Times* article a year later described the fallout:

> As Mr. Daly had expected, business boomed at World following the C.A.B. decision. In the first two months after the carrier started its first service from Los Angeles and Oakland to Baltimore and Newark in April 1979, 75 percent of the 380 seats on his six DC-10 jetliners were occupied.[54]

Daly saw himself as a capitalist cowboy, "the Wyatt Earp of the airline industry," according to the *Times*. He said he was David to the big airlines' Goliath, and even ran that image in a full-page newspaper ad exhorting consumers, "If you want lowcost airfares to stay alive, then fly with World Airways. After all, it's your fight, too."

To the *Washington Post* in the summer of 1980, Daly described himself as "one who's unselfish, has a definite code of morals, and adheres to them." He saw his fight as rooted in "recognition of the freedom, or rights of the individual, against all odds."[55] Indeed, World embodied the swashbuckling maverick that a deregulated industry finally allowed. He ignited famous bidding wars on coast-to-coast travel that made headlines.

In March of 1982, he made his most surprising headline, "Low-Cost Airline Now Seeks Fares Curb It Once Opposed." Daly explained that ticket prices for years "were too high in the transcontinental markets, and World did something about it to the public's advantage and our own; now they are too low, and I will not remain silent, even though our proposal may offend deregulation purists."[56]

The company declared the fare wars were "disastrous and completely irrational." World's lawyer told the *Times,* "If [the fare war] continues through September, then you probably won't have all these guys to kick around anymore." Neither the Reagan administration nor the Congress would go along.

Labor troubles and the changing market continued to plague the company until Daly's death in 1984. Months later, the company dropped its scheduled routes and returned to cargo and charter flights, which it does to this day.

But World's dramatic turnabout on the issue of price controls demonstrates clearly the business mind-set toward regulation. Daly knew the status quo in 1967 was blocking a golden market opportunity, which was why the major carriers wanted to preserve the regulations.

Daly's earlier rhetoric was altruistic sounding. "The fares were just too high," he told the *Times* in 1980, "Poor people couldn't afford it."[57] Truly, of course, Daly's interest in driving down rates was the profit motive, which in those days coincided with the consumers' interests.

Once he was entrenched, his interests changed. He now argued that heightened regulation benefited consumers because the fare war would destroy the industry—the exact fallacious arguments his rivals made against the entry of World into the industry.

Deregulation unlocked the door, and Daly charged through it. Once inside he called on government to lock it again. Such is often the nature of regulation: a fence that protects big business from competition. Is it any wonder that big business often helps build that fence?

8

The War against Tobacco

Why Philip Morris Is Leading It

There is a place in America where few venture without good cause. Millions drive through it every day, always with their windows rolled up, but that's never enough to keep out the stench. Maybe it's the swamp, poisoned for decades with mercury. It might be the smokestacks, or the trash, or Jimmy Hoffa, who is said to lie under the football field. The view is hardly an attraction, either, with nothing to see but factories, power plants, marshes, and highway. Yet, northern New Jersey was the choice location for an extraordinary event in the spring of 2003. Residents of the Big Apple actually started crossing the Hudson at night for a drink. On April 1, 2003, Mayor Bloomberg's smoking ban went into effect, outlawing smoking in nearly every bar or restaurant in the five boroughs. It was enough to make a New Yorker seek out the shores of New Jersey, where a smoker could be free. It was also enough to send Philip Morris packing, some surmise. After the city passed the smoking ban, the cigarette maker announced it was moving to Virginia for cost reasons.

While Philip Morris felt unwanted in New York, the company was feeling the love in Chicago. That same week, 37 state attorneys general, at the request of Philip Morris, filed a brief in a Madison County, Illinois, court imploring the judge to go easy on the tobacco giant. The judge had just imposed a $10 billion penalty on Philip Morris for allegedly deceiving customers about the health of "light" cigarettes. More to the point, the judge had further set the cost of the appeal bond at a whopping $12 billion. If the judge didn't reduce that amount, the state attorneys general argued, it would "severely threaten public health and safety programs in numerous states."

While New York Mayor Michael Bloomberg righteously declared he was saving lives by banning cigarettes from bars, the chief law enforcement officials of 37 states were arguing that driving Philip Morris out of business would be bad for public health.

The attorneys general got their wish, and the judge cut the appeal bond almost in half. Philip Morris, their shareholders, and the state governments breathed a collective sigh of relief. These were the same state governments that only a few years before had sued the company for unprecedented amounts. Such was the strange partnership forged between state government and Big Tobacco.

Few Americans know that Big Tobacco, perhaps the most vilified of all industries, has one of the coziest relationships with government. For that, we can thank the 1998 tobacco settlement, the so-called Master Settlement Agreement (MSA) between the states and the four biggest tobacco companies. In exchange for settling all the state lawsuits filed in the 1990s, the companies promised huge annual payments to state governments. To safeguard the new revenue stream, the states passed laws protecting Big Tobacco from smaller competitors. Critics have called the MSA, "one of the most effective and destructive cartels in the history of the Nation."[1]

Mississippi Smoking

Tobacco's new partnership with government began in the early 1990s, or so the story goes, at Baptist Memorial Hospital in Memphis, Tennessee, the same hospital where Elvis Presley was pronounced dead. Mississippi trial lawyer Michael Lewis had visited the mother of his paralegal, who was dying of lung cancer. Lewis was reportedly enraged by the experience, blaming the tobacco industry for the scourge of lung cancer. Honed as a litigator, Lewis turned his mind toward new strategies for suing Big Tobacco—but how?

Countless sick smokers or grieving widows of smokers had sued tobacco companies over several decades, but juries consistently found that smokers had assumed the health risks knowingly when they started smoking. Big Tobacco was undefeated. If individual plaintiffs could not beat Big Tobacco, maybe a stronger opponent could take them down, Lewis thought. His paralegal's mother might be no match for Philip Morris, but the State of Mississippi would be.

Luckily for Lewis, his chum from Ole Miss, Mike Moore, was Mississippi's attorney general.

Not long after leaving Baptist Memorial Hospital, Lewis called Moore with an idea: Could Mississippi sue the major companies in order to recoup the Medicaid costs of treating smoking-caused illnesses? Moore—a fiery populist politician from the mold of old-fashioned southern Democrats—answered with an enthusiastic yes. Moore recruited another old friend—legendary plaintiff's attorney Richard "Dickie" Scruggs who had made his name and fortune filing asbestos lawsuits.

On May 23, 1994, Mike Moore, in his official capacity as the attorney general of Mississippi, defied the explicit orders of the governor and filed a lawsuit in state court. The suit named as defendants the four major tobacco companies, which collectively controlled 98 percent of the domestic cigarette market. Moore's suit alleged that the tobacco companies had gained "wrongful enrichment," at the expense of the government, which had paid the health care costs of some Mississippians struck ill by smoking.

Tobacco companies, Moore argued, had for years denied that smoking was harmful even though their studies had found otherwise. The companies in response had always pointed to the government-mandated warning labels that had been on the packs for decades. Memos written by industry executives and later acquired by trial lawyers in the 1990s were a smoking gun on the charge that Big Tobacco was downplaying the harm of their product.

But Moore and Scruggs were not just after money for the Magnolia State. The two flew around in Scruggs' private Lear Jet from state capital to state capital enlisting other state attorneys general to file similar Medicare/Medicaid suits.

About three months after Moore filed his suit, Minnesota's attorney general, Hubert H. Humphrey III, filed a similar suit, followed by West Virginia, Florida, and then Massachusetts. In early 1996, Maryland, Texas, and Washington state all filed copycat suits.

In the abstract, hiring private lawyers to sue Big Tobacco ran the risk of wasting the states' money. After all, Big Tobacco had always won, and the trial lawyers the states were hiring were the most expensive in the country. But Scruggs and his colleagues tried to make it easy for the state

government officials, at least on the financial level. The private lawyers all
agreed to aid in the lawsuit on a contingency basis. That meant that if tobacco kept its winning streak going, the states didn't have to pay the private lawyers a dime. If the cigarette companies paid up, however, the
lawyers would get a hefty share.

For the lawyers going after tobacco, the lawsuits were something of a
religious crusade, judging by their rhetoric. In 1996, Mike Moore said the
tobacco industry had "lied and killed 425,000 people a year."[2] His allies
called the companies "merchants of death."[3] Countless lawyers referred to
them as "the devil." Dickie Scruggs called the litigation "war."[4]

But the *war* soon became a *deal*.

Smoke-Filled Rooms

Joe Rice usually wore his hair long, his silk shirt open, and often went without shoes. He was a native of North Carolina who lived and worked at a law
firm in South Carolina. On March 18, 1997, Rice found himself in a place
no plaintiff's attorney had ever sat before—across the table from an impressive assembly of lawyers representing Big Tobacco.

Indeed, Rice was alone in the room with four of the biggest corporate
lawyers in the country: Meyer Koplow, Herbert Wachtel, Arthur Golden,
and J. Phil Carlton. But Rice was up to the task. Like Scruggs, Rice was another crafty trial lawyer from the South. But where Scruggs was a crusader,
Rice was a businessman. *American Lawyer* magazine compared the two:

> Unlike the more visible Dick Scruggs, who has always talked about
> beating the tobacco industry with near-religious fervor, Rice is re-
> garded by the people in this litigation as more mercenary than mis-
> sionary. He is a cold-eyed dealmaker with the mind of an accountant.[5]

The same article quoted a law partner saying of Rice, "All you need to
know about Joe is that he was the business manager of the law review." In
other words, Joe Rice wasn't the man to come up with big ideas. He wasn't
the man to lead a public and national crusade, like Scruggs or Moore. But
this long-haired accountant of a lawyer was just the man to call on when
you wanted to cut a deal.

The March 18 meeting lasted four hours. A month later, a similar group
sat down in Crystal City, Virginia, the corridor of hotels and shopping malls
situated across the Potomac River from Washington, DC. The meetings continued through the spring.

By June 1997, there was a deal. Befitting Joe Rice's reputation, it was more of a business deal than a legal settlement. It was "an accounting exercise," in the words of Harvard scholar Kip Viscusi.[6] More to the point, Rice's deal was a draft bill for Congress.

The bill would have required the tobacco companies to pay nearly $400 billion to state governments over 25 years, and granted the Food and Drug Administration (FDA) the power to regulate tobacco. In exchange, Congress would grant immunity from more lawsuits and protection from upstart competition.

Geoffrey Bible, CEO of Philip Morris, toured Capitol Hill lobbying for the resolution. Congressional leaders took up the resolution but reworked the deal beyond recognition. By April 1998, when the Senate Commerce Committee passed its version of the bill by a 19-to-1 vote, it looked nothing like what Rice and the tobacco companies had agreed to the year before. The tobacco giants withdrew their support, and even staged a National Press Club event where R.J. Reynolds President Steven Goldstone denounced the bill in its new form. With industry now against it, the bill died, proving that when it came to "sticking it to Big Tobacco" nothing happened without the approval of Big Tobacco itself. Philip Morris and R.J. Reynolds were not helpless whipping boys in this settlement deal—criminals caught, cuffed, and at the mercy of the government. They were partners with the states, working to find a mutually beneficial agreement. Toward that end, Joe Rice once again sat down with the tobacco lawyers in June of 1998.

Round Two and the Master Settlement Agreement

Joining Rice and the tobacco lawyers a second time around was a handful of state attorneys general. Their goal was to reach an agreement like the one crafted the year before but one that excluded Congress. The lawyers wanted a national deal, but if the federal government wouldn't be involved, the lawyers needed each state. Eventually they succeeded. While four states ended up settling individually, the attorneys general of 46 states plus the District of Columbia and Puerto Rico all filed tobacco lawsuits and so earned a seat at the settlement table with Joe Rice. The negotiating was not easy, though, with all of the competing personalities and interests involved.

Political scientist Martha Derthick described one critical problem: "Within the industry, the main source of tension was how to protect against competition from upstarts."[7] Indeed, this protection was the main prize

Rice knew he could offer the companies, even if he had to get creative. In the end, this second round of negotiations succeeded and yielded an enduring partnership between big business and big government.

The centerpiece of the MSA was the "damages" the tobacco companies would pay, not to smokers or their descendents but to state coffers.

As soon as each state finalized the MSA by getting court approval of a "consent decree," the tobacco companies would make an initial payment of $2.4 billion. The sheer size of $2.4 billion is hard to grasp. As a point of comparison, imagine the goliath annual payroll of the New York Yankees. Add to it the almost-as-large Boston Red Sox payroll. For good measure tack on the payrolls of the New York Mets, the Los Angeles Angeles, the Philadelphia Phillies, and the St. Louis Cardinals. Keep adding until the payroll of every single Major League Baseball team in 2005 is included. The final figure would total about 10 percent less than the $2.4 billion Big Tobacco paid as the initial payment.

Put another way, imagine coming home and finding a suitcase packed with $1 million on your front step—that's 100 stacks of 100 $100 bills. When you go inside you see that your living room is stacked to the ceiling with identical suitcases, so that there are 2,400 suitcases, each with a million dollars. That's $2.4 billion.

But this 1999 $2.4 billion payment was just the *initial* initial payment. Over the next four years, the cigarette makers would pay "initial payments" of about the same size, adjusted for inflation—again, each year being able to pay every Major League Baseball salary and more.

That's just for starters.

On April 15, 2000, the tobacco companies, while still paying the initial payments, would have to fork over their first *annual* payment. Nearly twice as large as the initial payment, the *annual* payment was $4.5 billion—a sum that exceeds the total general fund budget of 20 U.S. states.

While the initial payments would last only five years, the annual payments, as the name would suggest, would continue every year, presumably until the end of time. And they would increase on a set schedule. In 2018, the scheduled annual payment from the tobacco companies to the states would be $9 billion. The official estimate of these annual payments put the 25-year price tag at $183 billion (though the companies would keep paying long after those 25 years).

The premise of the state lawsuits was the Medicaid costs of treating sick smokers. But the settlement payments bear little relationship to such alleged Medicaid costs. Indeed, in the negotiations in both 1997 and 1998 over the price tag of the settlement, the haggling was not over reimbursement costs but, rather, how much the companies could pay without going bankrupt. All parties dropped the pretense of trying to set straight the balance sheets—actual costs incurred were not much of a factor in the negotiations. Nor were the states trying to slay the "devil," fighting a "war," or vanquishing the "merchants of death," as Dickie Scruggs' or Mike Moore's rhetoric suggested. The lawyers and the tobacco companies were simply cutting a deal. (That deal, as it would turn out, was so rich for the states that they would need to keep Big Tobacco alive to ensure continued cash flow.)

These billions would go into a pot, and the MSA prescribed how the money would be divvied up among the states. Each state had an "allocable share"—that is, some percentage of the tobacco money that it would get.

If the suit were really about recouping Medicare and Medicaid costs, then the settlement would have allocated the money proportional to the smoking-related Medicaid and Medicare costs each state had incurred. But just as the overall cost of cigarettes to the country was never a serious consideration, the states' respective shares of those costs were not the determining factor in dividing the pot.

In general, larger states and those with higher health costs did get the most money. But those factors were just two of many in determining the states' "allocable share." In his own study, author Kip Viscusi, by multiplying the estimated health cost per cigarette in each state by the number of cigarettes sold in each state, estimated each state's portion of cigarette related health costs. According to his math, New York bore 15 percent of the smoking-related health costs, more than any state. Second place was California, shouldering 8.6 percent of smoking-related health costs.

But the MSA gave California and New York both 13 percent of the cash, which meant California got more than its share and New York got less. By Viscusi's count, Indiana was the most shortchanged state—it accounts for 3.6 percent of the nation's smoking-related health costs, but got only 2.1 percent of the total pot. Hawaii made out best, pulling in 0.6 percent of the tobacco money while incurring only 0.2 percent of smoking-related health costs.

Viscusi's data suggests that the payouts to the states were, like much of the MSA, more of a political and business deal than any real attempt at justice. "The national settlement was a political deal in which the attorneys general bargained for their piece of the largesse," wrote Viscusi.[8]

A third portion of the settlement openly reflected the political nature of the deal. The "strategic contribution fund," into which the companies would start paying in 2008 was divvied up to "reflect the contribution made by states toward resolution of the state lawsuits against tobacco companies." For example, Virginia would get $6.5 million a year from this fund, compared to Washington state's $49.6 million. Once again, this fund suggests that what was going on in this deal was not really a matter of recouping Medicare costs, but dividing up a pie and cutting deals.

The companies would also spend $25 million each year for 10 years in order to create an educational foundation that would try to convince people not to smoke. The companies would fund this agency's ads for about $300 million a year for the first five years.

The attorneys general would also get their share. In 1999, the tobacco companies paid $50 million into the attorneys general enforcement fund, to help them enforce the terms of the deal. Also, the companies would give $150,000 each year for 10 years to a Washington, DC, organization called the National Association of Attorneys General (NAAG).

NAAG (a fitting acronym, one might say, for a bunch of government officials on an antismoking crusade) uses this money to coordinate all the attorneys general in their efforts to enforce the agreement. Sometimes, however, it appears that NAAG's job is mostly to keep the money flowing into state coffers—and this is the point of tension.

Despite Dickie Scruggs' rhetoric, and the talk of "going after Big Tobacco," the state governments that sued the companies soon realized that they had no interest in putting Philip Morris or R.J. Reynolds out of business. If the tobacco giants folded, the money would go away, and a huge source of revenue for the states would disappear. National Association of Attorneys General, then, charged with keeping the tobacco money flowing, became a guardian of Big Tobacco, and their actions since the settlement, as well as the details of the settlement, suggest they are doing a pretty good job on that front.

A Conflict of Interest

The four tobacco companies who were sued (and who comprised about 98 percent of the U.S. cigarette market) were labeled in the settlement as Original Participating Manufacturers (OPMs). These OPMs (Big Tobacco) became golden geese for the states, and so the settlement and the states guard them vigorously.

First, the MSA contained provisions allowing the big companies to lower their payments in some circumstances if their sales decreased. Under the "Volume Adjustment," provision of the MSA, the OPMs would owe the states less money if their sales dropped. Conversely, if the OPMs's sales increased, their annual payments would increase.

Similarly, the settlement provided for a "Nonparticipating Manufacturer Adjustment." A Nonparticipating Manufacturer (NPM) was a cigarette maker that was not "participating," in the MSA. These were the tobacco companies the states had never sued. Under the NPM adjustment, if the NPMs (small tobacco) gained market share, the OPMs (Big Tobacco) could reduce their payments.

So, the big cigarette companies were paying into state coffers money roughly proportional to the number of cigarettes they sold—in effect, the MSA imposed a tax on cigarettes without a single elected representative having to cast a vote to approve it. Economist, tobacco expert, and author Kip Viscusi called the settlement, "an unprecedented imposition of an excise tax on cigarettes that was sold to the public as a damages award paid by the companies."[9] To make it clear that the annual payments are tax payments, they are due every year on April 15.

This rough outline makes it clear: If Philip Morris or R.J. Reynolds lose business, the states lose revenue. But it gets worse. It did not take long for many of the states to spend all their annual tobacco money, but also much of their *future* tobacco revenues as well. By April 2003, when the Illinois judge handed down the $10 billion verdict against Philip Morris, states had collectively borrowed nearly $20 billion against future tobacco payments. If upheld, the judgment would drive the company into bankruptcy, Philip Morris officials said, reducing the states' tobacco bonds to junk bond status.

Clearly, there was a conflict of interest. The state attorneys general—the erstwhile crusaders against the large cigarette companies—became the protectors of Big Tobacco. Not only did the state attorneys general successfully lobby to reduce the appeal bond Philip Morris had to pay (Philip Morris won on appeal in December 2005), but they also worked to reduce the de facto excise tax's negative impact on Big Tobacco.

Technically, companies pay excise taxes, but the cost is really borne by the consumer because excise taxes increase prices. This is why duty-free liquor sold at the airport to passengers departing on international flights is so much cheaper—the price of a bottle of whiskey in the United States includes the price of the federal distilled spirits tax. Because cigarettes contain addictive nicotine, it is even easier for manufacturers to pass the tax onto customers, who are less likely to be driven away by a price raise.

But, in the world of whiskey, if the federal government imposed an excise tax only on the biggest distillers, it's not hard to guess what would happen: The small distillers could keep their prices the same, and drinkers would flock to the less expensive liquor. If the MSA only demanded payments from the participating tobacco companies, it would drive smokers to the NPMs, who, not paying the effective excise tax, could keep their prices at presettlement levels and still maintain a profit. This would be bad news for Big Tobacco, but it would also hurt the states.

The negotiators of the MSA were too shrewd to let Big Tobacco lose too much business. The states, the private attorneys, and the big cigarette makers designed the agreement in such a way as to preserve Big Tobacco's market share.

The only way to keep their customers from fleeing to the NPMs was to make the NPMs raise their prices, too. But the NPMs hadn't been sued and didn't owe anything under the MSA. The negotiators had to find another way.

Expanding the Excise Tax

The MSA prescribed that NPMs would be required to pay 35 cents per pack into escrow funds (that per-pack amount would rise with inflation). State governments would hold the escrow payments as a sort of insurance for any future lawsuits against these small tobacco companies—even though the lawsuits against Big Tobacco were all based on the notion that these companies had covered up the harmful and addictive nature of cigarettes for decades, while these small companies had never been accused of such deceit. After 25 years, the small tobacco companies could get their money out of escrow.

This escrow arrangement, in effect, would expand the excise tax on cigarettes to the NPMs. While the escrow payments were about equal per pack to the OPMs' annual payments, Big Tobacco's settlement payments were tax deductible while the little tobacco companies' escrow payments were not. This meant that the excise tax would be bigger on the little tobacco companies—who had never been sued—than on Big Tobacco.

The MSA spelled out this escrow plan, but that wasn't enough. The MSA was a legal agreement, and so it could not bind the NPMs nor could it create a new tax structure—only legislatures could do that. So, the lawyers got crafty. The MSA punished any state that didn't create this special NPM tax. If the tobacco payments shrank because the NPMs grabbed market share, the entire loss would be borne by states that hadn't enacted an NPM tax.

Predictably, all 46 states party to the NPM passed the escrow bill, prohibiting companies from selling cigarettes within their boundaries if they did not pay into the escrow fund.

But even the best laid plans of Rice and Scruggs can go awry. Under the escrow laws, small tobacco companies that sold only in one state were entitled to a quick rebate of most of their money. As a company expanded its business to more states, its rebate from state governments would decrease— another provision that induces the small companies to stay small.

But some state officials did not like the result. A *Winston-Salem Journal* article in May 2003 reported the unsettling news in the Tar Heel State. "The attorney general's office reported to a Senate judiciary committee that while Philip Morris pays 2 cents a cigarette to the state, the amount paid by non-participating manufacturers after their rebates in North Carolina ranges from 0.13 cents to 0.75 cents a cigarette."[10]

Quickly, the state moved to fix it. State Senator Linda Garrou proposed a bill that would prohibit the rebates, or as she put it, "close a loophole." The general counsel for the state attorney general put it this way: "The bill would basically put into parity the per-stick charge for the participating manufacturer and the nonparticipating manufacturers."[11]

The state would make sure that tobacco companies that were never sued, were never accused of wrongdoing, and in some cases didn't exist when the alleged deception and wrongdoing occurred, and certainly never participated in the settlement would pay the same damages as the Big Tobacco companies that had been hit for covering up the harmful effects of smoking.

Sometimes, the small tobacco companies being affected just like the "guilty" big companies had trouble understanding what they ever did wrong to deserve such punishment. Dan Norris, for one, was chewed out by a state lawmaker in Tennessee. His company, called Poison, Inc., is a NPM.

North Carolina State Senator Rosalind Kurita tore into Norris's brands in April of 2004. "They give themselves names that are enticing to children like Black Death and Grim Reaper, and they're advertising on T-shirts and in ways that the larger manufacturers can't any more."[12]

Grim Reaper cigarettes picture a hooded death figure on the pack, but Black Death is probably his more morbid brand. Norris's Gravediggers is perhaps a more poetic brand name, and Go To Hell cigarettes make even bolder claims about the eternal dangers of smoking than the other Poison, Inc., brands. Dan Norris is not hiding anything about his products or his company.

But to the state government, Grim Reaper cigarettes were a real threat—not because of the detrimental health effects to the citizenry from smoking them but because a NPM such as Poison, Inc., didn't pay as much into the state coffers as the OPMs. So, the states all passed laws making sure that the NPMs paid as much as the guilty parties, wiping out the rebates.

After the states saved Philip Morris from a devastating appeal bond and passed laws taxing their competitors, it sure looked like government was on the side of Big Tobacco. A September 12, 2003, memo on NAAG's letterhead confirmed that perception.

The memo, with "<u>PRIVILEGED AND CONFIDENTIAL</u>" written across the top, is from Vermont Attorney General William H. Sorell (the chairman of NAAG's Tobacco Committee) and Mark E. Greenwold, NAAG's chief counsel for tobacco to all attorneys general. It begins with a dire warning:"Increasing sales by NPMs will sharply reduce the next scheduled payments to all states and the MSA."

Later on, Sorell repeats:"One of the principal contributors to this revenue loss is the accelerating increase in sales of cigarettes by NPMs." Then, Sorell gives some suggestions:

> Attorneys General should consider how to share this information with other interested agencies of State government. . . . These results underscore the urgency of all States taking steps to deal with the proliferation of NPM sales, including enactment of complementary legislation and allocable share legislation and consideration of other measures designed to serve the interests of the States in avoiding reductions in tobacco settlement payments. . . . It should be stressed that NPM sales anywhere in the country hurt all States. . . . All states have an interest in reducing NPM sales in every State.[13]

And so it was official: The state governments would join forces with Philip Morris and R.J. Reynolds in quashing the little companies to keep the money spigot open and flowing, irrespective of the health effects of smoking. It seems the states were now dependent on their people's smoking habits.

Stunting Growth

Keeping the small tobacco companies *small* and protecting Big Tobacco's market share seems to be a major aim of the MSA. For one, the settlement offered any NPM that joined the settlement within 90 days of its completion in late 1998 all of the protections of the agreement (some protection from legal liability), with none of the payments. In exchange, the small companies signing on to the MSA were not allowed to grow by more than 25 percent. This provision, in effect, was a threat: "Stay small, or we'll tax the heck out of you."

Dozens of small tobacco companies have signed onto the MSA since 1998, achieving the status of Subsequent Participating Manufacturers (SPMs). But only those SPMs who joined in the first 90 days are free from the excise tax. These days, cigarette makers join the settlement to get tax deductions on their payments and to get protection from liability.

Manhattan Institute Senior Fellow Walter Olson criticized the settlement in a January 2000 article titled "Puff, the magic settlement." Olson wrote:

> The word for this process is *cartelization,* and the irony is that had cigarette executives met privately among themselves to raise prices, freeze market shares, confine small competitors to minor allocations on the fringe of the market, and penalize defectors and new entrants, they could have been sent to prison as antitrust violators—quite possibly by the very same attorneys general who sued them in this case (they'd also have faced tag-along consumer lawsuits filed by some of the same plaintiffs' lawyers). This way it's all legal.[14]

As an added bonus to Big Tobacco, the settlement drastically limits the advertising of all parties.

All restrictions on advertising work in the favor of the big companies, whose brand names are universally known. Cigarette advertising, many studies find, does far more to influence brand choice than to actually drive people to smoke or smoke more. Some studies find that cigarette advertising does nothing or nearly nothing to increase cigarette consumption. Others find that cigarette ads *do* make people into smokers. They all agree, though, that a major function of the ads is to win smokers from one brand to another. Money spent on advertising is largely spent to try to win customers from your competitors.

Author Kip Viscusi makes the argument in the language of economics:

> If the primary effect of advertising is to influence brand choice rather than consumption of a broad class of products, as a considerable economic literature suggests, then banning advertising or restricting it in important domains has the effect of locking in the current market shares to the extent that firms cannot advertise new brands.[15]

Everyone already knows Marlboro. If there were never another cigarette advertisement of any sort, Marlboro would do fine. The small companies, who might have something new or different to offer—or perhaps even a safer cigarette—are the ones who lose. Restrictions on advertising were part of the proposed FDA regulation of tobacco, and as could be anticipated Philip Morris supported the strict rules. Big business does like regulation.

Mr. Smith Goes to Washington

Young "Mr. Smith" is an honest guy. In his mid-20s, he had a devoted wife, a baby girl, a modest home in suburban Virginia, and a job as a legislative staffer on Capitol Hill. He's also a modest guy, and he wouldn't let me name him in this book.

Smith is a conservative, both socially and economically. He and his wife are practicing Catholics. Smith is a firm believer in low taxes and low regulation, and he got his start in Washington working for an antitax group. His boss on the Hill was a fairly conservative Republican.

Even with Republican control of the White House and Congress, conservatives like Smith often feel like the underdog in Washington. The mainstream media with its leftward tilt, together with the megaphone of Hollywood—make a right-winger, especially a young right-winger like Smith—feel a bit downtrodden. Thus, Smith welcomed the chance to meet with the much-maligned Philip Morris, or Altria, as the parent company was now known.

An Altria lobbyist was on the Hill to talk about a couple of issues, among which was expanding the authority of the FDA to regulate tobacco. It seemed to Smith that everyone was ganging up on Big Tobacco, from the press to the government prosecutors, and now the FDA was going to pile on, too? Smith did not smoke, but he believed in the free market and admired real capitalists. He was ready to lend a sympathetic ear.

Perhaps a bit naive, Smith was surprised at what he heard. Altria wanted Smith's boss to support greater federal regulation of tobacco. Their arguments were not shrewdly pragmatic or even political, Smith says. Altria's lobbyists lobbied for heavier federal regulation of its product with arguments that "came out of the Ralph Nader playbook," Smith would tell me days later over lunch at the Tortilla Coast, a Capitol Hill fixture.

It took Smith a little while to understand what was going on, but he soon figured it out. By lobbying for FDA regulation, Philip Morris might gain some goodwill within the FDA that would prove beneficial when the agency eventually takes control over tobacco. Such a philanthropic move might help win the friendship of liberal Democratic politicians who tend to be pro-regulation and antitobacco.

"But what about the costs FDA regulation would impose on Philip Morris?" Smith wondered, "wouldn't that outweigh these abstract gains in PR?" The costs, it turns out, are the key.

Philip Morris controls about half of the domestic tobacco industry. Altria's revenues of $81 billion in 2003 were many times the budget of smaller tobacco companies. Philip Morris could bear the costs associated with complying with greater federal regulation—hiring new lawyers, hiring new lobbyists, creating new labels, and so on—far more easily than its small family-owned competitors.

Also, the specifics of the proposed regulation would likely favor the big companies, as the first attempt at FDA regulation of tobacco, under President Clinton, showed.

On August 10, 1995, Bill Clinton appeared on stage at a live press conference in the White House with the president of the National PTA and the president of the American Medical Association by his side. He announced that he was doing what Congress wouldn't:

> Our children face a health crisis that is getting worse. One-third more eighth graders and one-quarter more tenth graders are smoking today than four years ago. One out of five high school seniors is a daily smoker. We need to act, and we must act now before another generation of Americans is condemned to fight a difficult and grueling personal battle with an addiction that will cost millions of them their lives.
>
> [T]eenagers are especially susceptible to pressures—pressure to the manipulation of mass media, the pressure of the seduction of skilled marketing campaigns aimed at exploiting their insecurities and uncertainties about life. When Joe Camel tells young children that smoking is cool, when billboards tell teens that smoking will lead to true romance, when Virginia Slims tell adolescents that cigarettes may make them thin and glamorous, then our children need our wisdom, our guidance, and our experience. We're their parents, and it is up to us to protect them.[16]

More precisely, Clinton meant that it was up to the FDA to protect all of America's children. The next day, FDA Administrator David Kessler officially proposed his regulations. Most of them were aimed at limiting tobacco advertising that could lure in children.

Clinton and Kessler were restricting advertising as an effort to protect children, but clearly the rules would limit the tobacco ads adults would see, too. Curtailing advertising aids those brands that already have broad name recognition and shelf space in corner stores—that is Philip Morris's brands.

Keeping kids from illegally buying a harmful product is a worthy aim. For many, it is even worth some losses in the realms of competition and free speech. But just where did Bill Clinton's FDA find the legal authority to regulate tobacco advertising?

The FDA has only the powers that Congress has authorized. In 1938, as part of the New Deal, Congress created the FDA to regulate food and consumer drugs—prescription drugs, over-the-counter drugs, and even vitamins. Subsequently, Congress has granted the FDA authority to regulate cosmetics and medical devices such as pacemakers.

But cigarettes are not food. They are not over-the-counter or prescription drugs. They are not vaccines, medical devices, dietary supplements, cosmetics, medicines, or any other kind of consumer product that Congress has authorized the FDA to regulate.

Antitobacco officials in the FDA, however, pointed out that there was a drug in cigarettes—nicotine. Sure enough, nicotine is addictive, but it is not a medicine or dietary supplement. Nor is it an illegal drug, and if it were, it would fall under the jurisdiction of the Drug Enforcement Agency and law enforcement.

So, how did the FDA claim authority over tobacco? The title of its *Federal Register* filing summed up the argument: "Nicotine In Cigarettes And Smokeless Tobacco Products Is A Drug And These Products Are Nicotine Delivery Devices Under the Federal Food, Drug, and Cosmetic Act."[17]

Nicotine, the FDA argued, was a therapeutic drug with "pharmacological effects," and that a cigarette was a "medical device," that functioned as a "nicotine delivery device." As Sam Kazman, general counsel for the free-market Competitive Enterprise Institute, would write, "Of course there's a basic question here: If tobacco is a therapy, what's the disease?"[18]

In 2000, the U.S. Supreme Court rejected Clinton's ploy. By a 5-to-4 margin, the Court ruled that, "it is plain that Congress has not given the FDA the authority to regulate tobacco products as customarily marketed."[19] The minority opinion argued that the plain letter of the law allowed FDA regulation of tobacco because nicotine's "mood-stabilizing effects" classified cigarettes as "articles (other than food) intended to affect the structure or any function of the body," which the FDA was allowed to regulate.

But Sandra Day O'Connor, in the majority opinion pointed out a self-contradiction in the FDA's claim to authority over tobacco. The FDA does not have *absolute* authority over medical devices. The agency can't require that such devices be beautiful, plentiful, or fairly priced, but only "safe" and "effective." In the whole process of making the rule, though, the FDA established that "tobacco products are unsafe." The proposed FDA regulations were not aimed at making cigarettes safer—that would have involved lowering the tar content or banning them altogether. Nor was the FDA concerned with making cigarettes more "effective" at delivering nicotine. The Supreme Court made it clear: If the FDA wanted to regulate tobacco, it would need Congress's go-ahead. That's where Altria's lobbyists come in.

In 2004, Congress was trying to finish a tax bill that would have ended a trade conflict with Europe. As typically happens in a bill's journey to become a law, this tax bill got loaded up with all sorts of unrelated provisions. One was a tobacco buyout, in which the government would end the convoluted program of government-imposed quotas for tobacco farmers with a one-time buyout of many tobacco farmers or investors who had bought the government-issued quotas. In the Senate, public health advocates and Altria convinced lawmakers to insert a provision authorizing the FDA to regulate tobacco.

In this battle, unlike with the MSA, the rest of Big Tobacco was not on Philip Morris's side. In July, R.J. Reynolds lawyer lambasted the proposal when it passed the Senate, saying it would "create an overwhelming competitive advantage for Philip Morris."[20]

The House leadership was not warm to FDA regulation, despite Altria's efforts in GOP offices such as that of Smith's boss. When the House passed its bill in October, FDA regulation of cigarettes was left out.

This was a defeat for Philip Morris. The *Richmond Times-Dispatch* carried a headline on the front page declaring, "No FDA control a setback for Altria." The article quoted an Altria spokesman speaking about the bid to give FDA control over tobacco, "We spent a lot of time and effort on it. We think it's very important to the industry as a whole. We don't have any regrets about pursuing it."[21]

But in the story of failed FDA regulation of tobacco is another shining example of the persistence of the misperception that big business wants less regulation. Senator Tom Harkin, Democrat of Iowa, said that Republicans had killed FDA regulation on orders from the White House. "I lay this right at President Bush's door," Harkin told the *Washington Post* at the time. "He concurred with big tobacco."[22] This *Post* article never mentioned that

Altria—the embodiment of Big Tobacco, controlling half of the market—did not concur with the president.

Harkin was either defining Big Tobacco to mean everybody besides the company that controls nearly half of the cigarette market, or he hadn't done his homework. Altria lawyer Mark Berlind had made it clear that the company was not ambivalent on FDA regulation of tobacco, calling for, "soup to nuts regulation of the entire industry," adding, "we think that the FDA should be involved in all of that."[23]

And 2002 didn't mark a sudden pro-regulation turnaround for Philip Morris, either, according to *Slate* reporter Samuel Loewenberg, "Philip Morris actually began its campaign to get an FDA stamp of approval right after the Bush administration took office, according to lobbyists who do work for the company."[24]

Altria's 2004 annual report states clearly the position of Altria Group (ALG) and Philip Morris USA (PM USA). Their third-quarter 2005 report goes further:

> ALG and PM USA endorsed federal legislation introduced in May 2004 in the Senate and the House of Representatives, known as the Family Smoking Prevention and Tobacco Control Act, which would have granted the FDA the authority to regulate the design, manufacture and marketing of cigarettes and disclosures of related information. The legislation also would have granted the FDA the authority to combat counterfeit and contraband tobacco products and would have imposed fees to pay for the cost of regulation and other matters. The legislation was passed by the Senate, but Congress adjourned in October 2004 without enacting it. In March 2005, bipartisan legislation was reintroduced in the Senate and House of Representatives that, if enacted, would grant the FDA the authority to broadly regulate tobacco products as described above. ALG and PM USA support this legislation.[25]

While the FBI, the Customs Service, the IRS, and other law enforcement agencies all currently work to prevent black-market cigarette sales and cigarette smuggling, Philip Morris saw a benefit from empowering one more agency—the FDA—with that job, helping protect the company from competition, illegal or legal. Giving tobacco more layers of protection than most products (at taxpayer expense) would be yet another boon that FDA regulation would provide to Philip Morris—a boon, in this case, shared by other tobacco companies.

FDA regulation of tobacco was one more example of regulation help-ing the biggest companies at the expense of consumers, competitors, and taxpayers.

A Nicotine Patch for the States

Turning attention back to the MSA, what happened to all that money? Most of it went to state governments. The original lawsuits were about re-couping lost money due to state Medicare and Medicaid costs with pay-ments apportioned—supposedly but not really. So did the money go into state Medicare or Medicaid funds? Did they go to taxpayers or insurance companies that bore the cost of cigarette-related health costs?

The answer, no matter how you look at it, is no. The money, in most cases, went straight into the hands of state lawmakers. The scene in state capitals after the tobacco settlement resembled children let loose in a candy shop. "This is going to be pretty much a feeding frenzy," said one Albany legislator.[26]

In 2003, states spent 36 percent of their MSA money covering "budget shortfalls," according to the General Accounting Office (GAO), and another 8 percent on "general purposes." States spent 7 percent on "infrastructure." That means that at least 51 percent of the tobacco money in 2003 went to pay for roads, lawmaker salaries, parks, grants, and other government activi-ties. Less than a quarter of the money (24 percent) went to health programs, and 4 percent went to education. Most interesting, in 2003, the states spent only 2 percent of the tobacco money on programs to fight smoking.[27]

To be fair, some of the settlement money (from other payments besides the annual payments) did go toward private efforts to curb smoking, and many states already had antismoking programs in place. But the tobacco money was basically treated like general revenue, showing once again that the MSA was just a big tax hike on smokers, passed without a single vote.

While lawmakers got this "free money," without having to pass a tax hike, the lawsuits also promised to boost the political careers of the state at-torneys general (another nickname for NAAG was "National Association of Aspiring Governors"). For the most part, however, these prosecutors failed to climb the ladder. In Mississippi, Attorney General Mike Moore launched a campaign for governor shortly after the settlement but then bailed. In Minnesota, Attorney General Hubert H. Humphrey III lost to wrestler Jesse "The Body" Ventura in his 1998 gubernatorial bid. In Massachusetts, A.G. Scott Harshburger also got his party's nomination, but he fell in the 1998 race for governor. Republican Carla Stovall also tried to parlay her tobacco suit into a promotion to the governor's mansion in 2002.

The two tobacco attorneys general who won came from opposite ends of the tobacco wars. In North Carolina, Mike Easley, who was a reluctant participant in the lawsuits, won the governorship in 2000. In Washington, Christine Gregoire, one of the most dogged opponents of Big Tobacco, won a razor-thin election for governor in 2004.

All of these candidates ran their races with a little help from their friends, the recently filthy-rich trial lawyers. If these lawyers' future political races were read as referenda on the MSA, the people did not approve.

Trial Lawyers Get Rich

The settlement, in large part, was a transfer of wealth from smokers to wealthy trial lawyers. The lawyers in the states that settled outside of the MSA made out the best, according to author Martha Derthick, who reports, "Florida's lawyers received $3.43 billion; Mississippi's, $1.43 billion; and those of Texas $3.3 billion." Among the MSA states, "in the first year or two, the legal teams in each state would receive hundreds of millions of dollars."[28] Dickie Scruggs and Peter Angelos, however, stand above all other lawyers when it comes to cashing in on the tobacco suits.

Yale Law professor John Langbein, before a Manhattan Institute panel in 1999, described Scruggs' winnings this way:

> Mr. Scruggs is a historic figure. His picture is going to go in the legal history books, along with Justinian and Lord Coke. He's going to be there for having had the unbelievable nerve to demand billions upon billions of dollars and then to actually to get it, or at least come very close.
>
> The idea of charging this kind of money in connection with a legal system is unheard of, not only in our own legal tradition, but anywhere else. When Europeans hear these numbers, their jaws hit their desks. No well run polity needs to pay $8 billion or $40 billion to facilitate the ordinary functions of government. To pay this kind of money to private entrepreneurs for what is basically a public function is extraordinary, unprecedented, and deeply unprincipled.[29]

The most spectacular case of lawyers' fees, however, happened in Maryland, and it involved the owner of the Baltimore Orioles, Peter Angelos.

Angelos is a colorful man. He gained attention in early 2000 when an Orioles official announced that the team had a policy of discrimination in its hiring practices. The *Washington Times* reported, "The Baltimore Orioles refuse to sign players who defect from Cuba, saying they believe it is bad for relations between the United States and the communist country."[30]

Angelos had befriended Cuban dictator Fidel Castro and did not want to do anything "that could be interpreted as being disrespectful or . . . encouraging players to defect," according to a team official.[31] Despite his respect for the Communist leader, Angelos appears to believe firmly in the American dream of getting filthy rich.

In 1999, in exchange for his services on behalf of the Free State, Angelos demanded 25 percent of Maryland's tobacco money—about $1.1 billion. State lawmakers were not pleased by the notion of sharing so much of their largesse, and so they voted to cut Angelos's payday by half. When Angelos complained in late 1999, State Senate President Thomas Miller defended the state's actions, explaining to the *Washington Post*, "Mr. Angelos, in my opinion, agreed to accept 12.5 percent if and only if we agreed to change tort law, which was no small feat. We changed centuries of precedent to ensure a win in this case." In the end, Angelos agreed to a paltry $150 million.

The trial lawyers didn't just put their money in the bank. In 1998, even before MSA payouts, the *New York Times* reported: "Since 1995, lawyers from 13 firms with tobacco cases have made nearly $3 million in political contributions, the vast majority going to Democratic Party committees or candidates."[32]

From November 2000 through September 2005, Peter Angelos, his wife, and his son—who are also lawyers in the practice with Peter—have given over $2 million to politicians, almost all of it to Democrats. In the same period, Scruggs has spent $327,000 on politics, mostly giving to Democrats. Joe Rice, as is fitting for a dealmaker, has split his many thousands more equally among the parties, but still favoring Democrats.[33]

Winners and Losers

It's not hard to pick out the winners and losers in the MSA. First, the smokers lose big. They now have to pay significantly higher prices for cigarettes, making them both poor *and* sick. Smokers, for the most part, are lower-income individuals. The Oral Cancer Foundation reports that, "Smoking prevalence was higher among adults living below the poverty level (32.3 percent) than those living at or above the poverty level (23.5 percent)."[34] The MSA, then, is a regressive tax, disproportionately affecting the poor.

Second, the competition suffers. The small tobacco companies that now pay damages for a wrong they've never been accused of—often paying more per pack than their big competitors pay. These upstarts are also threatened with penalties if they have the nerve to expand.

Third are the taxpayers, who by some arguments might be the real victims in the states' lawsuits—after all, they were the ones forced to pay the Medicare and Medicaid expenses of sick smokers. Almost none of the tobacco money went to tax breaks or even into health funds that would cover future cigarette-related health costs. States addicted to tobacco money have borrowed against future payments, which may never come to be, or which force them into an unholy alliance with Big Tobacco to keep them alive and well. The MSA has made state governments more profligate, which will cost taxpayers in the end.

The biggest winners are Philip Morris and the other original parties to the MSA. Tobacco expert Jack Calfee agrees, saying, "the MSA has turned out pretty good for them." Many of their competitors are basically prohibited from expanding, while others are paying damages for a wrong Big Tobacco committed. Restrictions on advertising further limit competition and enhance Big Tobacco.

Clearly, the private trial lawyers made out pretty well, earning unimaginable riches by hiking taxes and helping create a business cartel. The attorneys general did okay, with a couple of them now holding governorships.

The "war against tobacco" turned out to be one more example of big business and big government ripping off the consumers, the competitors, and the taxpayers.

9

You Get Taxed,
They Get Rich

Why Big Business Loves High Taxes

The governor was on friendly turf. On stage, with his jacket off, and a PowerPoint slideshow behind him, he was in his element: a capitalist among capitalists. "I spent twenty years in business, two in politics," he said to reassure the men and women in suits before him.

On January 16, 2004, he was asking his state's Chamber of Commerce for support in an effort that would shape his legacy, and he was getting good vibes. "I like speaking to business groups," he told the *New York Times,* "because they get it." Sure enough, he found he didn't need to twist any arms—business already backed his plan. He was asking them to use their lobbying power to win over the legislature, which would not be easy. "My strategy is simple," he told the Chamber. "My strategy is you."[1]

Four months later, the governor's strategy came together. On the strength of big business's support, Democratic Governor Mark Warner passed and signed the largest tax increase in the history of Virginia.

The story of the five-year effort by Virginia's business leaders to hike all sorts of taxes is eye opening but not extraordinary. Big business frequently advocates higher taxes for many reasons.

Virginia's pro-tax businesses had many motivations. For one, the leading businesses in Virginia thrived on government money. Other businesses
were "feeding the alligator" of state government hoping it would get full
before it came after them. The road to the tax hike took some detours, but
it ended where most big ripoffs end: with another notch in the belt of big
business and big government, and another loss for taxpayers, consumers,
and competitors.

The Beginning of the Road

Governor Mark Warner introduced his tax-hiking budget in early 2004, and
big business helped it become law later that year. But, if you ask former Virginia Republican Party Chairman Pat McSweeney, he will tell you the
whole thing started in the 1970s.

McSweeney has been around Virginia politics longer than almost any
other living person. In a telephone interview, he reminisced to me about
the 1950s, and the good relationship conservative politicians had with the
state's business leaders. "We had a very conservative coalition," he told me,
explaining that the people most active on Richmond's political scene were
the ones who were most wary of Richmond's potential power. "Many of
these guys were self-made businessmen, but all of them wanted government out of the way."

As McSweeney tells it, the folks making the most noise in Richmond
"wanted government to stay out of the way, abhorred debt, and genuinely
worried about the stifling effect of higher taxes on job creation, capital for-
mation and even the average middle class family."

But "a new breed" of politicians came to Richmond in the 1970s, he
said, inserting the state government a little more in Virginians' lives and businesses. In McSweeney's narrative, this was the prologue to the current dynamic, where the big government types in Richmond have a symbiotic
relationship with the big business types throughout the state.

Once government started getting more involved in everyday life and in
business, the people running the businesses had to pay attention. "It creates
this self-perpetuating cycle," says McSweeney. "Once a businessman realizes
he has to play politics, he plays politics. He realizes more government can be
good for his business." Of course, as government grows, the incentive
heightens for business owners to turn away from customers and toward
politicians. State Senator Ken Cuccinelli calls this a "vicious circle."

McSweeney says the business–government partnership truly flowered in the governorship of Chuck Robb from 1982 to 1986. The two powers started to look to one another for political and financial help. The politicians saw in business both an engine to drive the bold plans they had for the state and a source of campaign funds. The businesses saw the politicians as offering protection from unwanted government interference, but also in stabilizing the unpredictable market. Government also represented a deep well of contract awards.

But these friends of big business have not had uninterrupted control of the governor's mansion. The 1997 election brought in a man who at least talked like one of McSweeney's old conservative friends. That man was Governor Jim Gilmore.

Gilmore, to be sure, belied his conservative message by increasing general fund spending by 41 percent over four years,[2] but he never lost his conservative instinct. By 1999, Gilmore earned the nickname "Governor Gridlock" for his unwillingness to increase taxes for the sake of building more roads. Every newspaper, politician, businessman, and businesswoman agreed: The traffic in Northern Virginia, around Washington, DC, was unbearable, and something had to be done. Gilmore agreed, but said that raising taxes was not on the table. One editorial assailed his "anti-tax absolutism."[3]

Many of Gilmore's fellow Republicans in the state legislature—mostly the more senior members who were part of the now-old "new breed" of the 1970s that McSweeney described—assailed the Governor for his firm position against tax hikes. In his 2000 budget, Gilmore offered $2.5 billion in new road spending over two years, paying for it without increasing taxes.

This was not good enough for some around Richmond. A special transportation commission that Gilmore appointed returned a study calling for local authorities to raise taxes locally and spend the money on local roads. Around the same time, James Dyke Jr., chairman of the Fairfax County Chamber of Commerce made it clear he supported an increase in the sales tax.[4]

But Gilmore wouldn't budge. This was a confusing dynamic to many. It seemed that businesses were volunteering to make a sacrifice for the sanity of the state's drivers and the health of the state, but Gilmore was rejecting their offer. Wealthy developer Til Hazel had sounded that note, saying "At some point you have to get past the question of 'How is it going to affect me?' and look at the good of the state."

Local newspapers sounded confused. "Still, even with business support, tax increases remain poison to many politicians," wrote one Virginia reporter.[5]

But only a gullible observer would believe that Hazel, in supporting higher taxes, was looking beyond his own good and toward the good of the state. Sure enough, most people figured out why businesses, especially Hazel and his fellow developers, wanted higher taxes and highway spending.

Anyone looking for clues for the developers' motivation might want to take a drive down Interstate 66 to Exit 43, about 23 miles outside the Beltway. That will drop you onto Route 29 in a place called Gainesville. With accelerating expansion of the federal government driving up housing prices in the District of Columbia and the suburbs, the "exurbs" out I-66 are growing. Thousands of drivers every morning take Route 29 in Gainesville to I-66 to work in or around DC. But that part of Route 29 near Exit 43 was built to be a country road, not a major commuter route—and you can tell. Gainesvillians who depend on Route 29 say it takes them longer to get to I-66 than it does for them to drive the 30 miles into the city.

But take the local roads out a mile or two in the middle of the day, and you won't see commuters but big, red trucks with yellow lettering on the side, reading "William A. Hazel." These trucks move up and down the roads hauling dirt, trees, equipment, and workers to the dozens of developments that Bill Hazel is helping build.

Bill's older brother is John, who goes by "Til." Til Hazel owns many of the plots out in Loudon County, Virginia, and for years has planned to build more housing developments in the area. That part of Virginia has many advantages. The air is cleaner than inside the beltway, you're close to Dulles Airport and Civil War battlefields, and there is just more space.

But the traffic on Route 29 is a turnoff. Most people would reject a 90-minute commute if they had a choice. In other words, congestion on Route 29 was driving down the prospective value of the houses Til Hazel was building. If the roads were wider, and if there were more roads, people would be willing to pay more for the homes. The developers had dozens of developments like the ones at Interstate 66 and Route 29 scattered through Northern Virginia.

Like the homeowner who wants to make improvements on his house to increase his sales price, Til Hazel wanted to make his developments more desirable. While the homeowner might take out a loan or dip into his own savings, Til Hazel had a better option: get the taxpayers to pay for new roads around his properties.

Hazel and other business owners and developers launched a campaign in 1999 to increase taxes in Virginia for the sake of building more roads. They initiated an expensive public relations campaign playing on drivers' frustration with traffic. James Dyke at the Fairfax County Chamber of Commerce wrote:

> Foremost among [Virginia's challenges] is the tremendous stress placed on an inadequate transportation infrastructure system that is threatening our quality of life, as employees and parents spend more time sitting in traffic and less time with their families and jobs.[6]

Many groups throughout Virginia had been complaining about the traffic jams and calling for limits on new development, but Dyke and the business community had a different solution. "What we desperately need right now," Dyke wrote in a public letter to Governor Gilmore, "is a massive injection of cash into the process."[7] That means a tax hike.

If the problem was too many drivers on too few roads, some suggested, maybe hiking the gas tax and earmarking the revenues for road construction would address both ends of the problem, both encouraging car pools and "inject[ing] cash." Dyke disparaged that idea. Maybe if we need more roads, the drivers should pay for them—through tolls. Til Hazel scoffed at that idea.

The answer, the businesses all said, was a sales tax. Increase sales tax by half a penny per dollar, they argued, and spend the newfound millions on more roads. The business leaders lobbied the lawmakers in Richmond, but it was a hard sell. In 1999, for the first time in history, Virginia voters had elected a majority of Republicans to both the House of Delegates and the Senate in Richmond. While eager to help the businesses, these lawmakers were leery of hiking taxes.

In January 2001, responding to Governor Gilmore's budget, Delegate John Rollison, chairman of the House Transportation Committee, found a way to allow politicians to straddle the fence. Rollison sponsored a bill that placed a tax hike on the Election Day ballot in Northern Virginia, allowing voters in the region to raise their own sales tax for the sake of building roads.

For the next four years, one of Virginia's most interesting political battles would unfold. Amid the subplots, twists, and turns, one thing remained constant: Big business supported higher taxes.

Follow the Money

On Election Day, 2002, I walked into work prepared for a long day. As a political reporter, I would be pulling an all-nighter. When I got to my chair (just outside Bob Novak's door, allowing Novak to see whatever I was working on), I saw a flyer. It was from the building's management, but it had nothing to do with the rat problem (which was now mostly solved) or the elevator repairs (which were still ongoing).

The flyer showed a photo of bumper-to-bumper traffic and exhorted me to vote for the sales tax increase. Every chair in the building had one. Were the building managers concerned with how early we had to leave home in the morning or worried that we might sometimes be late to work? More likely, the building's owner, Charles E. Smith Management, was interested in getting taxpayers to build more roads to the company's land holdings throughout the DC area.

Sure enough, Charles E. Smith Management gave $25,000 to a group called "Citizens for Better Transportation."[8] Despite its name, Citizens for Better Transportation (CBT) was hardly a grass-roots group of angry commuters. It was, more or less, the political arm of the state's Chamber of Commerce. The only thing this organization did in 2002 was to lobby for higher sales taxes.

Data compiled by the nonprofit Virginia Public Access Project (VPAP) show just how much this tax hike meant to the Commonwealth's big business community. Citizens for Better Transportation raised and spent over $2 million—half of it from the Real Estate/Construction industry according to VPAP.

Citizens for Better Transportation's top benefactor was Myron Erkiletian of Alexandria, Virginia. Erkiletian's generosity covers the entire political spectrum: Republicans and Democrats, federal and state candidates, both inside and outside of Virginia. But never did Erkiletian invest as much in an election as he did in the effort to raise taxes in 2002. Erkiletian forked over $100,000. One of the largest construction companies in Virginia is Erkiletian Construction Corporation.

Erkiletian shared the top spot among CBT's donors with First Virginia Bank. First Virginia is a major home lender, which means that the more houses Hazel and Erkiletian build, the more business First Virginia can get. First Virginia is also the biggest auto lender in Virginia according to the *Washington Post*.[9] More roads, and more commuters living in the exurbs means more business for First Virginia.

Donors who gave $25,000 or more to this pro-tax group included the Northern Virginia Building Industry Association, the Virginia Transportation Construction Industry Association, the Washington Infrastructure Industry Association, Bechtel Infrastructure Corporation, Fairfax County

Chamber of Commerce, Virginia Association of Realtors, Til Hazel, Bill Hazel, and more than a dozen other builders and businesses.

Other pro-tax hike groups had similar financial bases. "Virginians for Better Transportation" was a much smaller group that in brought in thousands from construction companies and highway builders.

These business-funded groups spent $2 million trying to persuade the people of Northern Virginia to increase taxes. The antitax side was not so well heeled. The "Committee Opposing Sales Taxes for Transportation" raised less than $20,000, with half of its money coming from one realtor in Southeastern Virginia. The "Coalition Against the Tax Referendum" hauled in a total of $61,000, with no gifts of $25,000 or greater. A few business owners made smaller contributions, but the pattern was clear: The big money was on the pro-tax side.

Polls just before Election Day showed that the pro-tax forces had convinced most Northern Virginians. One survey in late October showed the Yes side up by six points. But the antitax folks took their cause to the ground. With almost no business support, antitax conservatives and antisprawl environmentalists joined forces against higher taxes for more roads.

In October 2002, the Virginia League of Conservation Voters, the Coalition for Smarter Growth, and the Piedmont Environmental Council issued a paper titled "The Sales Tax as Highway Robbery: Developers Making Us Pay for Sprawl."

Pointing to the pro-tax CBT, the antisprawl groups wrote:

> The CBT can be seen as a small but very lucrative investment for big business and big developer interests. Give $2 million to boost the sales tax. Get the taxpayers to pay $5 billion dollars of their money for infrastructure. Do nothing to change development locations and designs to reduce traffic, while having new bypass highways built near land held for speculative development. Then, make billions of dollars. We end up footing the bill.[10]

These antisprawl groups also wanted government to block the developers' building plans. Conservatives such as Ken Cuccinelli had more modest goals.

In 2001, Cuccinelli was a patent attorney and a father of five girls. By 2002, he was a state senator and a crusader against the tax increase.

When his Republican state senator resigned to take an appointment by the Democratic Governor Warner, Cuccinelli made a run for the open seat.

His antitax message caught the notice of the business community right away, but not in a good way. Cuccinelli's opponent in the GOP primary, Mike Thompson, quickly gathered over $10,000 in contributions from developers, the most from any industry. Thompson was no champion of higher taxes, but to the developers, he was better than Cuccinelli.

In the general election, the contrast was sharper. After winning the primary, Cuccinelli faced Democrat Cathy Belter. She raised $25,000 from developers—again, the most from any industry. For his part, Cuccinelli got $19,000 from businesses characterized by VPAP as "retail and services," businesses that would actually *pay* the proposed higher sales tax.

Cuccinelli won the special election that spring and immediately went to work with a small group of conservative lawmakers and activists lobbying against the referendum. They highlighted the self-interest behind the pro-tax businesses. "The developers are asking you to pay for their driveway," he told one crowd of taxpayers.

That characterization may be most true in the case of Albert Dwoskin. According to the October 2002 paper by the antisprawl groups, Dwoskin owned more than 230 acres along a new bypass and near Route 28, a road that would be expanded if the tax increase succeeded. The paper also reported that Dwoskin, through his various holdings and companies, gave at least $11,000 to CBT. That's a small investment if, in return, you get millions in free road improvements near your property.

Major newspaper editors were not blind to how the tax increase would enrich certain developers, but they agreed with the developers' message that easing road congestion would be good for the region. But the developers' credibility on this matter was suspect. The *Richmond Times Dispatch* raised that point in an editorial about the businesses funding the pro-tax cause:

> One can assume [the developers] do not support the referendum out of nothing more than an altruistic desire to make their employees' commutes more relaxing. Rather, they expect new road construction to make possible new development: more housing units, more stores, and more office space. If so, then the referendum will not "end congestion" or even reduce it. Congestion will decrease only if road space increases while the volume of traffic remains static. If traffic volume increases along with space, then Northern Virginia will find itself just as clogged as ever. There will be more of the dread "sprawl." Developers will make more money, of course—and residents will pay higher taxes.[11]

In other words, CBT promised less congestion, implying more roads for the same number of cars, but the forces behind CBT were really planning more roads for more cars—leaving just as much congestion.

But it didn't happen. The late poll figures proved to be a red herring. Northern Virginia voters, on November 5, rejected the tax hike by a margin of 55 to 45. The developers and politicians scolded the people of Virginia. "On Nov. 6, we all woke up and realized that our region still has a severe transportation crisis," wrote Michael J. Lewis, the new chairman of the Fairfax Chamber of Commerce. "So what are we going to do about that?"[12]

Sean Connaughton, a Prince William County politician who had supported the tax increase, figured that the developers would now have to pony up themselves. "The only readily available solution is to get the private sector to build some of these projects with the expectation that they could recover the costs," Connaughton told the *Washington Post*. "Is there interest out there to build some of these transit road facilities with tolls?"[13]

Connaughton was wrong. The developers had no intention of "building their own driveway," as Cuccinelli would put it. Their plan B was just like plan A in one respect: Hike taxes for more road money. It was very different in another respect: They would get the politicians—not the taxpayers and drivers—to approve the tax increase.

Big Business Wins Tax Increases

Virginia holds its elections for state government offices in odd-numbered years. Pat McSweeney says that the Democrats who ran Richmond for years realized it was hurting them to appear on the same ballot with the likes of George McGovern and other national Democrats, and so they moved the elections to odd years, meaning lawmakers in both chambers of the Virginia General Assembly were up for reelection in 2003.

That year, according to VPAP, developers gave more than $5 million to politicians—*after* the $2 million they spent on the referendum the year before. The second most generous industry was the legal profession, which gave half what developers gave.

The new legislature took office in January 2004, and that's when Governor Mark Warner launched his pro-tax-hike charm offensive on the Republican-controlled Senate and House. As he made clear in his January presentation before the Virginia Chamber of Commerce, he would need the support of the state's businesses in order to pass his tax hike.

The 2002 referendum showed that getting businesses backing for the tax hike was an easy sell. In January, the state Chamber of Commerce voted unanimously to support Warner's budget, which he estimated would raise taxes by $1 billion over two years. James Dyke, the former head of the Fairfax Chamber of Commerce, put his new business organization, the Northern Virginia Roundtable, squarely behind the tax increase.

Meanwhile, the Virginia chapter of the National Federation of Independent Business (NFIB) came out against the plan. NFIB's state director Gordon Dixon explained why his small business group would see things differently than the Commonwealth's big businesses. A *Washington Times* editorial paraphrased his argument thus:

> [L]arger companies can afford to hire lawyers and accountants to search for ways to lower their taxes. Small firms, by contrast, cannot afford to do so, and consequently, tax increases hit them much harder. Many small business owners, he said, include their business income in their personal income tax returns and would be hard hit by Mr. Warner's proposal to increase the top rate from 5.75 percent to 6.25 percent.[14]

Dixon's rebuke of the tax increase—and plea for mercy on small businesses—held little sway in Richmond.

By the spring, Warner had his way, and Virginians were paying higher taxes—thanks to big business and its unfailing financial and verbal support of the tax increases.

Big Business Profits from the Estate Tax

Readers of the *New York Times* Op-Ed page on Sunday, February 18, 2001, had quite a lot to enjoy. Sandwiched between Paul Krugman's and Maureen Dowd's anti-Bush screeds was a headline, "My Reason for the Pardons" by William Jefferson Clinton, explaining why he issued pardons to two convicted felons who fled the country before serving a day of their sentences. In the bottom right corner of the page was an advertisement: "If the estate tax is eliminated," the ad read, "someone else will pay. YOU."

President George W. Bush had just proposed his first budget. It called for ambitious tax cuts including elimination of taxes on inheritances. Critics of this estate tax call it the "death tax." Supporters of the estate tax point out that there is a large exemption, and so inheritances as big as $650,000 are not taxed at all. Only the very rich actually pay the estate tax, they argue.

It was eye-catching, then, that this pro-estate-tax ad was paid for and signed by William H. Gates, George Soros, Rockefellers, Roosevelts, and Paul Newman. These were the superrich, people who presumably would benefit from eliminating the estate tax. The group called themselves "Responsible Wealth." A *New York Times* article on the group paraphrased William Gates, the father of Microsoft CEO Bill Gates, saying, "if it were not for his full-time job, he would organize a group called Millionaires for the Estate Tax."

The article reported that one billionaire refused to sign the petition because it was too mild: investment mogul Warren Buffett. The *Times* article said of Buffett:

> [H]e had not signed the petition itself because he thought it did not go far enough in defending "the critical role" that he said the estate tax played in promoting economic growth, by helping create a society in which success is based on merit rather than inheritance.[15]

Opponents of President Bush would use these millionaires and billionaires as a tool to attack a proposed repeal of the estate tax. "If Warren Buffett can tell America that he just got a bonanza . . . and he thinks it's more important to give $1,000 to every family, I think that's pretty good thinking," John Kerry told PBS's *NewsHour* during the 2004 campaign. Kerry contended that repealing such a tax would benefit only the rich, and that even the second-richest man in America, Warren Buffett, thought the estate tax should be preserved.

Kerry implied that Buffett and Gates had special credibility to criticize estate tax repeal because of how rich they are. Kerry wasn't the only one who spoke that way. When Bill Clinton was preparing to veto a repeal of the estate tax in August of 2000, he said he supported a reduction but not an elimination of the estate tax. "[I]t's not fair to totally repeal it—like even Bill Gates has said, why are you going to give me a $40 billion tax break."[16]

In an article in the liberal *American Prospect* magazine in January 2001, liberal journalist Jonathan Rowe wrote "Warren Buffett, George Soros, and even Bill Gates . . . have urged that fortunes go toward charitable and public uses rather than just to spoiled heirs." His article, titled "Every Baby a Trust Fund Baby," suggested this was motivated by a "a responsible attitude toward their wealth."[17]

Deeper investigation suggests less noble motivations. Consider Bill Gates' Microsoft. It is a publicly held corporation. One difference between Microsoft and most small businesses is that Microsoft's owner will never die. Of course, the hundreds of thousands of shareholders will each die at some point, but passing their stock to their children will probably not be subject to the estate tax. Even if it is, shifting ownership of its shares will not affect the operation or structure of Microsoft.

In contrast, consider your favorite local restaurant for a moment. Perhaps the owner opened it 40 years ago and bought the building after 10 years, renting out the other units to other businesses. Now, his mortgage is completely paid off. The building's value (surely appreciated) plus the value of his equipment could add up to $2 million. When he dies, his son, who has been running the business for the past five years might owe $500,000 in estate taxes. But the business may not generate anything close to that much profit per year. The son will have no choice but to sell his inheritance—the business, the building, or both—in order to pay the taxes for receiving it. The estate tax, then, clearly favors publicly held or at least broadly held businesses over family-owned businesses.

The estate tax will never hit Microsoft, but it may hit its smaller competitors, who, in turn, might have to sell to bigger corporations (or developers). Burt Willey runs Systems & Software, Inc. (S&S), in Colchester, Vermont. His father founded the business in 1973. In 1990, along with his sister, Burt took ownership of the company, whose primary customers are utilities. S&S makes a product called enQuesta, a program that utilities use to track customers' payment and billing information.

Willey knew about the estate tax, and has tried to prepare his company for it, paying high premiums for insurance policies and taking other measures. "You constantly have to be thinking about if you die, what will happen to the company?" Willey told me in a telephone interview. "I find that not many people plan for that, because they're too busy running their business."

Willey says the estate tax was a consideration, while not *the* central factor, when he and his sister decided to sell controlling stake in S&S to a private equity firm called Accel-KKR. Accel-KKR seeks out well-run companies to buy. One advantage of being owned by Accel-KKR, Willey says, is to instill consumer confidence. Beyond receiving a stamp of approval from a well-respected private equity firm, S&S may have just won the gift of immortality. Since S&S is no longer owned by individuals who might die but instead by a venture capitalism firm, the estate tax will never disrupt the company. That security, says Willey, helps improve customer confidence.

Willey and S&S might be able to expand and thrive now that Accel-KKR has bought the majority of the company. But the estate tax imposes an added pressure on companies like S&S to sell and narrows the choices those small businesses have to determine their own future.

When corporate chiefs favor the estate tax, they might be "feeding the alligator." As the Responsible Wealth *New York Times* ad suggests, the loss in revenue incurred by repealing the estate tax would have consequences— possibly higher taxes in a form that could harm large corporations.

For Warren Buffett, though, the benefits of the estate tax are more direct. Warren Buffett's business is *buying businesses.* Bill Gates makes software and Paul Newman makes movies and salad dressing, but Warren Buffett makes money. He runs Berkshire Hathaway as CEO and principle owner. Berkshire Hathaway used to make textiles, but now they simply own other companies. Some familiar Berkshire Hathaway properties are GEICO, Dairy Queen, Fruit of the Loom, and the *Buffalo News.*

While Buffett is clearly an unusually brilliant investor, what he has done with this company has been straightforward in some ways: He buys companies that are worth more than the selling price. He buys things that will go up in value.

Anyone who has ever seen a going-out-of-business sale knows that one of the best ways to get a bargain is to deal with a motivated seller—a person or business that needs to sell in a hurry. In the case of a general store, a store-owner who has lost his lease might need to unload his merchandise before he loses the room to store it.

In the case of the *Buffalo News,* the motivated seller was the family who had just inherited the business, and was facing an estate tax bill. In 1873, at the age of 23, Edward H. Butler founded the newspaper that became the *Buffalo Evening News.* After his death, it passed to his son, Edward Jr. When Edward Jr. passed away, his widow Kate became the owner (spouses do not pay the federal estate tax).

According to Murray Light, a former top editor at the paper and author of the only history of the *Buffalo News* (as it is now called), Kate "had repeatedly rejected the advice of her attorneys that she take steps to minimize the tax consequences that would occur upon her death." Sure enough, when Kate died, the family felt it had no choice but to sell the paper. Buffett was happy to pay $32.5 million to own the publication, which soon was making $40 million per year.[18]

Reporter John Berlau has documented other motivated sellers facing the estate tax who have found a willing buyer in Warren Buffett. Among them are Dairy Queen, a Utah furniture store, and a Nebraska jeweler.

When the estate tax forces an owner to sell his businesses, it provides an opportunity for a bargain, but that opportunity is not available to everyone. While $32.5 million is a bargain for a newspaper that can return more than that per year, it is also a price that only the very rich can afford. When the estate tax puts a business on the market, it is a market that's open only to big business.

Beyond making it easier for Buffett to find bargains, the estate tax drives customers to his primary business interest: insurance, including life insurance. The estate tax has created an entire industry called "estate planning." Anyone with a business or large assets sooner or later needs to engage in estate planning, which involves hiring tax specialists, attorneys, and accountants. To avoid the estate tax, people create foundations and trust funds, give small annual gifts, skip generations and give to their grandchildren, and employ countless clever techniques known to those who make a living helping people avoid the estate tax. Two central elements of estate planning are life insurance and annuities. If the estate tax were eliminated, demand for life insurance and annuities would be lower.

Sure enough, as Berlau reports, one of Buffett's acquisitions, Safeco, offers "special life insurance programs that can help you continue your business after the death of a key employee or help your heirs pay estate taxes without selling your property." Clearly, the estate tax generates business for Safeco, which creates wealth for Buffett.

Frank Keating's embrace of the death tax reflects the life insurance industry's interest in keeping it alive. Keating was once the Republican governor of Oklahoma, touted by conservatives in 2000 as the best choice to be Bush's running mate. In 2002, Keating wrote: "I beleive death taxes are un-American. They are rooted in the failed collectivist schemes of the past and have no place in a society that values entrepreneurship, work, saving, and families."[19]

When he left Oklahoma City in 2002, Keating took a high-paying job as the head of the American Council of Life Insurers. Once in that position, he made it clear that he opposed complete repeal of the estate tax—a measure that Bush had promised in his campaign. The October 20, 2003, *National Underwriter* profile of Keating reported, "One area where Keating parts company with many of his fellow Republicans is that he is not in favor of abolishing the estate tax. He is a 'populist,' he said, and wants to keep the tax because 'we don't have a class system in this country.' "[20]

It is impossible to read Frank Keating's or Warren Buffett's heart and mind. While Buffett profits from the death tax, his support for it may truly be motivated by his dislike of a class system. Compounding the problem, Buffett's secretary told me, "he is not available for interviews on any topic." We don't know his true motivations, but we do know he is a very good businessman. From a business perspective, fighting to save the death tax makes sense for Buffett.

Tax Crusaders

Big businesses fighting for tax increases or against tax cuts is hardly new. In fact, in the major tax battles of the past quarter century, business regularly fought on the pro-tax side.

Ronald Reagan's legacy is not typically associated with tax increases, but sure enough, in 1982, Reagan proposed a $98.3 billion tax increase, the year after his tax cut, which budget estimates said would reduce revenue by $718 billion over five years.[21] Reagan's White House pitched the 1982 tax increase as a bill to "close loopholes" in federal corporate tax law.

Across Lafayette Square from the White House is a stately building that many tourists assume is a government agency. But the massive edifice houses the U.S. Chamber of Commerce, which is the largest business association in the world. In the summer of 1982, as Reagan's tax hike marched across Capitol Hill, the Chamber fought a civil war.

U.S. Chamber of Commerce President Richard Lesher walked point on the anti-tax-hike side within the Chamber. Marching behind him was a slim majority of the Chamber's board members. Commanding the opposing camp was the Chamber's chairman, Paul Thayer, CEO of LTV Corporation. Thayer, with the backing of 30 of the Chamber's 65 board members, supported the tax increase. They were not alone. The National Association of Manufacturers, the Business Roundtable, the National Association of Realtors, and American Business Conference were among other tax-boosters in the business world.[22]

Although Lesher won within the Chamber, Thayer won on Capitol Hill. The *Wall Street Journal* quoted Lesher afterward, saying, "I'd rather lose an issue than be on the wrong side of it."[23] He meant he would always oppose tax increases, even if it cost him—and it did cost him.

Because he went against Ronald Reagan, Lesher was now persona non grata at the White House. White House business liaison Wayne Valis told the *Wall Street Journal*, "We intend to work with the chamber, but only through Paul Thayer." The *Journal* quoted another top official—an anonymous Senate staffer—sounding the same note about Lesher: "With his totally intransigent stance on the tax bill, the Chamber very seriously wounded its ability to do anything up here."

Thayer had predicted this reaction from Congress and the White House, which is probably the main reason he supported the tax increase. The moral of the story: If people in the government want to raise taxes, it is best not to get in their way. This is often part of the reason big business favors tax hikes or regulations even when the regulations themselves provide no benefit or even small harm.

(As a footnote, Lesher did not stay "intransigent" on taxes for long, nor did Thayer's good grace with the federal government last. In 1993, the Chamber, under Lesher, supported Bill Clinton's tax increase.[24] In 1985, Thayer went to jail for obstructing justice in a federal insider-trading investigation,[25] showing that cuddling up to the government will only get you so far.)

The Business Roundtable, a similar organization to the Chamber, consistently showed an accommodationist side. In 1983, it called for a $250 billion tax increase, and again in 1985, it declared, "the time has come to consider a revenue increase."[26]

In 1993, when Democrats controlled the White House and Congress, there was even less will to oppose tax increases. Newly inaugurated President Bill Clinton called for higher taxes, and received full support from the business community. Columnists Rowland Evans and Robert Novak described the situation aptly in a March 1, 1993, column, "Clinton's Corporate Dependents." They reported that Chamber economist Lawrence Hunter "was thrown overboard" for opposing higher taxes. Apparently, Hunter had signed a letter objecting to an energy tax.[27] Hunter told that column, "This is the new collectivism. It looks very much like the corporate state. Some call it fascism."

Evans and Novak wrote:

> Integral to [Clinton's] plan is not to defeat business interests but to make them heavily dependent on government for survival. . . . Business leaders are asked to join the president's campaign for a program that increases the burden of taxes and regulation. In return, they are offered government dependency: subsidies, protection and cooperation. The takers are not reticent. . . . The desire to cut a deal permeates today's business mentality. . . . For business, the alternative to fighting redistribution and bigger government is to tap into the largess.

The columnists, however, were slightly off when they wrote of "the switch of the U.S. Chamber, long an impassioned advocate of the free market," as the Chamber has been far from steadfast in its opposition to tax hikes in the past.

Also during Clinton's first days, one particular CEO went on national television to advocate higher taxes. Dwayne Andreas, chairman of Archer Daniels Midland (ADM), called for a national sales tax (which wouldn't apply to food) and an increase in the gasoline tax. ADM, it turns out, sells food products and alternative fuels that enjoy special breaks from the gas tax.

The pro-tax politicians pointed to big business enthusiasm for tax hikes as conclusive evidence that the hikes were needed. Congressman Dan Rostenkowski, chairman of the Ways and Means Committee, which writes tax law, pumped up the 1993 tax hike by producing a list of "more than 50 major businesses" supporting the hike. Among the tax-hike advocates were Philip Morris, IBM, GM, GE, and Anheuser-Busch.[28]

"This proves that there's broad support for this bill throughout the nation," said Rostenkowski. "We seldom see taxpayers lobbying for a bill that will raise their taxes, but that is what is reflected in these letters."

On the state level, a similar dynamic occurs. In 1992, Douglas Bruce succeeded in amending the Colorado State Constitution, passing the "Taxpayer Bill of Rights" (TABOR), which prohibited any state or local tax increase unless voters approved. One of Bruce's chief opponents was the Denver Metro Convention and Visitor's Bureau—a sort of local Chamber of Commerce for the tourist industry, consisting of hotels, shops, and restaurants.[29]

Bruce was not surprised to encounter business opposition. In 1986, a similar ballot measure went down 62 percent to 38 percent, with the pro-tax side enjoying a 12-to-1 cash advantage, thanks largely to big business's contributions.[30]

Under TABOR, the state government could not hoard a surplus. If tax revenues were larger than expected, the state would have to cut taxes to return the cash to taxpayers. In 2005, in a third battle over TABOR, voters in Colorado eliminated that requirement by passing Referendum C, allowing the state to spend all surplus money instead of cutting taxes. Its companion measure, Referendum D, would allow the state to issue more debt, in the form of municipal bonds. Proponents of Referenda C and D, in short were opponents of tax cuts. Although pro-Referenda C and D activists correctly pointed out that the referenda would not, in themselves, hike taxes, Referendum C would prevent tax cuts that otherwise would have been automatic.

The campaigns for and against Referenda C and D were furious and expensive. Once again, the pro-tax side outspent the antitax side—this time $5.5 million to $2 million.[31] Once again, big business backed higher taxes, particularly the group "Vote Yes on C & D" (Referendum D failed).

The Denver Metro Chamber of Commerce spent more than $700,000 supporting the Referendum that would facilitate tax hikes. Colorado Health and Hospital Association spent $300,000, and Centura Health gave the pro-tax hike groups $195,000.[32] The HMO Kaiser Permanente donated $100,000 to "Vote Yes on C & D." Kaiser Permanente is technically a not-for-profit company, meaning it is taxed differently from most companies—no wonder tax hikes don't bother them. Both Safeway and Walgreens sent five-figure checks to the pro-tax activists, as did Coors Brewing Company. The Colorado Municipal Bond Dealers Association spent $60,000 helping the pro-tax referendum, which is not surprising considering that their entire business involves selling bonds backed by tax dollars. Also, their bonds are tax-exempt. Dozens of builders and contractors in Colorado forked over $10,000 to the pro-tax cause, and the Colorado Contractors Association spent $275,000 on the effort. The Realtor Issues PAC gave more than $70,000 to the well-organized "Vote Yes on C & D," likely considering that one reason people buy a home is for the tax benefit—a benefit that shrinks if taxes go down. The list of pro-tax businesses in Colorado in 2005 goes on and on.

The story was similar in California in 1978 when antitax activists put Proposition 13, which would limit property taxes, on the ballot. The "No on 13" Committee raised $1.7 million. Daniel A. Smith, who has written a history of such ballot measures titled *Tax Crusaders,* wrote:

> Over half of the money opposing the measure came in contributions of $1,000 or more. The big contributors [included] dozens of major corporations, including Ford, Rockwell International, Atlantic Richfield, Standard Oil, BankAmerica, Pacific Mutual Life Insurance, Pacific Gas and Electric, Pacific Telephone and Telegraph, and Pacific Lighting.[33]

In nearly every state where citizens have gone to the polls to vote on measures that would curb taxes or expand them, big business has funded the pro-tax lobbying effort. Big business justifies their support of higher taxes by arguing in these cases that higher taxes are good for the economy as a whole. In many cases—such as highway builders, tax-exempt businesses, or municipal bond dealers—it makes sense to assume that businesses see more concentrated benefits for themselves. Where Safeway has no problem with higher income taxes, the family that owns the corner store might feel differently.

While commentators often express surprise when big business supports higher taxes, it is not a rare occurrence. There are many reasons for a corporation to want higher taxes, and usually some blend of these reasons explains a company's pro-tax stance.

As Mark Warner and Bill Clinton have learned, when the forces of government and business join to increase government's slice of the pie, the taxpayer usually loses.

PART IV

GREEN: THE COLOR
OF MONEY

For the sake of saving the planet, American taxpayers and consumers are told to make all sorts of sacrifices—in the cars they drive, in the taxes they pay, and in the price of fuel and commodities. Hidden behind all the altruistic talk of environmentalism and conservation are two ugly facts: These "green" laws often don't make the air clearer or the water cleaner, and they usually are backed by some big business that stands to profit from them. The loser is the driver, the taxpayer, and the entrepreneur.

Clean air laws, clean fuel requirements, restrictions on mining, and other green measures usually find a key ally in industry. At the very least, someone gets rich off these laws. Some corporate-environmentalist alliances are formed out of political strategizing or for public relations benefit, but very often clever corporations see a way to profit off laws or regulations created in the name of saving the planet.

Aren't Environmentalist Laws *Good?*

If all "green" laws really did make the Earth better and cleaner, many Americans might argue they are worth the costs to the economy and the average family; most people would not see anything wrong with some corporation's angling to make money while improving the world. But environmental laws are often ill-conceived, and some bring benefit only in the short term or to a few corporations and politicians.

For example, the government once pushed a "clean" fuel additive on us called MTBE, and now they tell us MTBE is toxic. In the place of MTBE, governments on all levels are profusely subsidizing ethanol, a fuel made from corn, although it may be a pollutant in its own ways.

Also, environmentalist laws impose economic costs—costs that the consumer and the taxpayer ultimately bear.

How Does Big Business Profit from Them?

What if you could buy a worthless product and then magically give it value? That would be a good investment. This is often what lies behind corporate support for environmentalist laws. If you can make fuel out of corn or wind, but nobody wants to buy it, just get the government to mandate it. If you can cut your carbon dioxide emissions by 10 percent, it might or might not do anything to help the planet, but the right government action can make those cuts worth money.

Most observers portray tree-hugging talk by corporations either as public relations ploys or as uncomfortable realizations of undeniable truths (*"even* corporate America agrees we need to clean the air!"). In truth, big business's impetus to back environmentalist regulations is often nothing extraordinary: It is the profit motive.

Why Do I Care Who Gets Rich?

But the profit motive is not evil. Why should it matter if some business gets rich while helping save the planet?

Environmental issues are complex and difficult. Scientists disagree on the net effect of ethanol on the environment, the cause or magnitude of global warming, and hundreds of similar questions. Also, ambitious laws have dire consequences on both the planet and the economy. The ulterior motives of the people pushing a new law ought to be taken into account.

Just as we might listen with some skepticism when a coal company argues that burning coal poses little or no risks, we ought to be on guard when a company like Enron tells us we need new laws that will promote natural gas. Indeed, Enron was one of the prime supporters of the Kyoto Protocol on climate change, a treaty beloved by green groups worldwide that is aimed at stopping global warming.

This Part

In this section we see how some of America's biggest companies use questionable environmentalism as a way to get rich without having to try too hard. We see how the "good citizenship" of some corporations is just another investment, different only in that it is an investment in something for which there is no consumer demand. We learn why a refiner in California lobbied for strict new clean-fuel laws, and why they're laughing all the way to the bank today as the industry they've left behind flounders.

This section introduces you to the world's most successful moonshiner, who has made millions by making a fuel that some scientists argue is worthless. His success lies in marketing his commodity, not to consumers, but to politicians. And, oh yeah, his moonshine might cause pollution.

Finally, we explore the deep, dark, bowels of the erstwhile World's Leading Energy Company and show how environmentalism, government meddling, and corporate welfare combined to create a bubble that popped in the biggest bankruptcy in American history.

10

Environmentalism for Profit

How Bad Environmentalist Laws Give Your Money to Big Business

In June 1992, stretches of Los Angeles were still in ruins. Union Oil Company of California (Unocal) was miles away in El Segundo, but it still felt the effects of the riots following the Rodney King verdict weeks before. Tensions were high, bomb threats surfaced, and some of Unocal's neighbors closed shop for a few days during the riots.

California refiners like Unocal were having an all-around rotten summer in smoggy L.A. On May 22, the Organization of the Petroleum Exporting Countries (OPEC) had announced it would freeze oil production for the third quarter. Oil supplies had already taken a hit because Saddam Hussein's Iraq was now banned from exporting oil, and Hussein's armies had torched Kuwait's oil fields.

On top of all that, up in Sacramento, the California Air Resources Board (CARB) was finalizing its new rules—potentially costly mandates on refineries forcing them to make cleaner-burning gasoline. Unocal, though, was being a good citizen and actually helping CARB draft these stricter rules.

But, in the early days of the summer, some good news came into Unocal's offices from Washington, DC. It was a letter from the U.S. Patent and

Trademark Office (USTPO).[1] The USPTO planned to approve Unocal's patent applications. The central "invention" being patented was an efficient way to reduce harmful emissions (specifically hydrocarbons—molecules that, when they react with the air, become pollutants harmful to plants).

Unocal had figured out that among the many ways to reformulate gasoline to reduce the emission of hydrocarbons, it was most important to control the temperature at which the gasoline would vaporize. Gasoline contains many elements, and so different parts evaporate at different temperatures. The key to Unocal's discovery was that 50 percent of the gasoline should be vaporized between 180 degrees Fahrenheit and 205 degrees Fahrenheit (°F). As the scientists put it, the "T-50" should be at least 180°F and at most 205°F.

In November, CARB's final clean gasoline rules came down from Sacramento, and they happened to require that refineries make their summertime gasoline with a T-50 between 180°F and 205°F.

How did CARB come to the conclusion that T-50 was the key? Unocal had told them so. However, Unocal never told them that they were pursuing a patent on that exact method for reducing hydrocarbon emissions.

In February 1994, the USPTO granted Unocal the patent.[2] This meant that anyone refining oil to sell in California was, by law, using technology owned by Unocal. On January 31, 1995, Unocal announced that it was enforcing its patent rights, and demanding license fees from everyone who was using this method—meaning, *everyone* who was legally selling oil into California.

Ten weeks later, Exxon, Mobil, Chevron, Texaco, Shell, and other refiners sued in federal court to invalidate the patent. They were not about to pay licensing fees to Unocal in order to comply with a law that Unocal helped write.

But Unocal turned the tables on them, countersuing for patent infringement. All of these companies, Unocal argued, were using *their* technology to refine oil. Of course, any other process would have been illegal. The District Court found in Unocal's favor and required the original plaintiffs to pay Unocal 5.75 cents for each gallon it refined using the patented "invention." A federal appeals court upheld the ruling and the U.S. Supreme Court refused to hear the appeal.

Since then, Unocal has sued another California energy company, Valero, for copyright infringement, on the same grounds. The Federal Trade Commission has brought an action against Unocal, which is still pending in early 2006.

For its court victories so far, Unocal can thank the liberal Warren Court for its decision in a case called *United Mine Workers v. Pennington,* where big coal mines backed strict mine regulations that drove their smaller competitors out of business. The smaller mines sued, but the Supreme Court ruled that conspiracies in restraint of trade were protected as long as one of the co-conspirators, so to speak, was the government. In the light of *Pennington,* Unocal's official statements maintain its "right to petition government (as provided by the First Amendment) to secure legislation and regulations that may confer private gain."

The CARB rules were a double winner for Unocal. Before they even collected a dime in license fees or court-ordered back payments, Unocal already profited because the costly regulations they helped create drove their smaller competitors out of business—even though the rule granted smaller refiners a longer time to come into compliance (an exemption Unocal had lobbied against).

Shortly after the rules went into effect, a small Conoco plant in Santa Maria went under. A couple of months later, a Chemoil refinery shut its doors. In mid-1995, Pacific Refining, a small, independent refinery, closed its plant in Hercules, California. Others shuttered their refineries as well, reducing the choices California's gas stations had.[3]

This drove up oil prices, offsetting any new regulatory costs to Unocal and the other big refiners who survived and, in turn, were strengthened as their competitors fell. An *L.A. Times* article in the summer of 2005 summed it up this way:

California refiners are simply cashing in on a system that allows a handful of players to keep prices high by carefully controlling supplies. The result is a kind of miracle market in which profits abound, outsiders can't compete and a dwindling cadre of gas station operators has little choice but go along.

Indeed, the recent history of California's fuel industry is a textbook case of how a once-competitive business can become skewed to the advantage of a few, all with the federal government's blessing. "They don't have to collude, they don't have to form a cartel, they don't have to be monopolists," said Stanford University economist Roger Noll. "All they have to do is take advantage of the crazy rules."[4]

Thomas O'Malley, once the boss of refinery owner Tosco, explained how these new rules helped the big refiners. "My view for the industry was:

Why in the world would you fight clean fuels?" O'Malley asked, "Make no mistake about it, the more stringent you make specifications, those become barriers to entry. . . . Strong companies would have an advantage."[5]

As costs rose and the refiners shut down, Unocal also got out. In November of 1996, Unocal sold its entire California business, including the famous Union 76 gas stations, to Tosco, making Tosco the largest refiner in the nation. Unocal turned its focus to oil exploration, with regular income (5.75 cents a gallon) from the combined ingenuity of its scientists, lawyers, and lobbyists.

The refiners who survived still operate under the rules Unocal helped craft, and they still pay Unocal what amounts to rent. Because every refiner pays this rent, the extra cost is passed on to the consumers. This means that for each gallon of gasoline a California driver puts in her car, she is forking over more than a nickel to Unocal—as much as a dollar a tank.

So, CARB set out to clear the smoggy air in car-addicted California and ended up making Unocal rich. Why should we care as long as the air is actually cleaner?

We should care because any benefits from CARB's rules come with real costs. Gasoline prices are higher, leaving California families with less money left over for vacation or a night out. Higher gasoline prices also drive up the costs of shipping goods—everything gets more expensive. If you worked at a refinery that shut its doors, you also lost out thanks to CARB's rules. Money the oil companies would have spent developing their own new fuels or employing people instead went to lawyers and court fees.

In examining Unocal's role, it is important to separate the two parts of their scheme. Taking out a patent on a technology that the government is about to mandate may not be something to be proud of, and it may not be good for the economy, but it makes good business sense, is not illegal, and does not make government any bigger. But by actually lobbying the government to coerce its competitors into using its patent, Unocal becomes implicated in this infringement on consumer and business freedom.

Unocal's story is eye-catching but not unique. Although the media often portray the environmental policy debate as being a battle between friends of the Earth and friends of industry, big business is often the most effective advocate of environmentalist restrictions. Usually the businesses calling for environmental regulations stand to profit from those regulations. Examples of corporations seeing green—as in cash—in the environmental movement are not rare.

Paid Alarmists

It was 86 degrees in mid–December. Chris Horner, covering the UN conference on climate change as a freelancer, was rattling off another dispatch on how global warming was a myth.

The warm, dim room was a familiar backdrop for Horner, a hybrid lawyer–journalist. Reporters were arrayed among long rows of folding tables, facing a small television at the front of a depressing room, all hunched over their laptops amid a tangle of wires. Press assistants (many of them unpaid interns) from every group at the conference, littered every writer's tiny space with piles of handouts that usually just ended up on the floor, out of the reporter's way.

A kid from Greenpeace dropped a paper on Horner's desk that caught his eye. Horner's picture was on it, under the figure "$870,000." The flier called Horner and his colleague "paid skeptics." The think tank that employs them, the Competitive Enterprise Institute (CEI), had received money from ExxonMobil in what Greenpeace called a "cash-for-disinformation campaign." (Disclosure: The author finished this book under a journalism fellowship from CEI but has had no contact with, relation to, or input from any of its donors.) Future Greenpeace fliers would say that Exxon has given more than $15 million to anti-Kyoto groups and that CEI has pocketed $1.6 million.

The implication was clear, and the storyline was a familiar one: A corporate polluter hired some slick lawyers and bought off some media to spread lies in an effort to convince the world that ruining the planet wasn't that bad. The average reporter or editor loves this sort of story, and you can read it nearly every week in the major newspapers: What sort of deregulation did Dick Cheney's Halliburton friends buy? Whose money is delaying or weakening clean air or water standards?

The angle the media too infrequently see is that if global warming laws would hurt ExxonMobil, then they would likely aid some competitor. Horner and his allies say that these green laws are bad for the economy, but that doesn't mean they aren't gold mines for particular companies.

In looking for who would win with strict new laws to stop global warming, it makes sense to begin with one of the close allies of Greenpeace: the World Wildlife Fund/Conservation Foundation (WWF). The WWF takes money from countless large companies and corporate foundations. Chevron/Texaco, DuPont, Enron, Alcoa, Ford Motor, DaimlerChrysler,

Eastman Kodak, Getty, and dozens of other corporations all have foundations that give to the WWF,[6] which has now made global warming and environmental conservation a central battle.

Chevron's web site declares the company invests about $110 million per year in "renewable energy, alternative energy, and energy efficiency." Chevron has created special units of the corporation where scientists work on alternative fuel and power sources.

Fuel derived from the sun, hydrogen, or crops is called renewable fuel, contrasting it with fossil fuels such as natural gas, oil, or coal. Biomass, solar energy, and other renewables often create less pollution and less CO_2 and do not deplete finite reserves. The problem with renewable fuels is that they are not profitable. That makes these environmentally friendly investments by Chevron essentially *charity*, which gets Chevron good publicity.

The corporation's charity doesn't stop there. Chevron also gives away hundreds of thousands of dollars to nonprofits, including environmentalist groups such as Resources for the Future, the H. John Heinz III Center for Science, Economics & the Environment, Nature Conservancy, Earthwatch Institute, and the WWF.

The WWF, as part of its climate change agenda, has launched a new campaign called "PowerSwitch!" The point of PowerSwitch!, according to the project's web site, is to "get governments to cut CO_2 pollution produced by coal power stations and force a switch to cleaner, more efficient power." The WWF is working to restrict coal fuel and promote alternative fuels—just like the ones in which Chevron has already invested, but for which it cannot seem to find enough demand.

So, Chevron's executives do two "good things for the environment": (1) invest in unprofitable renewable fuels and (2) give to green groups such as the WWF. The WWF and other green groups just happen to lobby government to make that first Chevron investment profitable—driving up the cost of fuel for American families in the process.

These facts do not a conspiracy make. If Chevron executives really believe that renewable fuels can save the atmosphere and prevent global warming at a reasonable cost, there's nothing wrong with them pursuing those technologies. But the environmental activists often sound as if they are altruists and the other side is profit-seekers, as if that were a slur. In truth, there are profit-seekers on both sides of the debate.

Rob Routliffe works for DuPont in an interesting capacity. By training, he is not a scientist or a salesman. He is a lawyer and a lobbyist, and DuPont pays him to be a broker of something that has no real value.

Routliffe, based in Canada, trades in "Carbon Dioxide Equivalent" credits. Companies that emit carbon dioxide (CO_2) or nitrogen oxide (NO_x) can earn these credits if they emit less than a certain amount, called a "cap." If some other manufacturer or power plant has trouble meeting *their* emissions caps, they can buy the credits from someone like DuPont. This is called a "cap-and-trade" system.

The problem is that in the United States, caps on CO_2 or other greenhouse gasses are not mandatory. While companies do buy and sell these credits, the value is entirely in public relations—or speculation.

DuPont, for example, spent tens of millions of dollars upgrading factories to cut various greenhouse gases and has achieved a 65 percent reduction.[7] This investment, which earned CO_2 credits for DuPont, was probably beneficial for the environment and good publicity. In a 2004 presentation to the Business Roundtable, Routliffe identified two kinds of companies that might buy these credits: (1) "Public relations buyers" (companies that wanted to show a commitment to reducing greenhouse gasses, but couldn't yet make the reductions) and (2) "Speculative compliance buyers" (firms that expect the government to create a mandatory cap).[8] Those speculators, including DuPont, could not cash out on their investment as long as the credits were basically worthless.

The *Economist* reported that in 2004, "multinationals like DuPont are convinced that carbon constraints are coming anyway in America, and they want to make global preparations." When the magazine writes that DuPont is "convinced" that the United States will pass mandatory limits on greenhouse gasses, it is missing one angle of the story. DuPont is not merely *betting* on the outcome, like a sports fan putting money on a big game. DuPont is also *playing* in the game.

A critical part of Routliffe's job is to make CO_2 credits *worth something,* which is why DuPont needed a lobbyist to do it: Only government action can make CO_2 credits truly valuable. Routliffe traveled to London and helped the government in 2001 craft a law capping CO_2 and NO_x emissions and allowing credit trading.[9] With the stroke of a pen, guided by Routliffe's hand, DuPont's "holdings" (emissions credits) became cash cows. Routliffe is also active in lobbying the Canadian government to create mandatory emissions caps and trading systems.[10]

As companies like DuPont tried to set up the Chicago Climate Exchange, dealing in U.S. CO_2 credits, Routliffe encountered some difficulties. One reporter explained the problems:

> As for carbon trading outside of Kyoto or another regulatory scheme, one industry analyst predicted that participation will be spotty and

prices will likely remain low. "That is going to be a characteristic of any voluntary market. It's hard to get folks to volunteer to spend money."[11]

Routliffe's observation boiled down to saying: "It's hard to sell something that's useless." On another occasion, he proposed a solution: "It would have been a lot easier with active government involvement."[12]

The more nations that institute such cap-and-trade schemes, the more DuPont can sell the "product" that it has already made. So, DuPont continues to lobby for such laws. In Washington, in 2004, DuPont assigned five corporate lobbyists to support environmental legislation including climate change bills.[13]

Also, they fund the WWF, which aggressively backs the Kyoto Protocol that creates a global policy forcing nations to institute exactly the sort of emissions caps that will make DuPont's investment in CO_2 credits pay off.

Charles River Associates, a private accounting firm, estimates that complying with Kyoto would cost the U.S. economy $225 billion every year.[14] That means lower wages and higher prices for all Americans—but a boon for DuPont.

Critics say that cap-and-trade schemes amount to a tax on energy, just a very complex one. A straightforward tax on CO_2 emissions would also discourage use of CO_2 and provide an incentive for companies to switch to cleaner fuels while requiring fewer regulations and less lobbying and wrangling over exactly how the credits will be parceled out.

A CO_2 tax is exactly what Paul Anderson wants. Anderson is the CEO of Duke Energy, and on April 7, 2005, he told a crowd: "I believe U.S. public policy on global climate change should encourage a transition to a lower-carbon-intensive economy through a broad-based, mandatory approach. And, I believe the best approach is a carbon tax."[15] Anderson continued:

> You can imagine the reaction I get when I say "carbon tax" in the halls of Duke Energy! One employee wrote me that as a shareholder, he couldn't fathom why I would advocate a position that would discourage use of our product by potentially increasing its price! Because, of course, a carbon tax would cut emissions by increasing the cost of fossil fuels in proportion to their carbon content—thereby encouraging both conservation and shifts to lower-carbon fuels.

A month after calling for a tax on CO_2 and a shift to "lower-carbon fuels," Anderson announced that Duke was merging with Cinergy, a midwestern energy company that depends mostly on coal—the highest-carbon fuel in the world. A few months later, Duke started selling off many of its non-midwestern plants, making Anderson's company more reliant on coal.[16]

To understand this behavior, check out a press release from Cinergy in May of 2004. The release mentioned that Cinergy's Indiana unit, PSI, had "invested hundreds of millions of dollars to comply with federal and state environmental rules regulating nitrogen oxide power plant emissions."[17] Cinergy wasn't bragging. The purpose of the press release was to announce that the Indiana Utility Regulatory Commission had approved Cinergy's request to raise electricity rates about 8 percent—describing the clean air costs was a way of justifying the price hike to consumers.

Indiana's power sector is heavily regulated, and the state has granted PSI a monopoly in parts of the state. If you live in Plainfield, Indiana, and you want power, you need to buy it from PSI. In exchange for this monopoly protection, the state government controls what PSI can charge. If the state makes PSI spend more cleaning up pollution, PSI just raises its prices with the state's permission.

Duke Energy now owns PSI, meaning Duke has a monopoly in parts of Indiana, and in many other regulated power markets. A CO_2 tax would raise Duke's costs, but so what? In a free market, PSI's customers could drop PSI for someone charging less—maybe a nuclear power company that pays less in CO_2 taxes. But if you are a government-protected monopoly selling something your customers probably can't do without—such as electricity— then higher taxes roll off of your back and soak the customers below you.

From the perspective of PSI and Duke's other regulated power plants, there's nothing harmful about a CO_2 tax or *anything* that adds to your over-head. There would be a real cost to the customer, though. Anderson argues that higher energy prices are a worthy sacrifice in the battle to prevent global warming. If you believe that the CO_2 from power plants truly poses a serious risk to the planet, you might agree. But Paul Anderson isn't really convinced of that, as he made clear in the same talk in which he advocated a CO_2 tax.

"Even if science proves that climate change isn't a major problem," Anderson said, "a carbon tax is a 'no regrets' policy that still results in less CO_2 emissions and greater energy conservation." No regrets, that is, except for the family who has less spending money thanks to Anderson's tax.

In May 2005, General Electric (GE) hopped on the bandwagon with a new initiative they called "ecomagination."[18] The idea, promulgated through expensive ad-buys and public relations campaigns, was that GE would invest more in cleaner sources of energy and reduce the greenhouse gas emissions from its own operations. Perhaps to reassure shareholders, GE CEO Jeffrey Immelt said at ecomagination's launch party, "it's no longer a zero-sum game—things that are good for the environment are also good for business." That's great. If GE can help the planet and help its bottom line at the same time, more power to them.

But one has to wonder whether Immelt really believes his ecomagination plan is a profitable one. The hoity unveiling of the initiative, complete with wine from solar-powered vineyard and organic canapés, was not held at the company's corporate headquarters in New York. Instead, it was in Washington, DC, on Pennsylvania Avenue—the same street as the White House and the Capitol. Immelt made it clear that another element is necessary to make ecomagination profitable. "Industry cannot solve the problems of the world alone," he told the solar-powered-wine-sipping guests, "we need to work in concert with government." That same day, Immelt met with Senator John McCain, a Senate champion of mandatory CO_2 caps, and Bush's environmental advisor James Connaughton.

Ecomagination involves investing in certain fuels and technologies, and then working with government to make those fuels or technologies mandatory. Fuel mandates or caps are not just restrictions on what factories or power plants can use—they also bind you as an energy consumer. If your power company uses more expensive fuel, you pay higher prices for your electricity. If you have a choice between companies and you believe windmills and solar power is important enough, you might go with the clean power company and sacrifice a few bucks a month. But ecomagination doesn't stop there. It wants to *force* you to use or subsidize alternative fuel sources, however unproven they are. Good corporate citizenship for GE involves limiting your freedom and driving up your prices.

Chevron, DuPont, Duke, and GE all stand to profit from heavy-handed government environmental laws, and they are not alone in corporate America. For some reason, the media largely ignore the fact that environmentalist regulation and legislation will be profitable for some businesses. But the media do focus on how free-market policies benefit other businesses.

On November 27, 2005, *Washington Post* reporter Juliet Eilperin penned a preview of a meeting the following week in Montreal to discuss strategies for implementing the Kyoto Protocol.[19] Eilperin quoted and cited a handful of government and nonprofit types talking about the need for mandatory limits on greenhouse gases. For balance, she ended the piece by citing research scientist Roy Spencer, "who does not believe the climate will warm as rapidly as many computer models predict," as Eilperin put it.

Spencer opposes government measures to limit energy use. When she quoted Spencer, she made sure to mention that he "contributes to the free-market online journal Tech Central Station, which is in part funded by oil companies opposed to mandatory carbon limits."

An academic opposes government restrictions on energy use and the reporter feels the need to mention he occasionally freelances for a web site that gets some money from companies who oppose these restrictions and who will likely see decreased profits in government intervention. Fair enough. But what about turning the tables? What about the environmentalists she cites?

The article mentions that Senator Joseph Biden has endorsed a proposal to impose mandatory emissions cuts, but leaves out that one of Biden's best sources of political contributions over the past six years is the DuPont Corporation, who supports greenhouse gas laws and has invested in CO_2 credits. Employees of the company gave more than $16,000 to Biden from 2001 to the end of 2005,[20] likely more than Tech Central Station has given Roy Spencer.

Eilperin quoted eager environmentalist David Doniger from the Natural Resources Defense Council (NRDC). The NRDC has received nearly a quarter-million dollars from Citigroup Foundation over the past decade.[21] Citigroup, the parent company, in 2004 invested $23 million in a factory that makes wind turbines—an investment that would clearly be worth more if the government began attaching a monetary value to emissions reductions. Citigroup has also invested in other renewable energy and "clean technology" according to its web site. Still, Eilperin did not write: "Doniger's group is funded by a banking corporation that stands to profit from restrictions on greenhouse gas emissions." Not wanting to engage in mind reading, we ought to presume Biden and Doniger favor green laws because they think they are good for the planet. Similarly, men like Spencer believe that free-market approaches to environmental issues will be even better for all people. If a free-marketeer's indirect corporate funding is worth mentioning, so is an environmentalist's.

A few explanations are in order. First, there is no reason to believe that the WWF or NRDC are interested in anything other than saving the planet. Although they don't share Greenpeace USA's policy of rejecting corporate cash, these groups show no signs of "selling out" their principles on conservation. Indeed, there's not great pay in the nonprofit world, and so most environmental activists are idealists making a sacrifice for what they believe is a good cause. The same is true on the other side of the fence. The legions of libertarian activists opposing these rules are not exactly raking it in, either.

What DuPont, Chevron, and Citigroup accomplish with the help of the WWF may be good for the planet. No one should forget, though, that there are many costs to forcing factories, power plants, and minivan-driving mothers to reduce emissions: Emission reduction raises the cost of energy (and thus of nearly everything else in the world, which can stunt the development of poor nations), endangers American sovereignty, and may have unforeseen environmental impacts. Environmentalists respond that the benefits outweigh these costs.

When considering arguments regarding energy and the environment, the public ought to bring the same sort of skepticism to the green arguments from which some company stands to profit, as it does to the opposing arguments by Horner and his allies from which some other company hopes to get rich.

Finally, it must be noted that it was 86 degrees in mid-December at the UN conference on climate change because the conference was in Buenos Aires, Argentina, where December 21 is the first day of summer.

What's Good for General Motors

"My, what a beautiful evening," exclaimed President Lyndon Johnson from the podium in the Grand Ballroom of New York's Plaza Hotel. It certainly was. For one thing, three of the guests, Mayor John Lindsay, Mrs. Charles Engelhard, and Mrs. Henry Ford II, were regulars on the official annual "best-dressed" list published in the *New York Times*.

It was LBJ's farewell address, and it brought together an interesting crowd that included Republicans and Democrats alike. The guests included Senator and failed vice presidential candidate Edwin Muskie of Maine, minerals magnate Charles Engelhard, and Henry Ford II.[22] The lives of these three men were already crossing, but in the coming years they would intersect to form another example of environmental profiteering.

This story starts with an expert in ladies underwear, runs through a failed presidential bid and tumultuous South Africa, and ends the largest ever bailout of an American company.

The central characters in this tale—besides the socialites at the Plaza that night in New York and General Motors President Edward Cole—are the chemicals carbon monoxide (CO) and nitrogen oxide (NO_x). When CO enters the lungs, it goes into a person's bloodstream where it displaces oxygen. When the CO gets to the brain, it's deadly. NO_x is less deadly, but it causes smog and acid rain. Internal combustion engines burn almost everything in gasoline, but these two pollutants survive the combustion, come out of the tail pipe, and go into the air.

After playing a quiet number 2 role on the doomed Democratic ticket running against Richard Nixon and Spiro Agnew in 1968, Senator Ed Muskie was already running for president. He needed an issue, and his chairmanship of the Subcommittee on Air and Water Pollution gave him an obvious choice: He would propose a bold round of amendments to the current clean air laws.

A year after LBJ's farewell, Muskie was moving clean air legislation and holding hearings. Anything he did on the issue that winter was drowned out, though, by Edward Cole, president of General Motors (GM).

On January 14, 1970, Cole, addressing the Society of Automotive Engineers, said: "It is my opinion that the gasoline internal combustion engine can be made essentially pollution-free. This is a goal to which General Motors is devoting extensive resources and we are confident it can be achieved."[23]

For this to happen, Cole also declared that the industry would have to switch to unleaded fuel. This came as a shock, especially considering that it was GM that invented leaded fuel, through a subsidiary called Ethyl.[24]

Jerry Flint, the *New York Times* reporter covering the speech searched for an explanation, opining in a straight news story: "[Cole's] emphasis on cleaning up the gasoline-powered internal combustion engine was probably an effort to head off attempts to ban the engine and force the auto makers to produce electric or steam-powered cars."[25]

Flint's interpretation was certainly not wholly wrong. Corporate executives who fear damaging regulations often seek a compromise of more benign government interference. But Flint would have had a more straightforward explanation for Cole's words if he knew what was going on inside GM labs.

General Motors scientists had just completed a 50,000 mile in-factory "road test" for cars equipped with a new device: the automotive catalytic converter. Doing something like an alchemy trick, the converter took in CO, NO_x, and harmful hydrocarbons, spitting out water, harmless nitrogen gas, and CO_2.

The key was the metal *catalyst*—the scientific term for a material that, without being altered itself, facilitates a chemical combination. The catalytic converter was hardly a new idea. One of the scientists, Dick Klimisch, had been using the same technology for years making women's underwear. Getting a catalyst to work in a car, though, was seen as a daunting task.

"The exhaust system of a car is a nasty place," Robert Mondt, one of the other scientists who worked on the converter for GM, tells me. "We couldn't believe it," said, Dick Klimisch after the road test. "The conventional wisdom was that we'd never get [the converter] to last so long."[26]

General Motors was not the only carmaker pursuing the converter. Ford and Chrysler were, too. The difference was the composition of the converter. Ford and Chrysler were pursuing a "monolith" style converter, which used a long, wavy surface coated in a catalyst. General Motors instead used tiny beads, with countless microscopic hills and valleys, coated in platinum. The GM model exposed more platinum to the exhaust, creating more catalysis and thus cleaner emissions in the end.

Also, GM was simply a bigger company with better research and development. "At the time we were in a very good financial situation. We just had more money," Mondt told me in a phone interview.

With momentum provided by GM, Muskie moved ahead. In September of 1970, his clean air bill passed the Senate 73–0, which, in effect, mandated new cars come equipped with a catalytic converter.

This was bad news for Ethyl, the company (which GM had recently sold off) that made tetraethyl lead, used in leaded gasoline. R. V. Kerley, an Ethyl executive, had a temper tantrum the day after Cole's speech. "Who kills the most people yearly?" he ranted reporters at a press conference. "The automakers, not the leaded gasoline."[27]

It was also bad news for Ford and Chrysler, who were lagging GM in developing an affordable, durable catalytic converter. While all three carmakers had talked up the importance of cleaning up car fumes, GM was the most outspoken.

It was very good news for another guest at LBJ's farewell address: Charles Engelhard. Engelhard owned platinum mines in South Africa, and he not only would supply the metal that would serve as the catalyzing agent but also actually build the whole interior structure of the converter for GM. Ford, too, would sign contracts with Engelhard.

Engelhard was a good friend of the Democratic Party, being one of LBJ's biggest funders. Platinum prices in 1970 were falling toward $100 per ounce. The price quickly shot up to $300. In 1980, platinum would peak at nearly $1,100 per ounce.

The autumn of 1970, it would turn out, was the peak of Muskie's career. His presidential race and his clean air bill both soon got sidetracked.

Muskie's bill granted the Environmental Protection Agency (EPA) the authority to postpone implementation of the auto emissions standards, and soon the Big Three unified behind pushing for a delay.

Chrysler President John Riccardo said the rules, set to be implemented in 1975, would put him out of business. He called on Detroit to lobby Washington to change the regulations and push back their implementation date. Ford stood by Chrysler, and the two tried to unify the industry to delay the new rules.

General Motors foiled that plan. On page 25 of the September 12, 1974 *New York Times* GM ran a full-page ad headlined, "General Motors believes it has an answer to the automotive air pollution problem." The page featured four diagrams and dozens of paragraphs extolling the virtues of and the need for the catalytic converter. By 1975, all U.S. cars had the converter.

Why was GM any different from Ford or Chrysler? For one, GM had learned its lesson battling Ralph Nader over the Corvair in the 1960s: Rather than battle government might, it often makes most sense to go along and get along.

Second, GM was the biggest of the Big Three. They could afford to shell out for the platinum far more easily than Ford or Chrysler could. As witnessed repeatedly in the history of business, one big company, such as GM will be willing and able to add to its overhead if it means that their competition, such as Ford and Chrysler will suffer, too. As an added bonus, the carmaker American Motors had to buy its converters from GM, who was able to build quickly a factory just for making the converter casings.

A 1978 *Wall Street Journal* editorial explained it:

> In an economic contraction . . . the weakest and poorest are crushed the worst. Of the auto industry Big Three Chrysler is at the bottom of the pile. Anything the federal government does to the industry in general is felt most by Chrysler, next by Ford, and least by General Motors. The rich can better survive a squeeze because they are rich.[28]

So, Muskie, Engelhard, and GM won, while Ford and Chrysler lost. The result was as expected: Car costs went up, hurting consumers and costing the Big Three, but none as much as Chrysler. By 1979, Chrysler was on its last legs, and so it came crawling back to Washington. The story ends with an infamous affair of big business and big government: Washington bailed out Chrysler with subsidized loans to keep it from going under.

Again, Senator Muskie's laws probably made the air cleaner in the short term, but this story shows another angle to the environmental movement.

The laws helped GM strengthen its dominance of the market. American consumers almost lost a carmaker that otherwise was profitable. Instead, they lost their tax dollars to a mega-bailout, but only after new car prices went up.

Standing to profit from a law doesn't disqualify a company from commenting on it. It should merely increase the skepticism with which the lawmakers, the public, and the media listen to these interests—a skepticism that mostly only goes one way these days.

This story also points toward another cost of environmental legislation. Requiring the catalytic converter had real costs for the public, besides the price of cars. When new car prices go up, drivers are more likely to hold onto their old jalopies, which are dirtier and less fuel efficient in many ways. In 1990, revisiting the catalytic converter debate, reporter Michael Weisskopf described the resultant emission from a catalytic converter as "harmless carbon dioxide." Try telling that to the folks clamoring for the Kyoto global warming treaty.

At the time Muskie's rules went into effect, unleaded fuel required more crude oil per mile than would leaded fuel. This increased our dependence on Middle East oil and added incentives for oil drilling. Lead had also served as an octane enhancer, to reduce engine knocking. The catalytic converter required a new octane enhancer, and so the compound MTBE filled that role. Today, MTBE is thought to poison groundwater and possibly cause cancer. On another front, we must wonder whether the massive platinum mining harmed South Africa's environment or exacerbated the plight of the oppressed blacks in that country.

Finally, the time and money spent developing a good catalyst certainly paid off in making the air cleaner in the short term, but did it preclude other experiments and developments? We will never know if GM might have invented a hydrogen-powered car, freeing us from petroleum altogether, if it had not been forced by law to solve the emissions problems by 1978. Considering all of these costs, green arguments coming from every corner warrant more examination than they receive.

"It's a Bonanza"

Business Week in July 1992 reported on new emissions standards that cost car owners dearly, but pleased many businesses. Chester Davenport, chairman of Envirotest Systems said, "It's a bonanza," about the new rules, predicting a tripling in the company's revenues.[29]

Sure enough, Davenport got rich and sold the company in 1998. He's now extremely wealthy and has given over $200,000 to Democrats since 1992,[30] months after the EPA standards drove business his way. Davenport contributed to the presidential runs of environmentalist candidates Al Gore and John Kerry.

The same *Business Week* story tells of Standard Motor Products, Inc., "a $550 million-in-sales auto-parts maker in Long Island City, N.Y." that also stood to profit from the rules. "It's what's known as the untapped repair market," the company's vice president for marketing said.

Nearly $15,000 of Nick Rahall's campaign cash in 2004 came from coal-mining interests—either mineworker unions or mine owners. During debate on an energy bill in April 2003, the West Virginia congressman sponsored an environmentalist-backed measure that would have prohibited coal mines larger than 160 acres on federal lands.

The average size of a new West Virginia coal mine in 1998 was 450 acres,[31] but those mines would have been unaffected by Rahall's provision. It happens that 100 percent of coal mines in West Virginia are on privately held land, according to the Bureau of Land Management, while western mining, mostly in Wyoming, happens overwhelmingly on federal land.

Congressional Quarterly's *CQ Today* reported that "Rahall was joined by environmentalists and Eastern state lawmakers who did not want to see large swaths of public lands opened up to coal mining."[32] Thus, we see another alliance of environmentalists and one group of big businesses—eastern coal miners—against another group of big businesses—western coal miners.

Enron was the most influential supporter of the United States' adoption of the Kyoto Protocol. Today, a handful of companies are jockeying to profit from it, hoping above all that they can pressure the United States to join this global regime of emissions control.

Federal aide for ethanol—fuel derived from corn—is also in the name of the environment. Its benefits to the planet are dubious, but not its benefits to some large corporate farmers.

It is important to remember why we care who supports which law. If all environmental laws were good for the planet and its inhabitants, it would not matter who was getting rich off them. But land conservation out West hurt settlers. Catalytic converters increased oil consumption. California Air Resource Board's regulations drastically consolidated the refinery business in California and may have stunted new technological development. All of these laws added to the cost of living for Americans. One could argue that increased costs that accrue to the few are a detriment to peoples all over the world. If Americans give more money to the government or to specific companies such as GM, they spend less on other goods and services.

No one should assume environmentalist arguments are always altruistic, if sometimes naive. Often, they are shrewd. Often, the tree huggers are trying to squeeze out a few bucks.

11

Enron

A Big-Government Scandal

S pring means rebirth and new hope, and nowhere is this truer than in the world of baseball. For anyone who has ever played the game, the April air is intoxicating—crisp with the scent of new grass and rich with the smell of the damp, reawakened soil beneath it.

On Opening Day, they say, every team is undefeated, and everyone is in first place. For the fans, who throughout the winter tried to console themselves with football or basketball, Opening Day has loomed like a promised land since the February day the morning news reporter first uttered those tantalizing words: "pitchers and catchers reported today . . ."

And for the die-hards, the season-ticket holders, or those who swoop up seats whenever possible, your team's first game at home—with a sold-out crowd, red-white-and-blue bunting along the stands, and the pomp and circumstance of a coronation—is the greatest party of the year.

Rarely was a home opener more electric than on April 7, 2000, in Houston, Texas.[1] The Astros' fans were watching their first baseball since Atlanta's John Rocker got Houston's Ken Caminiti out to eliminate the Astros from the playoffs on October 10, 1999. But, also, Houston fans were enjoying their first baseball under the blue sky since 1964.

The new Houston stadium, with its retractable dome left open on this 79-degree night, was replacing the Astrodome as the Astros' home field. The city was buzzing. After the Houston Symphony played the National Anthem, army Golden Knights parachuted down from a helicopter to unfurl the stars and stripes. The 41,583 fans saw the Astros raise the pennant to mark their 1999 division championship.

All the pomp and circumstance, and the beautiful new ballpark added to the nerves any ballplayer would feel in a home opener. Even for the visiting team, the Philadelphia Phillies, the night was intense. The Phillies' young slugger Scott Rolen said "it was electric." And 23-year-old Phillies pitcher Randy Wolf, felt the jitters, too. "The butterflies were everywhere," he said.

At one point, as Wolf was preparing to bat, he looked up into the stands and saw two faces he recognized. Although, Wolf didn't know it, this father-and-son pair had been at the first game at the Astrodome in 1965: former President George H.W. Bush, and Texas Governor, George W. Bush. "I was pitching in front of a past president and maybe future president, and the first inning it felt like my first major league game," Wolf said.

In addition to the Bushes, the crowd included the commissioner of Major League Baseball, Bud Selig, and U.S. Senator Kay Bailey Hutchison. The *Houston Chronicle* reported that, "Hall of Famer Nolan Ryan was back for another appearance, but this time he didn't throw out the first pitch. Still doesn't want to wear out the arm, you know." Instead, the honor of throwing out the ceremonial first pitch went to a local businessman, who was also an old friend of the Bushes: Kenneth Lay, CEO of Enron.

Three players that day hit home runs to left field, drawing fans' attention to how close the fence was—a measly 315 feet from home plate. Center field was even more remarkable, with an unusual hill sloping up to the fence, and a flagpole planted in the field of play. Right field, however, was notable, not for what happened there on Opening Day, but for what wasn't there—or more precisely, what used to be there, just beyond where the right-field bleachers now stood.

In a scene starkly contrasting the glamour of Ken Lay's pitching debut, the Mackay family spent Thanksgiving of 1997 packing up their industrial supply company near Houston's Union Station.[2] Gayle Mackay, a 60-year-old widow who ran the company that her family had owned for 27 years, was moving out, after the city of Houston told her less than a month before that she had to go. The city was condemning her property through its power of eminent domain, demolishing it, and turning it into a part of a new ballpark—Enron Field.

Mackay's neighbor Billy Marlin also refused to sell his building that housed a bail-bond business. While Houston's government was doing the actual evicting, a private group had made them the offers they literally could not refuse. The Harris County Public Facilities Corporation was the buyer. The group's leader was Kenneth Lay.

Lay headed a group of private investors that helped front millions of dollars to build Enron Field. These deep pockets, however, had some help in building the stadium from the taxpayers, who forked over $180 million to build Enron Field.[3] Lay lobbied hard to get the referendum passed hiking taxes to build the stadium.

And so, on the first game at Enron Field, as Ken Lay christened the ballpark he helped build, Enron's stock was climbing and it would hit $90 a share in just a few weeks. Enron, which called itself the "World's Leading Energy Company," would also provide the power to run the ballpark. Things looked great for Lay.

But not for long. By the 2002 season, the stadium was no longer named Enron Field, Lay was out of a job, Enron was bankrupt, and he and many of his associates would soon face prosecution. Just as the company's health had been a charade, so was Lay's posture as a free-market capitalist.

Enron Field was built mostly by tax hikes and with the brutal big government tool of eminent domain—both of which Lay had advocated. With its roots in big government, Enron Field was a fitting image for the company whose rise and fall captured America's attention.

While much of the media portrayed the Enron saga as the bitter fruit of an unfettered free market, it was, ultimately, an unholy big-government-big-business scandal that resulted in a huge ripoff. Enron never would have risen as high as it did without the aid of heavy-handed government regulation and generous corporate welfare. Despite the free-market rhetoric spouted by Lay and his cohorts, the company often lobbied for and profited from big government.

Most analysts use the term *deregulation* to describe the setting in which Enron thrived, deceived, and then collapsed. But in nearly every corner of the Enron tale, we can find the fingerprints of big government.

An Enemy of Free Markets

As the whole world turned on its head in September 2001, things were going particularly badly for Enron.

The company had been forced to admit that many of its "assets" were basically imaginary, and it had billions in debt that it had hidden. Enron's prosperity was an illusion, conjured by clever accountants and executives operating under the mantra that the company's stock price trumped all else. When the facade lifted, the stock price plummeted, and hundreds of employees lost their life savings. The company had other headaches, too, including a disastrous power project in India and a hangover from failed electricity deregulation in California that led to rolling blackouts.

Ken Lay placed some phone calls in the hope of finding a lifeline for his sinking company. He phoned two members of George W. Bush's cabinet: Commerce Secretary Donald Evans and Treasury Secretary Paul O'Neill. Lay also called Federal Reserve Chairman Alan Greenspan and White House advisor Larry Lindsey. As one reporter put it, "Lay wondered whether the government might provide assistance."[4]

Ken Lay had already gotten many favors from Washington. For starters, during Vietnam an old professor of his pulled some strings along the Potomac and got Lay a job at the Pentagon, instead of on a boat in Southeast Asia.[5]

Lay understood well that doing good business meant maintaining good relations with Washington. In fact, Lay's career first got on the fast track in Washington, where he served in high positions at the Federal Power Commission and the Interior Department. Ken Lay, in a way, got his start as a regulator.

Never forgetting the importance of government, Enron greased the skids in Washington. Between 1989 and the company's bankruptcy, Enron and its executives doled out nearly $6 million to federal politicians. The company favored Republicans, but still sent about $1.5 million to Democrats running for federal office.[6]

Authors and *Fortune* reporters Bethany McLean and Peter Elkind, in their Enron book, *The Smartest Guys in the Room,* wrote: "For local politicians, getting an audience with (and donation from) Ken Lay was practically a rite of passage." In 1999, Enron spent $37 million on government affairs.[7] What did Enron do with this influence? The media and Enron's loudest critics claim that the company paid the government to stay away so that it could run free in a deregulated laissez-faire economy.

In November 2001, California State Senator Steve Peace, a Democrat, said, "it should be apparent to all observers that the kind of market Ken Lay promoted operated under the same principles that his company operated under. It's a kind of anarchic capitalism, in which there are no rules and no referees."[8]

In January 2002, a *New York Times* reporter called Lay, "A man with a doctorate in economics and an evangelical belief in free markets."[9] *Newsweek* described the company's collapse by claiming, "Enron's beloved free market did it in."[10]

A liberal *San Francisco Chronicle* columnist argued that, "the Enron scandal makes it clear that the unfettered free market does not work." The writer added, "also, Enron makes that whole Ayn Rand 'Fountainhead' thing look a little silly, too. Who is John Galt? Ken Lay."[11] A British magazine opined, "the Enron scandal may mark the last chapter in politicians' obsession with unbridled free markets."[12]

The moral of the story, according to these writers, is that free markets cause Enrons. Yes, free markets do have a tendency to catch and ferret out fraud and deceit where the policing powers often miss it, meaning the free market had a lot to do with Enron's fall. But free markets had little to do with Enron's rise—a rise which came about almost exclusively under big government. Lay's desperate calls to the White House are a good starting point. They were not calls for more deregulation, for tax cuts, or for looser rules. Lay was calling to ask the government to do *more* to help his company. This time, the White House refused, saying poorly run businesses going under is part of the free market. "Companies come and go. It's part of the genius of capitalism," said O'Neill.[13] Bush took flack for that, with Senator Joe Lieberman calling the White House's laissez-faire stance "cold-blooded."[14]

If the government had been a bit more cold-blooded, Enron might never have risen to the heights that made its fall so painful. Were government smaller, Enron might not have been able to play the games that proved so costly.

Jerry Taylor, a Cato Institute scholar, said it well in the *Wall Street Journal*:

> On balance, Enron was an enemy, not an ally of free markets. Enron was more interested in rigging the marketplace with rules and regulations to advantage itself at the expense of competitors and consumers than in making money the old fashioned way—by earning it honestly from their customers through voluntary trade. Indeed, Enron would probably still be a small-time pipeline company were it not for the statist conceit that consumers are better off under the regulatory boot of government than with the invisible hand of the marketplace.[15]

The media cannot be blamed too much for believing Enron and Ken Lay were capitalist swashbucklers. Lay and his sidekick Jeff Skilling sure sermonized like free-market evangelists, frequently singing the praises of laissez-faire. But they didn't walk their talk. They begged before Congress for more corporate welfare, subsidies, tax breaks, and complex regulations.

Ken Lay's failed appeals to the Bush administration for some sort of bailout also shatter the myth that Enron got from Washington whatever it wanted. Indeed, Washington spurned Enron on a few major issues. On one occasion, Enron lobbied hard for a federal bill pre-empting all state regulations on power, and reregulating the whole national electricity market. That dream, probably Enron's most cherished prize, never came close to fruition.

The second-biggest hope of Enron died on December 12, 2000, the frigid day that the Supreme Court ended Al Gore's recounts in Florida, ensuring Bush's election. Enron's unattained dream was the ratification of a treaty aimed at stopping global warming.

Kyoto: Good for Enron Stock, Bad for Energy Customers

On April 21, 2002, Al Gore assailed George W. Bush on Earth Day. Gore blasted Bush for rigging things to advance "Enron's agenda,"[16] (the company's name was by now a curse word). Gore also went after the president for withdrawing the White House's signature from the Kyoto Protocol on global warming—a treaty Bill Clinton had signed but never submitted to the U.S. Senate for ratification.

The attack followed the same old theme: Big business has too much influence, which obstructs environmentalist measures such as Kyoto. But Al Gore knew what "Enron's agenda" really contained.

On August 4, 1997, Ken Lay was at the White House with some other energy industry chiefs to meet with Gore, Clinton, and Treasury Secretary Robert Rubin. The White House wanted input before heading off to Kyoto to help draft the protocol. According to the *Washington Post*, "Lay, in a memo to Enron employees, said there was broad consensus in favor of an emissions-trading system." Lay was one of the advocates.[17] Four months later, Lay boosted the Kyoto Protocol in an Op-Ed, calling it "a tremendous opportunity to stimulate realistic climate solutions."[18]

Was Ken Lay trying to save the planet? Not quite. Columnist Robert Novak put it this way: "Lay saw Kyoto's green as the color of money."[19] The protocol, Lay explained in one e-mail, would "do more to promote Enron's business than almost any other regulatory initiative outside of restructuring the energy and natural gas industries in Europe and the United States." At another time, Lay wrote that Kyoto would be "good for Enron stock."[20]

How would a leading energy company profit from a global program of mandatory caps on emissions, especially considering that they had increased holdings in coal-fired power plants? The reasons were many and (especially by Enron standards) simple.

While Enron was an energy company, it was mostly in the business of dealing energy—not making it. Jeff Skilling, described as the brains of Enron under Lay, did his best to make Enron an "asset-light" company. Skilling's Enron would be an energy trader more than anything else.

One of Skilling's most successful creations was Enron Online—an on-line trading desk for commodities. Through Enron Online, the company made money by being the middleman. In a similar way, much of Enron's business was buying and selling energy—usually not *making* or *delivering* the energy. Enron largely was a broker. Enron traded natural gas, they traded electricity, and if the Kyoto protocol was ratified, they planned to trade carbon dioxide (CO_2)—sort of.

If the United States joined the Kyoto protocol, Congress would require factories and power plants to reduce their CO_2 emissions, the gas blamed for causing global warming. Most likely, Congress would create a "cap-and-trade" scheme whereby power plants would have *caps* on the amount of CO_2 they could emit. If a plant came in under the cap, it would earn CO_2 credits. These credits would allow the plant to exceed the CO_2 cap in the future, and "pay for" the excess emissions with the credits. If the plant had no need for the credits for future excess emission, it could sell the credits to another factory—one that feared it might exceed its CO_2 cap.

Under such a scheme, anyone could buy credits whether or not he or she owned a factory and simply sell the credit to a plant—or even to another speculator. It's not too hard to imagine a robust trade in CO_2 credits blossoming under Kyoto. Enron, the premier energy trader at the time, saw profits in becoming the premier emissions trader.

In another way, Enron would profit from Kyoto. Enron, as Lay built it, was a natural gas company—it owned natural gas pipelines and primarily dealt in natural gas. When it comes to reducing CO_2, natural gas is far cleaner than coal or oil. Kyoto restricts CO_2 emissions, thus multiplying the incentive to buy natural gas, driving up its price. Enron now liked Kyoto for the profit potential in the emissions credit trading possibilities it offered and for the higher natural gas prices that would result. How could it get better?

How about coal-fired plants in countries that would not have to follow Kyoto? Rebecca Mark, another Enron principal, would find Kyoto to be a nice boon. Mark trotted the globe, building power plants in Venezuela, Mozambique, and all parts of the developing world. Many of these plants were coal-fired power plants—exactly the type Kyoto would target.

Kyoto's drafters, however, knew that switching to "cleaner" fuels would be costly, and did not want to impose those costs on poorer countries, many of which were just emerging from poverty. Kyoto's restrictions, accordingly, only apply to about 35 countries (most of Europe, plus Canada, New Zealand, Japan, and Australia). The African, South American, and South Asian countries where Mark was building coal-fired power plants would be mostly untouched by Kyoto.

The Kyoto Protocol would shut down many coal-fired power plants, but not Enron's. Of course, Enron would love this—its competition in the energy industry might be harmed, and Enron's third-world power plants would pay less for their coal.

Enron never gave up on Kyoto. Even when George W. Bush, who opposed Kyoto, took the White House, Lay sent emissaries to the administration to lobby for it. One of his friends in January 2001 reported back to Lay that Treasury Secretary-designee Paul O'Neill had promised to push for Kyoto ratification within the Bush cabinet.[21] But George W. Bush would not push to ratify Kyoto, despite Enron's pleadings.

This situation made political liberals uncomfortable. On the environmental front, Kyoto was the grand prize for liberal Democrats and activist groups. The most common charge against Bush and Cheney is that they do the bidding of big business. The biggest, baddest business in 2001 was Enron. Yet, Enron was on the Left's side on Kyoto, and the Bush administration rebuffed them. Much of the Left's mythology about Bush, business, and the environment was threatened by the stubborn fact that Enron tirelessly supported the treaty.

Lay's environmentalism ran deep. He served on the board of a green group called Resources for the Future. Enron launched the Enron Renewable Energy Corporation, which dealt in alternative energies such as solar and wind power. Tom White, CEO of this new company, supported Clinton's anti–global-warming plan.[22] White's investment in renewable resources also made various green subsidies available to Enron.

One element of Bill Clinton's environmental agenda was a proposed energy tax, also called a British Thermal Unit (BTU) tax. Ken Lay, according to Cato Institute's Jerry Taylor, demonstrated an "outspoken embrace of Clinton's proposed BTU tax."[23]

Enron's charitable arm also heavily funded environmentalist groups who lobbied for tight restrictions on CO_2 and pollutants. Between 1996 and 1998, the Enron Foundation gave just under $1 million to the Nature Conservancy,[24] a green group which author Ron Arnold writes "receives millions in government funds and uses tax money to forward its own agenda of nationalizing private land at a profit."[25]

Slate columnist Timothy Noah wrote in 2001 that Lay was making Bush a little greener:

> Kenneth Lay, a close Bush friend and major campaign contributor, has been in the vanguard of businesses active on global warming. The chairman of Enron Corp., Lay stands to gain substantially from carbon control, not only as the largest North American trader of natural gas (less polluting than oil and coal) but because of the company's burgeoning energy-efficiency business.[26]

Too bad for Enron, Bush was never green enough to jump on board Kyoto.

The California Gold Rush

The power business in California has three main parts. It starts with the generators—the businesses that turn coal, oil, natural gas, or water into electricity in power plants. The power plants do not sell the power directly to you or your neighbors, though. They sell the power to utility companies. This sale of electricity from the generators to the utilities is called *wholesale*. The utilities, in turn, sell it to residences and businesses in the *retail* power market. Thus, the three main players are the generator, the utility, and the consumer.

The process by which the power gets from utilities to users (homes and businesses) is called *distribution*. More important to the Enron tale is electricity's movement before it reaches the retail level. Electricity's journey from the power plants to the utilities (and any pre-distribution detours) is called *transmission*.

Enron was a power generator—but only barely. Enron also had a few contracts to distribute electricity to a few individual customers. Mostly, Enron was an asset-light middleman—it bought and sold electricity between generators and utilities or other suppliers. A 2001 *Business Week* cover story on Jeffrey Skilling gave him the corny but accurate title, "Power Broker." The article said Enron was "more akin to Goldman Sachs than Consolidated Edison."[27]

In 1998, California deregulated electricity—but not really. The state allowed new players to enter the market and removed price controls at the wholesale level. In order to protect customers from spiking electric bills, though, Sacramento did not deregulate the state's retail market. While most of the reporting on Enron claimed that the company was a fierce advocate of complete deregulation of electricity, the true story is a little different.

Retail electricity deregulation in California allowed companies like Enron to enter the market. Before 1998, only three utilities—Pacific Gas & Electric, San Diego Gas and Electric, and Southern California Edison—were allowed to deliver electricity to Californians (they also generated electricity), and they didn't compete with one another. Deregulation opened the market to competition.

But *deregulation* is a bad word for what the California government did with its electricity market. Wisconsin's former Public Service Commission chairman looked at California's tangled web of rules, mandates, and limits and said, "none of this should be called deregulation."

What California tried, and Enron "gamed," was really *reregulation*. It was freer than the old system, but in such a way that called for even more government meddling and rules. Not only did the complex rules allow Enron to get rich, it also led to the price spikes, the energy shortages, and the blackouts that Californians suffered in 2000 and 2001.

Stanford University professor and Hoover Institute scholar James L. Sweeney wrote in the fall of 2002, "The financial crisis . . . *was* the direct result of California's regulatory actions. It was not the result of *deregulation* but rather of overly stringent *regulation*."[28]

The complexity of California's new rules played to Enron's advantage. Enron was more deeply entrenched with government than any other company, as was Ken Lay's style, with a huge government affairs budget and "lobbyists by the bushelful."[29] Remember, Ken Lay practically got his start as a regulator, at a young age holding fairly senior energy-related positions at the Interior Department and the Federal Power Administration. Competing in the energy industry would be impossible without intimate knowledge of regulation and close ties to federal and state officials.

But Enron didn't just take advantage of the complex rules it was given. Enron helped *draft* the regulations—and not by pushing more "anarchy." First,

Enron asked the California government to prohibit utilities—the companies who had been delivering power to California consumers for years—from generating electricity. The state, in the end, forced the utilities to sell half of their generating capacity. California's deregulation opened up the market of electricity delivery, but with strict conditions on some of the players.

This government mandate helped Enron by breaking up the energy supply chain and forcing everyone to come to the trading floors for energy—trading floors that Enron managed. The mandate hurt the utilities, and hurting one's competitors is almost always a boon. It hurt consumers because it eliminated one of the ways the utilities could stabilize prices. If you both produced and delivered electricity, you hedged against a drop or a spike in wholesale prices, being both a buyer and a seller.

Not content with managing the energy trading, Enron lobbied for another government favor and got it. In line with Enron's demands, California required the companies that controlled the electric grid—the wires and substations over which the electricity traveled—to allow all other companies access to their grid at a controlled price. Now Enron could buy and sell electricity at whatever price it wanted, but its competitors *had* to let Enron use their infrastructure at a government-set price.

Enron wanted mandatory, price-controlled grid access so badly that any other considerations took a back seat. Back in Washington, on February 16, 2001, Curtis Hebert, the interim chairman of the Federal Energy Regulatory Commission (FERC) wrote to Ken Lay, telling the CEO that he wanted to stay on as permanent chairman and asking for Lay's support. Hebert, after all, was critical to blocking the wholesale electricity price controls Enron also opposed (a case where Enron was free market).

Enron's priorities, however, were different. The *Washington Times* reported after Enron's collapse, "Mr. Hebert said Mr. Lay refused to back him because Enron wanted mandatory open access to power transmission and he opposed that."[30] Lay snubbed Hebert because Hebert wanted the government to get out of the way of the energy market.

California Games

Gray Davis's governorship was one of the most disastrous governorships in the history of the country, as the unprecedented recall election in 2003 showed. The blackouts in the summers of 2000 and 2001 were among the lowlights. Davis, as any good politician would, blamed big business.

To some extent, the blame was well placed, as Enron and other power companies played games with electricity that hurt consumers. But government regulations made the power games possible.

The most sinister-sounding Enron power game in California was "Death Star," (one Enron employee, disturbed by that name, came up with an alternative, "Cuddly Bear"). Both Death Star and another Enron game Load Shift used a rule that the Independent System Operator (ISO; the minute-to-minute manager of California's power grid) made about the transmission line and "congestion."

Power lines, sort of like water pipes, have a finite capacity: Only so much electricity can travel over a particular wire or set of wires. In a truly deregulated market, if many power companies wanted to transmit electricity over the same set of wires, the owner of those wires could raise the price it charged the power companies to use the wire. But California was not a free market. Enron had successfully lobbied the state to control grid prices.

So, no matter how high the demand for a certain transmission route, the price would stay low. Without market pricing, congestion became a problem. It was another case of price controls creating a shortage—in this case, a shortage of transmission capacity. So, the ISO created a patch to fill the hole that state law had made. The ISO charged a "congestion tariff" to companies transmitting electricity across congested lines. The proceeds from this tariff would go to any company who worked to relieve the congestion.

Under Load Shift, Enron might schedule an electricity transmission over a certain route for a Tuesday, with the expectation that the route would be full to capacity. On Tuesday, Enron would cancel that transmission and pocket the congestion-relief payment.

Because the companies who actually *did* ship the power over that line had to pay the congestion tariff, the price of electricity would go up. But if Enron had not scheduled the shipment in the first place, the line might never have been "congested" at all. Of course, Enron never planned to deliver the power, and so it only scheduled the delivery in order to create the congestion and then get paid for relieving the congestion—a scam that could only work under California's weird rules. In a free market, congested power lines would also raise electricity prices, but in a free market, Enron couldn't create false congestion because there would be no payoff for doing so. The weird regulations and Enron's savvy at exploiting them combined to raise customers' prices and Enron's profits. Enron used regulation to ripoff regular people.

Death Star involved another way of relieving congestion. Unlike with water pipes, electric-line congestion can be alleviated by transmitting power in the opposite direction of the congestion. If the lines became clogged with too much electricity flowing south from San Francisco to Los Angeles, the ISO would pay congestion-relief money to anyone sending electricity north from LA to San Francisco. To get this money, you could generate power in LA and ship it north.

But why would you do that? The congestion on the LA-bound lines signaled very high demand in LA, and so anyone producing power near LA would be best served selling it into LA.

Enron, on many occasions, though, scheduled power shipments against congestion in order to receive the congestion-relief money. The company would schedule a transmission from LA to San Francisco for which the ISO would pay Enron. Then, Enron would schedule a transmission from San Francisco into Oregon, where it would be outside the regulatory reach of California. From there, it would schedule transmissions down to Las Vegas. Finally, Enron would schedule transmission from Las Vegas into LA.

When the FBI indicted the man who is said to have invented Death Star, the complaint alleged:

> Although the Death Star strategy required Enron traders to arrange many energy schedules, in reality, Death Star did not directly cause electrons to flow because the electrons were scheduled to flow in a loop. As a consequence, [an unnamed Enron employee] stated that no congestion on the transmission lines was actually relieved by Death Star although Enron received congestion relief payments.[31]

While Enron lobbied for and profited from strict regulation of the grid in California, the company's stance was different elsewhere. Cato Institute's Jerry Taylor wrote:

> While most legislators got a full dose of Enron's regulatory agenda, some were hearing from the company that, well, grid owners should be left alone to do as they wanted. Those legislators, however, came from regions where Enron had managed to buy the transmission systems in question before the debate was settled. So officials from Texas, Louisiana, and various parts of South America in charge of the gas pipelines that Enron had bought were hearing one story while the rest of the political world was hearing another.[32]

Taylor calls this "regulatory opportunism." Enron, naturally, lobbied for government intervention when it thought bigger government would profit Enron. Then the company made the opposite arguments when it thought the free market would serve it best.

Subsidizing Enron

John Schwartz, the *New York Times* reporter who claimed Ken Lay had an "evangelical belief in free markets" should have been on Capitol Hill on March 23, 1995. In the early spring every year, the annual appropriations process gets underway with each subcommittee of the Appropriations Committee holding hearings on the different programs under its aegis. On that day, the Foreign Operations subcommittee discussed two parts of the federal government that subsidize U.S. exports, the Overseas Private Investment Corporation (OPIC) and the Export-Import Bank (Ex-Im).

The subcommittee hearings are dull affairs. Most of the congressmen and congresswomen are usually absent, and the "crowd" consists of a couple of reporters for obscure trade publications and few others. This was the scene on March 23, 1995. On that day, Ken Lay—John Galt, according to one *San Francisco Chronicle* writer—begged for bigger government.

Lay told the subcommittee that Ex-Im and OPIC needed to do even more than they were already doing. Lay said, "As other competitive factors (such as experience gaps) become less salient, and as bid processes increase the pressures on project costs and margins, financing is becoming absolutely pivotal."[33] Lay was talking about government loans or government-guaranteed loans.

Translated, Lay was saying, "we no longer can compete based just on our merits—we need government help." On another occasion, he personally asked then-Governor Bush to lobby in favor of OPIC and Ex-Im, calling them "critical to U.S. developers like Enron."[34]

More precisely, this corporate welfare was critical to Rebecca Mark's vision of Enron. Mark was an Enron executive who planned to take the company into the poorer countries of the world, where she saw a lack of reliable energy as the chief obstacle to serious economic development. Despite his occasional free-market sermons, Lay was unabashed about feeding at the federal trough. When Mark got her own company—at first named Enron Development Corporation (EDC), and later Enron International

(EI)—it lived high on government largesse. EDC/EI, went on a rampage, signing power deals around the world, often without consideration for how they would build or run the pipeline or power plant. "When they found a deal, they did a deal," one former Enron executive said. "It was buckshot all over the globe."[35]

Mark and EI racked up unthinkable debt. McLean and Elkind explain it this way:

> the assumptions Enron made to justify its deals assumed that nothing would ever go wrong. Of course, the banks financing the deals were making the same assumption; this was a mania, after all. But building energy projects in poor countries—often run by dictators and where capitalism was still a new concept—was absolutely fraught with peril, and it was absurd to believe that everything would play out according to plan.[36]

According to Jeffrey Skilling, EI is responsible for Enron's bankruptcy. Without a doubt, the federal government is responsible for EI. Federal agencies such as Ex-Im and OPIC subsidized Enron for more than $7 billion according to the Sustainable Energy and Environment Network (SEEN). Dozens of federal agencies spent taxpayer money to help Rebecca Mark fire her "buckshot" all over the world. One story from Vietnam illustrates Enron's dependence on big government and its creative accounting.

In 1997, Rebecca Mark's deputy, Linda Powers testified before a congressional subcommittee about OPIC and Ex-Im. Her message was similar to the one Lay had delivered three years before, but it had an edge.

> If programs like OPIC were not available, we would have no choice but to move our sourcing to other countries where financing is available. . . . [I]t is a clear and demonstrable fact of life and should definitely not be underestimated by policy-makers who care about U.S. jobs.[37]

It was a direct threat from Enron to Congress: Keep our subsidies coming or we will ship jobs overseas: hardly evincing an "evangelical belief in free markets."

But preserving Ex-Im was not enough. Enron wanted the government to *expand* Ex-Im. Specifically, Enron wanted to do business in Vietnam— a communist country that Ex-Im and other agencies were forbidden to finance. If Ex-Im wouldn't subsidize Enron's projects in Vietnam, Powers said, Enron would turn to France for subsidies.

Months later, President Clinton lifted the ban on U.S. subsidies to Vietnam. Soon, the United States Trade and Development Agency granted nearly $400,000 to study the feasibility of an Enron project in Vietnam. After the U.S. taxpayers spent that money, and Enron spent $18 million, Enron cancelled the project.

This was an unmitigated loss for the taxpayer, but Enron counted it as a gain. In one of its classic maneuvers of creative accounting, Enron executives listed as an *asset* the $18 million that it had spent on a project that was going nowhere—money that clearly should have been counted as a loss. Such accounting tricks helped drive up Enron stock despite the lack of true worth.

Floating coal-fired power plants off the coast of the Dominican Republic exemplify Rebecca Mark's Enron. In the mid-1990s, Enron partnered with another energy company to build power plants on barges off of Puerto Plata. In 1994, the World Bank, which is a U.S. government-supported body, loaned more than $130 million to the project. In 1996, the taxpayer-supported U.S. Maritime Administration gave a $50-million guarantee on loans to build the barges. The British government helped out, too.[38]

Once all this taxpayer money was invested, everything started going wrong. When Enron and its partners raised the prices on power, the people refused to pay. The Dominican government instead stepped in and started paying part of the tab—$5 million per month. When the price got too high for the government, the power companies turned off the lights, sparking deadly riots.

It gets worse. The coal-burning barges (just the kind Enron and Kyoto were trying to drive out of business in the United States and Western Europe) were close to a sea-front hotel whose customers did not like the soot settling on their meals. The hotel sued. By the summer of 2000, Enron had collected only $3.5 million on the $95 million that it had invested.[39]

The tawdriest episode in Enron's affair with big government took place in Maharashtra, India, involving a power plant called Dabhol. The story of Dabhol started with a meeting, took seed with some corporate welfare, and blossomed into "the biggest fraud in India's history," as prizewinning Indian author Arundhati Roy characterized it.[40] It ended with U.S. taxpayers contributing $20 million to the figurative Enron relief fund.

Suppose They Built a Power Plant and Nobody Came

Rebecca Mark kicked off her job by courting the Indian government. She spent a whole day with a delegation of Indian officials in early 1992.[41] By June, Enron and the state government of Maharashtra had an official understanding on paper—Enron would build a new power plant there. The two parties signed a contract in December 1993, but there were still negotiations to be had before things could be set in stone.

In all their dealings with India, Mark and Enron had a partner—the U.S. government. The hub of Enron's federal support was the Commerce Department's "Advocacy Center"—a war room for advancing the overseas interests of American corporations—in this case, Enron, GE, and Bechtel. The Commerce Department would pull in a motley crew of government agencies, all of whom would work alongside Enron in the hope of opening the floodgates of the Indian power market to American companies.[42]

Sure enough, the aid came from all corners of Washington. In September 1994, Ex-Im agreed to loan $302 million to the Dabhol Power Company (DPC), of which Enron owned 80 percent. OPIC also offered up $318 million in support, including insurance and loans.[43] The deal was soon final, and the bulldozers and cranes got to work.

The fine print was a gold mine for Enron. The Maharastra government had promised to purchase large quantities of energy at a high price. This caused price hikes on a population that could hardly afford it and that did not take very kindly to such things.

In March 1995, as construction began on the plant, Maharastra voters went to the polls and emphatically voted out the local ruling party. The winners were politicians who had campaigned against foreign corporations, promising to "push Enron into the Arabic Sea." The new coalition government appointed Gopinath Munde, an outspoken critic of Dabhol, to lead an investigation of the project.[44] Enron had to be troubled by this, considering that the Maharastra government was the only customer Dabhol had.

The media and the new politicians alleged bribery, wondering aloud if Maharastra could pay Enron what it had promised, and generally cried foul. Major Indian newspapers editorialized against the power plant, and locals rioted against Enron. In August 1995, the local government ordered Enron to cease and desist.

But the U.S. Government kept laboring for Enron. Bill Clinton's Energy Department and Treasury Department leaned on India to let Enron have its way. After six months of negotiating and pressure, Enron's Dabhol plant was back on track—for the moment. OPIC increased its amount of insurance on the plant to $392 million.[45]

While there were still problems, George W. Bush's administration kept up the drumbeat. In April of 2001, Secretary of State Colin Powell told India's foreign minister, "failure to resolve the matter could have serious deterrent effect on other investors."[46]

In May 2001, the Maharastra government—Dabhol's only customer—said it would no longer pay the bills. The plant ground to a halt. The $900 million investment by Enron, and the nearly $650 million in U.S. taxpayer financing, were now for naught. Soon, the Indian government seized control of the plant, and OPIC (read: "U.S. taxpayers") was forced to pay GE and Bechtel $64 million in insurance payments. In 2003, Bank of America, a lender to the project, pocketed $28 million in taxpayer cash to cover its losses. But Enron still had a claim on OPIC, and in April of 2004, U.S. taxpayers paid $20 million to GE and Bechtel so that they could buy out Enron's equity. This meant taxpayer money was helping the bankrupt company pay its debts.[47]

Then, there were the other banks whom DPC (the consortium of Enron, Bechtel, and GE) left hanging. They were out $138 million now that DPC couldn't pay them. OPIC picked up the tab.

The U.S. government then sued India and reclaimed most of the money (over $220 million) it had paid out to the corporations that had sunk money in Dabhol—good news for American taxpayers, but possibly bad news for American diplomacy in this tumultuous part of the globe.

Subsidized "Buckshot"

Enron is famous for creating the illusion of profits and assets by financial juggling. Authors McLean and Elkind wrote that "to a staggering degree, Enron's 'profits' and 'cash flow' were the result of the company's own complex dealings with itself." To an upsetting degree, the U.S. taxpayer served as the unwitting middleman in those dealings.

Enron owned 49.25 percent of a Venezuelan power company called Accroven.[48] In late 2000, after Enron had already peaked, Accroven wanted to buy "engineering services & process equipment" from certain exporters in the United States. The exporters turned to Ex-Im, and secured $132 million in direct loans.[49] This meant U.S. taxpayers would lend the money to Accroven (half-owned by Enron), so that Accroven could buy the services and equipment. Who was the exporter?

Enron. Yes, Enron was selling services to Enron, and to facilitate the sale, the U.S. government extended cut-rate subsidized loans to Enron. It wasn't the only time.

Ex-Im loaned $250 million to Trakya Electric in Turkey in 1995 and 1996, to finance Trakya's purchase from, among other companies, Enron.[50] Enron owned 50 percent of Trakya. Subsidizing this deal doesn't "create American jobs." It only transfers wealth from working Americans to Enron.

Sudan's government is notoriously brutal. The government has slaughtered its own people in the Darfur region in droves, with some estimates ranging as high as 400,000 deaths, and Osama bin Laden reportedly found sanctuary in Sudan.

The U.S. government bars American companies from doing business in Sudan. But the China National Pipeline Corporation (CNPC) doesn't take orders from Washington. It is working alongside the Sudanese government, building an oil pipeline through the country, enriching the government. China also helps arm Sudanese soldiers.[51]

Enron and the CNPC formed a partnership in 1999 to build a pipeline in China. The U.S. Department of Commerce's Advocacy Center worked to seal the deal. Enron and the CNPC signed their Memorandum of Understanding on a trip to China sponsored by the Commerce Department and led by Commerce Secretary William Daley.[52] While the U.S. government won't let you do business with Sudan at all, it will subsidize deals you might do with Sudan's business partners.

In March 2002, the Institute for Policy Studies documented the depth and breadth of the U.S. government's complicity in Enron's rise and fall. The report began:

> Many public officials have described Enron's demise as the product of corporate misbehavior. This perspective ignores a vital fact: Enron would not have scaled such grand global heights, nor fallen so dramatically, without its close financial relationships with government agencies.[53]

The report added together the financing and government support for Enron projects from U.S. agencies, the World Bank, and foreign versions of the Ex-Im or OPIC and found $7.219 billion in public financing for Enron, coming from 21 different agencies. One final detail: In 2001, Rebecca Mc-Donald, former Chairman and CEO of Enron Global Assets, was on the advisory committee of the Ex-Im.

Enron's global exploits—many of which are actually still going on—might never have happened were the federal government not active in promoting them. Had EI been more modest, Enron might never have racked up the debt or played the accounting games that it did. If the Ex-Im and OPIC did not exist, the Enron scandal would have been far, far smaller.

This is Not the Debt You're Looking For

Andrew Fastow, an accountant with a devotion to *Star Wars,* climbed quickly through the ranks of Enron, becoming its chief financial officer and winning the CFO Excellence Award from *CFO Magazine.* Fastow is now the symbol of what was wrong at Enron. According to the standard account, he was chiefly responsible for the accounting games, the special purpose entities (SPEs), and the fraud that is now Enron's legacy.

While Jeffrey Skilling is said to have succeeded through his mental powers and his will, Fastow got by, one could say, by using the Force—or some similar sort of magic. He could make debt vanish, revenue come out of a hat, and assets appear from thin air.

The basic form of Fastow's trickery was to "sell" Enron assets while never losing control of them. Selling a debt-ridden asset had three virtues. First, the sale brought in revenue. Second, the sale lowered the total amount of debt on Enron's books. Third, by officially separating a *part of Enron* from *Enron,* any business that the company did with itself, between these two units, could count as sales and profits. Of course, such maneuvers only created "wealth" on paper, and not in any real sense.

Fastow pled guilty to fraud, and he expects to serve 10 years in federal prison. But most of his accounting games that hid Enron liabilities or artificially inflated its earnings were, in fact, legal. Indeed, they were even within the standards of the accounting industry.

As with the rest of the Enron scandal, if we look at Fastow's schemes and scams, we find the government's fingerprints. Fastow's tricks were complex with many layers, twists, and wrinkles. In understanding his work, it will be helpful to begin—as Enron prosecutors have—with a simple example, involving the sale of some barges.

"Wanna Buy a Barge?"

Daniel Bayly is now in jail. His friends say he's there because of a single five-minute phone conversation he had with Fastow in December 1999. Bayly never worked at Enron. He was a veteran banker at Merrill Lynch, but federal prosecutors said he was an accomplice in Enron's fraud—and a jury agreed.[54] Bayly might or might not be blameworthy or truly guilty, but he certainly played a role in a dirty deal.

We now know that much of the vaunted economic growth the United States enjoyed in the 1990s was a house of cards. The dot-com boom proved to be a bubble, and it popped in 2000. In the late 1990s, stock prices had very little to do with underlying economic reality. But to corporate management, stock prices often were more important than economic reality. At Enron, this was explicit. An in-house risk-management manual made clear that Enron's risk management was "directed at accounting, rather than economic performance."[55] Indeed, it sometimes seemed that everything at Enron was directed at accounting performance.

And so, as the end of 1999 approached, Fastow became the makeup artist for Enron—trying to make it look prettier to Wall Street than it really was. He did a good job, as evidenced by one of his e-mails, which read, "Q4 1999: 8 days/6 deals/$125 million."[56]

One of his late 1999 deals involved Daniel Bayly and Merrill Lynch. Enron owned some power plants on barges near Lagos in Nigeria. In December 1999, Enron sold those barges to Merrill Lynch. What would Merrill Lynch want with barge-mounted power plants? Not very much, apparently: Merrill sold them back to one of Fastow's special purpose entities a few months later.

Federal prosecutors say that the point of the whole deal was fraud. Enron got to book the revenue from the sale as profits, padding its annual reports, and helping drive its stock prices even higher. Merrill got to keep Enron's business as an investment banker, and got to turn a tidy profit on a no-risk deal with Enron. In joking e-mails just after they bought the barges, one Merrill banker wrote to another, "wanna buy a barge?"

Bayly maintains he never acted with intent to defraud anyone. The *New York Times* reports:

> Mr. Bayly's lawyers contend that he neither structured nor approved the deal and that he had always believed that a third party would buy

the barges. In an appellate brief . . . , they argued that Mr. Fastow, who did not testify during the trial, had never guaranteed during his call with Mr. Bayly that Enron would buy the barges from Merrill Lynch.[57]

So, why is Dan Bayly behind bars? The *Times* quotes one lawyer who says, "Dan Bayly was part of a massive fraud perpetrated on the public and he knowingly mislead investors." But if talking on the phone about the deal makes Bayly a criminal, where does that leave the U.S. government?

Enron's very presence in Nigeria has U.S. government fingerprints all over it. In November 1999, a month before the barge sale, and before Nigeria had signed a contract with Enron, Houston Mayor Lee Brown went to Nigeria to press Enron's case.[58] In 2000, Bill Clinton focused his Africa trip on Nigeria and their power sector. Clinton's Commerce Secretary William Daley visited Nigeria in 1998.[59] Finally, OPIC and the International Development Agency subsidized Enron's Lagos barges.[60]

But Enron's accounting games go deeper than such sales and actually predate Andrew Fastow.

False Security

Champagne corks were popping in the 31st-floor conference room at Enron, and it was still midday—on a Thursday. But Jeff Skilling had cause to celebrate. It was not an earnings target, a new stock high, a new hire, or a new deal inked. Skilling was toasting an announcement from Washington.[61]

From the beginning, Skilling had been pushing Enron to use a new method of accounting called "mark-to-market" accounting. Under traditional accounting, Enron could not book profits from a project like Dabhol until money actually started coming in the door. Under mark-to-market accounting, however, once Mark signed the Power Purchase Agreement, Enron could write down as an asset all the future revenue from the deal. While perfectly legitimate in many cases, it is not hard to imagine how mark-to-market accounting can be a tool for misleading Wall Street: In order to increase its assets, a company only needs rosier estimates about a current deal.

On January 30, 1992, Skilling popped the champagne corks to celebrate a notice from the Securities and Exchange Commission (SEC) that Enron could legitimately use mark-to-market accounting. This decision by the SEC may have been the cornerstone of making Enron what it became.

Authors McLean and Elkind describe how this use of accounting, combined with an obsession with Wall Street, could transform a company into an insatiable beast:

> The most dangerous problem of all is the very thing that makes mark-to-market accounting seem so seductive in the first place: growth. When the initial deals are cut and all the potential profits are immediately posted, a company using mark-to-market accounting appears to be growing rapidly. Wall Street analysts applaud, and the stock rockets upward. But how do you keep that growth rate up? True, you're still receiving the cash from past contracts. But you can't count it in your profits, because you've booked it already. It's as if you have to begin every quarter fresh. If you did one deal last year, in order to show growth you have [to] do two the next and four the quarter after that and eight after that and on and on. And if you're promising Wall Street that your earnings will increase at a 15 percent annual clip, well, soon enough you're on a treadmill that becomes faster and steeper as the company gets bigger.[62]

So, when the SEC allowed Enron to use mark-to-market accounting, was it the sort of laissez-faire, "anarchic capitalism, in which there are no rules and no referees," that some of Enron's critics charged? Not exactly. There *was* a referee—the SEC—and if it said it was okay, what company or investor would disagree?

The SEC acts as a stamp of approval. It tells investors, in effect, "you don't need to worry, Uncle Sam has checked out this company, and it is above board." It is still up to the investor or mutual fund manager, of course, to decide whether the stock will go up or down, but on the questions of honesty, transparency, and accuracy, the SEC is the judge.

Whenever the government takes up the work of calling a business or a product safe, legitimate, and honest, a new hazard is created. Individuals no longer feel the same need to do the due diligence themselves. As long as the government does its job well, this is a blessing to most consumers—the time they would spend researching the trustworthiness of a company can now be spent with their families or playing golf. But when government makes mistakes, consumers are probably worse off than if there was no government watchdog at all.

Congress created the SEC to boost investor confidence in the stock market after the stock market crash of 1929. As the thousands who lost millions of dollars in Enron stock can testify, investor confidence in Enron was a little *too* boosted.

For Enron, the federal government judged that this risky way of accounting—an accounting method that helped spawn Enron's manic deal
making and book cooking—was just fine. Accounting firm Arthur Andersen
went under, in large part because it signed off on some of Enron's games.
But the SEC, which also gave Enron the green light, is still going strong.

A central character in Enron's final act was shortseller Jim Chanos.
Shortselling is a clever, but standard, Wall Street move that enables investors
to make money by betting a stock will go down. Here's a simplified way of
understanding Chanos's shortselling: Chanos believed Enron was overpriced, and so he borrowed some Enron stock, and then sold it. Now he was
at risk—if Enron stock went up, he would need to buy it at that higher price
so that he could give it back to the original owner. If the stock plummeted,
though, Chanos could buy it back much cheaper than he had sold it, return
it to the owner, and walk away with the difference. Professional shortsellers
spend their days looking for stocks that are overpriced. That makes them the
most motivated people in the country to find chinks in the armor of highly
esteemed companies. Chanos was the one who tipped off the *Fortune* magazine reporters who helped reveal Enron's true position. Shortsellers kept
Enron from playing their games any longer.

Enron might have been caught earlier had there been more shortsellers
on the scene. But Washington discourages shortselling with regulations such
as the "uptick rule," which permits shortsellers to unload their borrowed
stock only after it has gone up. Other government rules like that, aimed at
keeping stock prices high, help companies like Enron stay overvalued.

Jedis of California

Enron could no longer hide its precarious position in October and November of 2001 when the company announced it was restating its financials from
1997 to 2001. Enron was setting straight some accounting that had previously
been a little bent. The restatements centered on Fastow's Special Purpose Entities. These were partnerships, nominally separate from Enron, used to ware-
house debt or liabilities, or otherwise help Fastow make Enron look good.

The accounting changes in the fall of 2001 centered on a few SPEs that
Fastow named after Star Wars characters. These SPEs were the offspring of a
relationship between Enron and an agency of the California government.

The California Public Employee Retirement System (Calpers) is one of
the largest investors in the world. It holds the pensions of 1.4 million em-

ployees or retirees of the California state government, and their families.[63] Its portfolio reached $200 billion at the end of 2005.[64]

Calpers is a retirement fund, but it is also the government. Calpers is an independent agency in the California government, as its web site's domain name www.calpers.ca.gov would suggest. The state treasurer is an ex officio member of Calpers's board, and the governor appoints some board members while the legislature picks others.

In 1993, Enron and Calpers formed a team and called it Jedi. Jedi stood for Joint Energy Development Investment, but was also just a nerdy Star Wars joke by Fastow. Jedi started with $500 million, half of which was Enron stock and half of which was the retirement money of California's public employees.[65]

Jedi was its own entity—not officially a unit of Enron. But when Jedi would make an investment—buying a pipeline or part of a power plant, say—Enron would estimate the future value of the deal, and immediately mark half (Enron's portion of Jedi) of that down as profit on the day the deal was signed. But Enron only owned half of Jedi, so the company did not include Jedi's debt on its balance sheets. It's easy to see how this SPE, combined with mark-to-market accounting, made Enron look much better off than it was.

Again, however, the insatiable beast created by mark-to-market accounting reared its head. Even if Jedi's investments were making profits every year for Enron, Enron couldn't put those new profits in its quarterly reports, because it had already accounted for *all* of Jedi's future profits when the deal was signed. Once all of Jedi's money was invested, Enron needed a new way to feed the beast that was Enron's books.

So, in late 1997, Fastow made Jedi II, twice as big as Jedi. Once again, Enron approached Calpers, asking to go dutch on this new set of investments. Calpers agreed, but only if it could cash out on its original Jedi investments. But if Enron took the rest of Jedi off Calpers's hands, Fastow would need to add Jedi to its books, defeating the purpose of the SPE.

So, Enron needed some third party to buy half of Jedi from Calpers, and the two agreed on a price of $383 million. But nobody was biting. If Enron couldn't *find* a buyer, Enron would *make* a buyer. Enter Chewbacca—or Chewco as the new SPE, spawned in November 1997 was known.

Chewco, being just born, had no money, and so it borrowed $383 million. But banks don't just lend brand-new companies $383 million. So, Enron made it easier for the bank by guaranteeing the loan—if Chewco couldn't pay back the bank, Enron would.

Chewco's existed solely to own half of Jedi, keeping Jedi off Enron's books. That meant *Chewco* had to be off Enron's books. Under accounting rules, an SPE like Chewco could be moved off a company's books if somebody else owned 3 percent of it. So, if nobody would buy up half of Jedi, Enron now needed someone only to buy up 3 percent of Chewco's half of Jedi. Fastow needed to find $11.5 million in independent investment—and soon. Enron wanted to launch Jedi II before the end of 1997.

In that short time frame, Enron couldn't find someone to invest in even 3 percent of Chewco. Enron also needed Chewco to be controlled by someone other than Enron. Fastow wanted his wife's family to take up that job, but Skilling balked.

Instead, one of Fastow's deputies at Enron, Michael Kopper, became Chewco's manager. Kopper created his own institutions, called Big River Funding, LLC and Little River Funding, LLC. The "Rivers" would be the 3 percent "outside" owners of Chewco that would allow Fastow to move Chewco (and thus Jedi) off the books. Of course, the Rivers didn't have $11.5 million sitting around, and so they, too, had to borrow the cash.

But Barclays investment bank leant the Rivers the cash only after they agreed to set up a "reserve fund," which could guarantee repayment to the bank. Where did the reserve fund get its cash? From Chewco.

Chewco's financing, believe it or not, gets even more confusing, and it is unnecessary to go any further into its twisted bowels here. The key is that the whole purpose of Chewco was to keep Jedi off Enron's books. Chewco was supposedly an independent entity, but more than 99 percent of its money was in loans secured by Enron.

Auditors later determined that Chewco didn't qualify as an off-the-books SPE. For one, the Rivers were really controlled by an Enron employee (though he later transferred control to his gay lover),[66] and almost all of the Rivers' money was borrowed from and collateralized by Chewco—another dizzying circle.

Creating Chewco and moving it off the books may be where Enron crossed the line. Enron's special investigation of itself in late 2001 reported, "Chewco is, to our knowledge, the first time Enron's Finance group (under Fastow) used an SPE run by an Enron employee to keep a significant investment partnership outside of Enron's consolidated financial statements." The investigation also reported, "Chewco played a central role in Enron's November 2001 decision to restate its prior period financial statements."[67]

Without Calpers, neither Jedi *nor* Jedi II would have existed. Without both Jedi *and* Jedi II, Chewco never would have existed. Without Chewco and the Jedis, Enron's books may not have been so cooked.

Hair of the Dog That Bit You

On February 19, 2002, two of America's most obscure Winter Olympians generated one of the Games' most thrilling moments for the United States. Vonetta Flowers and Jill Bakken, the second-string women's bobsled team for the United States won the gold medal in a stunning upset.[68]

The win was not only dramatic; it was historic. Flowers became the first black athlete to ever win gold at the Winter Games. The two also helped snap a pretty impressive streak the next day when they made the front page of the *New York Times:* For the first time in 42 days, the Enron scandal was not mentioned on page A-1.

Enron's collapse was easily the biggest event in the business world in 2001 and 2002. Those days, the business pages sometimes read like a police report. The aftershocks of Enron included scandals at WorldCom, Global Crossing, Tyco, and of course, the extinction of Arthur Andersen.

Near the end of Enron's streak in the *New York Times,* on February 10, a small blurb about the company appeared on the *Times'* cover. The headline: "Enron fall creates a race to regulate."[69] This was utterly predictable. Enron was a problem, and so Congress was determined to fix it.

On the political front, the reaction was equally unsurprising. Democrats highlighted Bush's closeness to Lay, and some in the party tried to make the 2002 elections about Enron—hence the angry talk about "unbridled free markets," and "anarchic capitalism." At the 2002 California Democratic convention, delegates wore pins bearing Dick Cheney's name, with both E's replaced with Enron's trademarked "crooked E."

Prescribing more government intervention in response to the Enron scandal is a bit like the folk lore that says that the hungover drunk should cure himself with "the hair of the dog that bit you"—or more alcohol.

Sure enough, Congress plowed ahead and made new laws, specifically Sarbanes-Oxley, placing new requirements on all publicly traded companies. The law holds CEOs and CFOs strictly responsible for the accuracy in all reports that the company issues, and requires thorough record keeping and auditing.

In May 2005, the *Economist* described the measure this way:

the statute, carried along by rage and the desire of Congress to do something dramatic, ranged wider than was necessary. . . . Its daunting requirements on managers, with the threat of severe criminal penalties to back them up, are imposing substantial costs, direct and indirect, on American business.[70]

The costs, of course, disproportionately fall on smaller businesses. Naturally, there is much business to be made helping companies comply with the strict new law.

Congress's determination to use big government to try to fix a problem caused by big government was an example of either stubborn hubris or unflappable optimism, depending on your bias. Energy regulation done wrong, detailed accounting rules tacitly approving deception, and generous subsidies for dealing with oneself may have been part of the problem, most of Washington reasoned, but we can fix that with *good* regulations, *better* accounting rules, and *the right* subsidies.

Sure enough, Congress reauthorized the Ex-Im weeks after Enron's collapse.

While government may never quit trying to solve every problem, CEOs might be able to take a lesson from the Enron tale. Enron was built on government subsidies, complex and artificial rules, and environmental regulations. This formula may work for a while, but ask Ken Lay today: It will catch up with you.

12

Ethanol and Archer Daniels Midland

Corporate Moonshiners on the Dole

One day in early 1972, a man walked into the West Wing of the White House with a package and entered the office of Rose Mary Woods, Richard Nixon's personal secretary. Woods and the man exchanged pleasantries, never mentioning the envelope—an accordion folder full of cash—that he left on her desk. Woods immediately had the envelope sent down to the White House basement and locked in a safe whose combination was known only to Woods, her assistant, and the president.

The folder was filled with $100 bills—1,000 of them, Woods later estimated to the Watergate Special Prosecution Force.[1] Rose Mary Woods had never met the man before, but knew him to be Dwayne Orville Andreas, the chairman of Archer Daniels Midland (ADM), the largest agribusiness in the world.

This was not Andreas's first $100,000 gift to a presidential campaign. The chairman had contributed the same amount four years earlier—to Nixon's opponent, Hubert Humphrey (a contribution for which Andreas would be indicted but later acquitted). When a separate $25,000 Andreas donation ended up in the bank account of Watergate burglar Bernard

Barker, Humphrey (the godfather of Andreas's son) responded, "Let's put it this way: Dwayne Andreas has friends in both parties."[2]

Andreas describes his political contributions as "good citizenship." Considering that a huge portion of ADM's profits come from businesses that are subsidized or specially protected by the U.S. government, the cash to politicians—more than $4 million by some counts—could also be seen as good investing.

Archer Daniels Midland's main asset is corn, which sounds benign enough. Some of the corn they grow ends up on dinner tables around the world. Some ends up feeding cattle. But ADM turns some of the corn into alcohol and syrup. In those forms, they take the place of gasoline and of sugar, respectively.

The corn-based fuel is ethanol. The corn-based sweetener is corn syrup. Together, they constitute nearly half of ADM's business. Without big government intervention to ADM's benefit, neither product would exist. Archer Daniels Midland's gain is the taxpayers' and the consumers' loss. Your taxes fund some of ADM's welfare, and pro-ADM regulation drives up the prices you pay for food and gasoline. What helps ADM may also hurt the soil and the air.

Ethanol allies defend the subsidies by saying that ethanol is cleaner than petroleum. In many ways this is true, but not in all. In fact, the Clean Air Act would have banned ethanol if ADM's friends in government had not given it a special waiver.

Finally, at least two scientists argue that producing one gallon of ethanol requires more energy than that gallon will yield. In other words, all of the fuel for the tractors, power for the ethanol-processing plants, and other steps of ethanol production use more energy than the product can provide.

Archer Daniels Midland may be the most offensive case of corporate welfare and rent seeking. Looking at Dwayne Andreas's political activities it is hard to believe ADM is merely a passive recipient of corporate welfare or even a lobbyist who nibbles away at the edges of policy. Outward appearances suggest that many government programs exist *because* Andreas has supported them. Without government favors, ethanol may not exist. That's why Andreas's "good citizenship," which spans both parties and eight presidents, is so important. Indeed, for half a century, Andreas made sure he was close to the people at the top.

In history class, most kids see a black-and-white photograph of Harry Truman, the day after Election Day 1948, holding up the embarrassing

Chicago Tribune headline, "DEWEY DEFEATS TRUMAN." Of course, as it turned out, any Election Night joy in the Dewey camp gave way to agony. For Truman, the emotional journey went in the opposite direction, from despair to triumph. For Dwayne Andreas it was no big deal—he won either way.

Andreas had been friends with Thomas Dewey since Dewey was the governor of New York. Back then, Andreas pitched Dewey on the virtues of soy protein, one of ADM's products. Dewey soon made sure food in New York state institutions included soy protein.[3]

After Dewey's surprise loss in 1948, Andreas still did fine. During Truman's presidency, Andreas once acted as an envoy from the United States to Argentina to help convince Juan and Eva Peron to participate in a famine relief program. When Dewey left public life, Andreas hired him as his personal attorney. In that position, Dewey convinced Andreas to start giving away a lot of his money, including a decent amount to politicians. Andreas let Dewey decide which Republicans to help. For the Democrats, Andreas asked Hubert Humphrey for guidance.[4]

Andreas's friendship with Humphrey ran deep. In the 1950s, Humphrey brought Andreas with him to the Soviet Union, where he met with Khrushchev before the two flew to Yugoslavia to hang out with Tito. Andreas helped convince Humphrey, as a senator, to change the rules of the federal "Food for Peace" program, a Cold War tool, to allow the shipment of prepared foods, not just raw foods, which would get ADM more of the action.[5]

Of course, Andreas also supported the man who ended Humphrey's political career, Richard Nixon. Nixon and Andreas stayed close. Andreas helped convince Nixon to open trade with China so that ADM could sell wheat to the Communist power.[6]

When Jimmy Carter left peanut farming for public life, Dwayne Andreas bought his peanut farm. When Ronald Reagan considered meeting with Gorbachev at Reykjavik, Andreas helped convince him the meeting could be fruitful.[7] Both Bill Clinton and Bob Dole were tight with Andreas, with Andreas contributing nearly a quarter-billion to Dole over the years.[8]

Iowa's senators, Republican Chuck Grassley and Democrat Tom Harkin, are perhaps the oddest couple in the upper chamber. Grassley is conservative, and Harkin is one of the most liberal senators. They share close ties to ADM, and both fiercely defend subsidies for ethanol.

These two are not alone—everyone who goes to Iowa seems to catch ethanol fever. New Jersey Senator Bill Bradley, who had called ethanol subsidies "highway robbery" and a "sweetheart deal" as a senator,[9] came to Iowa as a presidential candidate in 2000 and announced he supported special favors for ethanol.[10] In the 2004 primaries, Democratic caucus voters saw similar contortions from Senators John Kerry, Bob Graham, and Joe Lieberman, who had all voted against ethanol mandates in 1994,[11] but abstained from a vote on a similar measure in 2003[12] when they were wooing Iowa voters.

While Iowa farmers may profit from ethanol, nobody benefits like ADM does. In 2004, ADM's corn-processing section (whose profits are about half from corn syrup and half from ethanol) yielded a $661 million profit, accounting for 41 percent of the company's total profit.[13] ADM's 2004 Annual Report says the company has the world's "largest market share in both high fructose corn syrup and ethanol."

Makin' Their Way, the Only Way They Know How

In the early days of this country, a huge Kentucky county on the Ohio River began gaining a reputation for producing a product that was a true American original: corn whiskey. Bourbon County has since been broken up into many smaller counties, but bourbon whiskey is still a favorite throughout the country and perhaps the most uniquely American contribution to the world of liquor.

Making bourbon was once a backyard business or hobby for countless families, but the whiskey excise tax (which led to the Whiskey Rebellion in 1794) consolidated the bourbon industry to only a few distilleries, many of which still thrive today. Prohibition relegated the process of distilling to backwoods hideouts and made it impossible to find the space to age the whiskey. The result was moonshine, which, in contrast to the distinctive red color of the oak-barrel-aged bourbon, was clear—hence the nickname "white lightning." Today, moonshining is nearly extinct compared to its past glory, but the legal bourbon industry thrives, and the process of making corn whiskey hasn't changed too much over the years.

The farmers pick the corn, dry it, and grind it into corn meal. The corn meal is mixed with water, at which point it is called *mash*. Adding yeast then spurs the crucial process of fermentation—the conversion of the sugars into alcohol. The next step, distillation, separates the alcohol from the mash.

One key factor in distillation involves hydrogen bonds, though the Kentucky settlers may not have explained it that way. Chemically, heat evaporates water, but that's not the whole story. Any liquid has an inherent dispersion force, with the electrons of each molecule pushing every other molecule away. This force would immediately turn liquid into gas, were it not for a contrary cohesive force holding the molecules together.

In the case of water, the cohesion comes from hydrogen bonds. Hydrogen's unique atomic makeup (with only one electron) makes hydrogen unusually adept at bonding to other molecules. In water (H_2O), a hydrogen of one water molecule sticks to the oxygen in another water molecule. Heating water excites these molecules, magnifying their dispersion forces, until, at 212 degrees Fahrenheit, the dispersion overcomes the strength of the hydrogen bonds, and the water turns into vapor.

But alcohol has a different chemical makeup. It contains hydrogen and oxygen, but also carbon. Carbon gets in the way of hydrogen's bonding work, and so alcohol's dispersion force has less to overcome than does water's.

As a result, alcohol evaporates at a lower temperature than water does. Distillers, then, will heat the mash to a temperature around 175 degrees Fahrenheit, which does not evaporate the water, but turns the alcohol into gas, and sends it up in the air. The gaseous booze is then captured, carried into another chamber, and condensed, leaving the corn meal and most of the water behind. Repeat this process until almost all the water is gone, and you've got pure rotgut.

In addition to making you blind, white lightning can also power your car. If you poured a bottle of grain alcohol into your gas tank, you could drive nearly as far on that as you could on a gallon of the gasoline they sell at the corner filling station. But if you've ever bought a jar of grain alcohol, you know it costs more by volume than the same amount of gasoline would.

This is the problem that ethanol faces. Cornell scientist David Pimentel, who studied ethanol in the Reagan administration and is now one of ethanol's most persistent critics, found in 2001 that an acre of corn yields about 7,110 pounds of corn, which can become about 328 gallons of ethanol. Just growing the corn and harvesting, before processing it into alcohol and distributing it, costs $1.05 per gallon, Pimentel estimated. In the end, it would take $1.74 to make a gallon, he said.[14] While this is cheaper than the *retail* price of gasoline today, it is still costlier than producing gasoline.

Different studies find very different results, but Pimentel is certainly not alone in finding that producing ethanol costs more than producing gasoline. A Congressional Research Service report from December 2004 reports that the wholesale prices of ethanol in a free market, "are generally twice that of wholesale gasoline prices." The average wholesale price of pure ethanol from March 2002 to February 2003 ranged from 94 cents to $1.33 per gallon. For gasoline, the average wholesale price (far cheaper than what drivers pay at the pump) was 65 cents to $1.03 for a gallon.[15]

In other words, ethanol can do the same thing gasoline can do, just more expensively. This is part of why financial analyst John McMillan said in 1996, "There's no question that ethanol would not exist without federal subsidies."[16]

Corporate Food Stamps

The federal subsidy, which according to one estimate reached nearly $10 billion between 1980 and 1995,[17] starts with a special targeted tax break. The U.S. Department of Transportation pays for highway construction and maintenance out of a special fund called the Highway Trust Fund. That fund is filled, not by income tax dollars, but by a federal tax charged on each gallon of gasoline. In this way, to some degree, the folks who are using the highways are also paying for them.

For every gallon of gasoline a refiner or distributor sells to a gas station, it must hand over 18.4 cents to the federal Highway Trust Fund. This tax, in the end, makes it more expensive to fill up your tank.

In 1978, we had an energy crisis, enflamed by OPEC withholding its supplies of petroleum. Congress passed a bill encouraging, through tax credits, development of domestic fuel sources. One provision of the Energy Tax Act provided a tax credit of 5.2 cents per gallon of gasoline that contained 10 percent ethanol. We call this mixture "gasohol."

The gasohol credit pushes refiners to buy ethanol. If a refiner buys a gallon of ethanol at the wholesale price of $1.33 and mixes it with nine gallons of gasoline, he knows that his gas tax bill will go down by 52 cents. The blender, in effect, is only paying 81 cents per gallon. The ethanol maker is pocketing $1.33. The extra 52 cents is, in effect, coming out of the Highway Trust Fund—if not for the special tax credit, the Highway Trust Fund would have more money.

In recent years, Congress has shifted the burden of this ethanol subsidy from the Highway Trust Fund to the general Treasury. The credit against the gas tax is gone, replaced with a 52-cent income tax credit for each gallon of ethanol a blender (typically either a refiner or a distributor) mixes with gas. For 2005, that credit went down to 51 cents per gallon.

Beyond the tax credits, the government protects the domestic ethanol producers with tariffs on foreign ethanol. In Brazil, farmers make ethanol from sugar (down there it's more like a rum-based fuel than a whiskey-based fuel), which is far cheaper. Additionally, Brazil subsidizes ethanol production. This means the Brazilians could undercut the midwestern corporate moonshiners. Accordingly, the federal government stepped in.

Washington slaps a 54-cent tariff on every gallon of ethanol sold into the United States. This effectively wipes out the tax advantage the foreign ethanol enjoys versus gasoline, thus eliminating any demand for imported ethanol.

The federal government uses the tax code to encourage gas companies to buy domestic ethanol but to discourage them from buying foreign ethanol. That's a pretty good deal for ADM and the other corn growers or ethanol plants. But Andreas's political influence, together with the general clout of the corn lobby, has managed to get even more favors out of desperate political leaders.

In October 1980, Jimmy Carter knew he was in trouble. Things were not going well in the Carter reelection campaign, as he trailed former California Governor Ronald Reagan in the polls.

On October 9, Carter's Agriculture Secretary Bob Bergland announced that his department would issue $340 million in special loan guarantees for the construction of 15 ethanol plants around the country.[18] The Carter administration directed many of these construction subsidies to states that were seen as key to the presidential election.

A few days after Reagan took office, the inspector general advised the new president that Carter had skirted official procedure and violated federal law in issuing the guarantees. Before Congress, one investigator testified that the loan guarantees never got proper review, but instead were "reviewed in a matter of days, some in a matter of hours."

Bruce Yellen, of the watchdog group Better Government Association testified:

> Two loan guarantees were approved for individuals who had contributed to the Democratic National Committee or the Carter

campaign. And 10 of the 15 guarantees went to states that were, at the time, considered critical to the president's reelection bid. These elements suggested that this last-minute rush was politically inspired, and our interviews with agency officials substantiated that point.[19]

In 1986, there was a different sort of energy crisis—one that threatened Andreas, and not consumers. The price of corn was going up, and the price of gasoline was falling. This made ethanol even more of a money loser. Andreas, once again, turned to the government.

In April, Andreas called his friend, Reagan's Agriculture Secretary Richard Lyng, informing him that his ethanol plants might shut down. A few days later, Andreas traveled to Washington and met Lyng at the Madison Hotel for breakfast. Two days after that meeting, Lyng announced a gift for ADM and other ethanol producers: The federal government would *give* ethanol producers free corn.[20]

This was not a mere tax incentive or a loan. This was a *gift*. The analogy would be an oil company suffering from low gasoline prices getting free crude from the government. It was a giveaway in the purest form. Earle Gavett, director of USDA's Office of Energy, estimated at the time that ADM would receive a majority of the $70 million in free corn. One gasoline industry lawyer called the program, "corporate food stamps for ADM."[21]

There Is No Such Thing as a Free Market

One central aim of this book has been to debunk the myth that "pro-business" and "pro-market" are the same things. Advocates of less government often are derided as doing the bidding of big business. Dwayne Andreas and ADM show more clearly than any other case how and why so many big businesses disdain free markets, and exist only because of a government willing to intervene in the economy. Andreas's own words show that while he certainly considers himself a businessman, he doesn't truly consider himself a player in the free market.

In a 1995 hearing before the Senate Agriculture Committee, Andreas spoke in favor of preserving agriculture export subsidies. In the preceding decade, ADM had benefited from more than $130 million in subsidized exports. Republicans had recently taken control of government in a dramatic revival of conservatism, and Andreas wanted to respond to all the free-market talk that was newly sweeping Capitol Hill.

"Well, let me tell you," he said to the committee, "when it comes to agriculture, there is no such thing as a free market." He explained that foreign governments subsidized their crops, and so ADM needed subsidies from the U.S. government—the same argument Boeing uses about Airbus. Only, in this case, the foreign agriculture companies lobbying for and receiving European crop subsidies included ADM's European affiliates.[22] On both sides of the Atlantic, then, ADM was receiving agriculture subsidies, and pointing to European subsidies it received as the reason it needed American subsidies.

On another occasion, under criticism for his government aid, Andreas spoke more bluntly. "There isn't one grain of anything in the world that is sold in a free market. Not one! The only place you see a free market is in the speeches of politicians. People who are not in the Midwest do not understand that this is a socialist country."[23]

Understanding, lobbying for, and influencing the laws that make us a "socialist country" has been the key to Dwayne Andreas's and ADM's success—and distinguishes Andreas from many of the other businessman in this book.

The government, beyond all of these efforts to *encourage* the purchase of ethanol or other ADM products, has gone so far as to *mandate* their purchase. When prices for something go too high, simple economics says consumers will simply stop buying it. The demand for a product will decrease as its price goes up, and consumers decide it's just not worth the money. In some circumstances, however, there exists "inelastic demand." Addicted smokers, for example, might be willing to pay almost any price to get a pack of cigarettes.

Ethanol enjoys some inelastic demand, too. The source of the inelasticity, though, is not addiction, but federal mandates. The energy bill passed in the summer of 2005 would require the consumption of four billion gallons of ethanol in 2006, rising to eight billion by 2012.[24] Very simply, consumers *must* buy what ADM is selling. The University of Missouri's Food and Agriculture Policy Research Institute estimated that the mandate will increase corn prices by 12.5 cents per bushel.[25]

Beyond Washington, ADM and other ethanol makers find subsidies in many state capitals. Andreas's home state of Minnesota, for example, pays ethanol producers 20 cents for every gallon they produce. Other states have similar programs.

The General Accounting Office (GAO) estimated in 1997 that the federal tax break had depleted the Highway Trust Fund by at least $7.5 billion and maybe $11 billion over the preceding 22 years.[26] Today, under the new tax break, ethanol subsidies are depleting the general fund at a time of deficit.

But ADM's chairman wants people to understand he opposes deficits. In 1993, days after Bill Clinton was elected promising voters a middle-class tax cut, Dwayne Andreas took to the airwaves to propose just the opposite. Speaking to Lou Dobbs on CNN, Andreas commented on the $4 trillion deficit:

> Well, Lou, there's an old Chinese proverb that says if you don't change your direction you'll wind up where you're headed. Our debt of $4 trillion, which is growing like a snowball, will lead us into a financial crisis unless something is done to change our direction, and I believe everything depends on whether the Clinton administration will have the courage to bite the bullet, give us some shock therapy, and make some major changes.[27]

Was Andreas pledging to swear off some of the millions in subsidies he received? Quite the contrary. He called for a tax hike. Specifically, Andreas called for a "a gas tax of $50 billion which would also improve our environment and would also save us a lot in our balance of payments, that would give us $50 billion." Of course, increasing the gas tax magnifies the value of the credit that ethanol receives, thus creating even more artificial incentives to purchase ethanol. For ADM, a gas tax hike would have the double benefit of driving more taxpayer money to the federal coffers (which are a major source of ADM's profits) and also more consumer money to ethanol.

But Andreas wasn't done. He also called for a new Value Added Tax (VAT), a sort of sales tax, like they have in Europe. The VAT, Andreas proposed, should apply to "all manufactured goods except food and medicine." ADM sells food. Once again, Andreas was saying raise taxes on everyone but ADM.

When Dobbs asked if Americans would embrace these tax hikes, Andreas responded: "I think it's time for America to face up to the fact that we have to accept the taxes that will keep our country solvent and preserve our democracy."

Why are federal and state governments so willing to subsidize ethanol? Andreas's clout is surely a factor, but what are the reasons these lawmakers give?

Like with most corporate welfare programs, the defense of ethanol subsidies is constantly shifting. In the 1970s, ethanol was supposed to provide a reliable source of energy amid OPEC shenanigans and the fear that petroleum might all but disappear. In the 1980s, as gas prices fell, ethanol advocates said that the American farmer was endangered and that ethanol subsidies might help. In the 1990s, Washington joined in the crusade to save the planet, and ethanol became a way to clean the air.

Under examination, all of these reasons begin to fall apart. Ethanol is not a legitimate source of energy, it is not broadly beneficial to American farmers, and it is possibly *damaging* to the environment. If we peel back the faulty justifications for ethanol subsidies, at the bottom we may be left looking at Dwayne Andreas and his campaign cash.

A Waste of Energy

Imagine you discover that your backyard is on an oil field. Only, the oil is very deep underground. So, you buy an oil rig and start pumping the oil to the surface. Now imagine the oil pump was powered by gasoline, like your car engine, and burns one gallon every hour. So, you go to the gas station and buy 10 gallons of gasoline—enough to run the rig all day.

At the end of the day, you've unearthed a few buckets of petroleum, and you take it down the road to the refiner. He tells you it is enough to make eight gallons of gasoline. You just wasted your day. After all, you started with 10 gallons of gasoline (that you purchased), and you ended with eight.

Such an enterprise, very literally, is a waste of energy. Burning fuel to make a smaller quantity of fuel makes no sense. At least two experts in energy and agriculture say that's what happens every day in the world of ethanol. Scientists vary widely in their calculations on the energy inputs and outputs of ethanol, and it will be years before there is consensus on this question, which was first raised in the late 1970s.

David Pimentel, a Cornell professor, was named to the Energy Resources Advisory Board (ERAB) during the Carter administration after he wrote an article in *Science* magazine in 1973 on energy inputs in agriculture—that is, how much fuel and energy is expended in farming.

While on ERAB, beginning in 1978, Pimentel headed a panel on the energy inputs of making fuels from different plants—biomass. Among these biomass fuels was corn ethanol. Pimentel's study took into account all the various energy inputs: The tractors burn gasoline during the planting, the weeding, and the harvesting. Irrigating the crops requires energy, too, to run the water pumps. Creating fertilizer is an energy-intensive process. Even tilling the land before planting and constructing the tractors and other farm equipment takes energy.

Once you have the corn, you still need to turn it into fuel. First, trucks ship it to a plant, which uses gasoline, again. The processes of sorting, grinding, soaking, drying, distilling, and containing the ethanol all require energy, typically from natural gas or petroleum. Corn mash must be distilled many times to obtain nearly pure ethanol.

One measure of energy is a kilocalorie (kCal). A pile of coal or a gallon of gasoline yields a certain number of kCals when burned. In a 2005 study, Pimental and Berkley professor Tad Patzek found that the entire process of producing a liter of ethanol (the planting, the shipping, the distilling, etc.) used 6,507 kCals. That same liter of ethanol, when burned, yielded 5,130 kCals.[28]

Exacerbating this problem is the fact that ethanol contains less energy than gasoline. The combustion when the sparkplug fires is weaker with ethanol than with gasoline. A liter of gasoline has an energy content of 8,400 kCals, compared to a liter of ethanol, which contains 5,130. That means that you can drive farther on a tank of gasoline than on a tank of ethanol.

Robert Mondt, one of the inventors of the catalytic converter and author of *Cleaner Cars: The History and Technology of Emission Control Since the 1960s*,[29] estimates in his book that it takes 1.4 gallons of ethanol to take you as far as one gallon of gasoline.

Although Pimentel's 2005 numbers are damning to ethanol, they paint the corn-fuel in a much better light than his original study did back in the Reagan years. Today, Pimentel says that making corn ethanol uses 29 percent more energy than it yields, while his original study had it using nearly 100 percent more energy than it yields. Improvements in farming technology, distilling, and fertilizers all help ethanol's case, but for nearly 30 years, Pimentel and other scientists have been arguing that ethanol is a waste of energy.

Corn-belt lawmakers did not like Pimentel's original study. Two senators ordered a GAO investigation of it, which found his methodology was sound and his conclusions fair. Taxpayers spent 20 times more money funding the GAO study as they did funding Pimentel's original study.

Many scientists disagree with Pimentel's findings. Some contrary studies have been funded by industry groups, such as the Renewable Fuels Association (which is largely funded by ADM), and many have been government studies. The Department of Energy has consistently maintained that ethanol is a net energy gainer, yielding a 35 percent gain. The disagreements arise from how to calculate the energy inputs: Do you count the energy required to build and maintain the equipment? Do you consider the energy required for irrigation only in some parts of the country or in all parts where corn is grown? The science is not exact, and the findings are not conclusive. But with such uncertainty, should the government really be subsidizing this product?

If Pimentel or Patzek are right, ethanol cannot possibly be the road to energy independence. An ethanol farm-and-distillery setup could not run on ethanol for the same reason our backyard oilrig was a waste of time and fuel. To make ethanol, you still need large quantities of other fuels, including gasoline.

Even scientists who reject Pimentel's findings and believe ethanol is an energy-gainer maintain that ethanol cannot provide energy security. In 2005, Marcelo Dias de Oliveira, Burton Vaughan, and Edward Rykiel Jr. wrote that if the United States wanted to switch to using all E-85 (a mixture of 85 percent ethanol and 15 percent gasoline), "by the year 2012, all the available cropland of the United States would be required for corn production."[30] Even worse, "by 2048, virtually the whole country, with the exception of cities, would be covered by corn plantations." (Of course, if nobody was allowed to live in the countryside or suburbs because ADM took their land by eminent domain to grow corn, demand for fuel would dramatically drop.)

To be sure, nobody can draw a definite conclusion from the varying studies. Taxpayers and drivers, however, might ask whether they should be subsidizing something that might or might not be literally worthless.

Even if ethanol is a waste of energy, or generates only a slight increase in energy, its defenders argue, it is still worth subsidizing. They defend the subsidies on the claims that it is good for the environment and good for farmers. After deeper investigation, these claims have their problems.

Clearing the Air?

Ethanol is touted as a clean fuel, but that claim is dubious. In fact, ethanol was on the verge of being outlawed by clean air laws in October 1992, when President George Bush, in a maneuver reminiscent of Carter's pre-election ethanol plant loans 12 years earlier, called for exempting ethanol from the Clean Air Act. Once again, Dwayne Andreas and ADM appeared to play a key role.

In the summer of 1991, the Environmental Protection Agency (EPA) played host to an unprecedented gathering. Leaders from the petroleum industry, the ethanol industry, government agencies, and environmental groups all sat down at what is called a Regulatory Negotiation (Reg-Neg).

The 1990 amendments to the Clean Air Act had set stricter standards for automobile emissions. Specifically, they addressed poisonous carbon monoxide (CO), and two types of emissions that cause smog: nitrogen oxide (NO_x) and hydrocarbons. Like most laws, the Clean Air amendments were fairly general, leaving it to the EPA to issue specific regulations that would implement them. The EPA chose to craft its implementing regulations through the Reg-Neg process.[31]

The eclectic group finally hammered out an agreement in August 1991, and the EPA implemented it in April 1992. Immediately, the ethanol industry, which had signed on to the agreement, raised a cry—the clean air rules might outlaw ethanol.

It turns out that, despite all the claims that ethanol is good for the environment, ethanol may be a net polluter in many ways. Ethanol *does* reduce CO emissions because it is an "oxygenate," which means it adds oxygen to the fuel, converting the CO into CO_2. But on the question of hydrocarbons, ethanol appears to make things worse.

The same fact that is crucial to ethanol makers and moonshiners in the distillation process is the key here. Alcohol's hydrogen bonds are weaker than those of water or even gasoline. That means alcohol is more likely to evaporate, both under high heat, and under normal temperatures.

A fuel's likelihood to evaporate is called its volatility and is measured by Reid Vapor Pressure (RVP). Volatility can be thought of as the net dispersion force, pushing outward on the liquid, with the consequence of turning it into a gas.

More volatile fuels send more hydrocarbons into the air, because before the hydrocarbons can be burned in combustion, more of them simply evaporate and float into the air. Adding 10 percent of ethanol to a fuel mixture increases the volatility and the RVP. That means gasohol sends more smog-causing hydrocarbons into the air.

The 1978 Clean Air Act included a maximum volatility for gasoline, as an effort to reduce hydrocarbons. This volatility standard would have outlawed ethanol. This was at the same time that Congress was creating the federal ethanol subsidy, though, and so lawmakers made a special exemption for ethanol. Gasohol would be allowed (and subsidized) although its volatility was higher than the standard legal limits. The final agreement of the 1991

Reg-Neg and the subsequent EPA rule, however, did not contain a full exemption. Gasohol would be held to the same standard as gasoline.

These rules sent ethanol's supporters into a frenzy. As Bill Clinton gained on him in the polls, including in the corn-belt, President Bush knew he had to act. In August, Bush went to the Illinois State Fair ready to propose an increase in the already generous subsidy for ethanol. Republican Governor Jim Edgar convinced him that would not go far enough, and so the president literally ripped that proposal out of his speech until he could craft a more appealing promise.[32]

In September, Minnesota Senator David Durenberger proposed a resolution in the Senate encouraging the White House to grant ethanol the exemption on hydrocarbons. Durenberger was retiring after an embarrassing scandal regarding unreported campaign contributions and improper expenditures, and, despite a legal defense funded in part by ADM's $10,000 contribution,[33] Durenberger would be convicted a few months later. His pro-ethanol measure, a nonbinding resolution, passed by voice vote.

Earlier that year, Dwayne Andreas had cochaired a fundraiser for the Republican Party, himself contributing $400,000 to the cause of reelecting George Bush.[34] On October 1, Bush announced that he would grant the special exemption the ethanol industry hoped for: Ethanol would be held to lower pollution standards than gasoline.

After Bush lost reelection, his proposed exemption entered limbo. A less skilled businessman than Dwayne Andreas might have been left out in the cold. But two months after the election, Andreas was at President Clinton's inauguration. Although Clinton arrived by bus, to display a populist image, the whole inauguration cost $25 million.[35]

Andreas contributed heavily to the inauguration, but he told reporters that although his business was directly affected by the government in many ways, his contributions or his closeness to the Clintons had nothing to do with ADM. "I'm here because I was invited," he told one reporter. "It has nothing to do with business. My business isn't affected."[36]

But his business *was* affected. Clinton ended up not following Bush's proposal to exempt ethanol from volatility standards, but instead, in the name of reducing CO, *mandated* increased use of ethanol rather than other oxygenate fuels. Clinton issued this rule not long after Andreas made a $100,000 contribution to the Democratic Party. A federal court later ruled that mandate was improper.[37]

The ethanol subsidies may harm the ground as well as the air. Subsidizing ethanol in myriad ways creates incentives for farmers to plant far more corn than can be consumed by humans and cattle. This encourages farmers to rely solely on one crop—corn—because the government is propping up its demand and supporting its price. (The federal government simultaneously applies downward pressure on corn prices through a completely separate corn subsidy, unrelated to ethanol.)

Farmers have long known that rotating crops—planting something different in a given field from year to year—is crucial to maintaining the health of soils. Planting corn year after year exacerbates erosion and depletes soil nutrients. David Pimentel, the Cornell scientist, maintains that corn is particularly destructive to soil health when planted exclusively.

If cars burning gasohol pollute the air, and farms growing only corn ruin the soil, it is only fitting that the middle stage—converting the corn into ethanol—would damage the environment, as well.

It turns out that ethanol plants can be criminal polluters. In 2002, 12 ethanol plants entered into a settlement with the Department of Justice, the EPA, and Minnesota. The plants lacked pollution controls mandated by the Clean Air Act and so had to pay small civil penalties and install the controls immediately.[38] Two days earlier, the Sierra Club had sued two midwestern ethanol plants for emitting illegal amounts of hydrocarbons.[39]

Marcelo Dias de Oliveira, disagrees with Pimentel and finds that ethanol is a net energy gainer, and can reduce CO_2 emissions, even considering the whole process of making ethanol. But looking at the full "ecological footprint," taking into account cropland used, water consumed, and other secondary factors to the ethanol process, he found that ethanol is a net drag on the planet. "The use of ethanol as a substitute for gasoline proved to be neither a sustainable nor an environmentally friendly option, considering ecological footprint values, and both net energy and CO_2 offset considerations seemed relatively unimportant compared to the ecological footprint."[40]

Additionally, some studies, done on mice, establish that prolonged exposure to ethanol could increase the risk of cancer.[41]

Clean Fuel, Dirty Water

If ethanol is found to be a carcinogen, or if the damage to the soil and the air turn out to be worse than any benefit ethanol provides in reducing CO, it will be a familiar story. America has already seen the federal government push an alternative "clean" fuel additive that turned out to be poison—methyl tertiary-butyl ether (MTBE).

The story of MTBE begins in the same place as the story of the catalytic converter—the January 14, 1970 announcement by GM President Edward Cole that GM would pursue an "essentially pollution-free" car engine. General Motors's catalytic converter wouldn't work with the predominant fuel of the day—leaded fuel.

The introduction of the catalytic converter, essentially mandated by clean air laws of the 1970s, meant the introduction of unleaded fuel. All gasoline is made in refineries by mixing many chemicals. A GM subsidiary called Ethyl had come up with the idea of adding lead to the fuel. Lead would increase the amount of pressure gasoline could withstand without spontaneously combusting. The ability to resist combustion under pressure is called *octane*.

Adding lead to fuel increased its octane. Octane is important because, in an internal combustion engine, the pistons compress the mixture of air and gasoline before the sparkplug fires. If some of the gasoline ignites under pressure, before the spark, it causes engine knock and reduces the efficiency of the engine. Lead helped keep the gasoline from igniting too early.

The catalytic converter, depending as it did on the exposed platinum, would be ruined if the engine's emissions contained lead. So, a new octane-enhancer was needed to replace lead. MTBE filled that role.

Methyl tertiary-butyl ether is a chemical compound made from methanol and butylene. Methanol, like ethanol, is an alcohol. But methanol comes from fermenting and distilling wood. Unlike ethanol, it is sweet. It also will kill you much more quickly if you drink it. It is used in antifreeze, windshield wiper fluid, and paint thinner.

Oil companies started using MTBE to increase the octane of their gasolines. Like ethanol, MTBE is also an oxygenate, and so it decreases CO in auto emissions. The 1990 amendments to the Clean Air Act mandated oxygenates in fuels, dramatically increasing the demand for MTBE.

But there are problems. Methyl tertiary-butyl ether does not break down very easily, and, containing methanol, it is poisonous. Some scientists say it causes cancer. This means that when MTBE gets into the ground—from leaky storage tanks or small spills—this poison eventually seeps into the water. Although it is still unclear how harmful MTBE-contaminated water is, many states have banned its use, only a few years after mandating it.

The story of MTBE is an illustrative one of how environmental policy works. Lawmakers and regulators saw a problem—CO emissions—and were willing to go to any length to solve it. Unfortunately, they may have introduced a brand-new carcinogenic toxin into our water by doing so. Are the mandates and subsidies for ethanol doing the same? Time will tell.

Transfer of Wealth

If ethanol is not a meaningful replacement for petroleum (Pimentel's research suggests that it is not), and if it is not good for the environment (the hydrocarbons, the soil degradation, and the plant emissions suggest that it is not), government policy mandating and subsidizing ethanol has one remaining defense: It helps the needy family farmer.

This defense has its problems, too. The most obvious problem is that ADM is hardly a small farmer struggling to get by. In 1981, when Pimentel's first study had just come out, and Carter and Reagan subsidies were piling up for ethanol, ADM controlled over 70 percent of ethanol plants in the United States.[42] On top of that, ADM owned much of the corn. Today, ADM is still the main beneficiary of ethanol subsidies.

Other farmers, who don't get nearly as much from the subsidies, suffer in the same ways most consumers do: higher gas prices and higher taxes. But some farmers feel even more pain. James Bovard wrote in 1995 "The primary effect of ethanol subsidies on agriculture markets, however, is to allow corn farmers to charge hog farmers and cattlemen higher prices."

Ethanol mandates and subsidies drive the price of corn higher than it would be in a free market. This hurts consumers, helps corn farmers, but more acutely hurts those for whom corn is an essential business supply—those who raise hogs and cattle. Bovard estimates (using USDA figures) that ethanol subsidies increase corn prices by 22 cents a bushel, thus costing hog farmers and cattlemen $1 billion. This drives up the price of pork and beef, further hurting the consumer.

The USDA's Office of Energy estimates that for each 100 million additional bushels grown for ethanol, the price for a bushel of soybeans would fall by four cents.[43] So, ethanol drives up the cost ranchers pay to feed their animals, and drives down the price soybean farmers can get for their crop.

As one final boon for ADM, the federal government has created a market for corn syrup—the sweetener used in soda and many foods in the United States. If you've ever had a Coke in Mexico, it tastes different. That is because it uses sugar as a sweetener. In the United States, however, the protectionist laws more than double the price of sugar. By denying consumers the sugar they want, the federal government drives Americans toward corn syrup—of which ADM is the number one manufacturer.

Politicians over Consumers

The case is strong that ADM makes a useless product in ethanol. It may cost more energy than it yields. It may pollute the air and destroy the soil. It is not only more expensive than gasoline but also less powerful. In short, left to their own will, Americans would not buy ethanol.

Yet, ADM is at the top of its industry, in no small part due to ethanol. How can you get rich making a product nobody wants? The answer lies in big government. Big government can give your buyers tax credits or subsidized loans. Big government can give you free corn. Big government can restrict competing products with regulations from which it then exempts your product. Finally, big government can mandate consumers use your product.

Archer Daniels Midland, because it was big, had access to government. Archer Daniels Midland lobbied government to play more of a role in the fuel and agriculture industry. That bigger government then helped ADM get bigger. Both big business and big government were constantly finding new justifications: energy security, engine knock, farmer welfare, and clean air.

The business's motivation, though, was always the same: profit. Archer Daniels Midland cannot be blamed for seeking profit. But is it moral to use the force of government to seek profit? CEOs argue that they would be betraying their shareholders if they passed up perfectly legal handouts for the sake of some free-market purity.

But Andreas, unlike many of the CEOs who profit from big government, has been tireless in winning favors and friends among the powerful. He has publicly and privately lobbied for laws that would enrich his company at the expense of consumers and taxpayers.

In any event, the blame more properly rests on the politicians, who, unlike CEOs, are supposed to answer to all the people. Richard Nixon, Jimmy Carter, George Bush, and all of the others were willing to auction off their constituents' wealth for the friendship and the campaign contributions of big business. In many ways, the country is poorer for it.

Notes

Chapter 1: The Big Ripoff

1. "Large Majorities of U.S. Adults Continue to Think That Big Companies, PACs, and Lobbyists Have Too Much Power and Influence in Washington," *Harris Interactive,* December 1, 2005, http://www.harrisinteractive.com /harris_poll/index.asp?PID=616 accessed March 20, 2006.

2. Campaign finance and lobbyist data from the Center for Responsive Politics, www.opensecrets.org.

3. Joel Bakan, *The Corporation: The Pathological Pursuit of Profit and Power* (New York: Free Press, 2004), p. 102.

4. Quoted in Arthur Meier Schlesinger, *A Life in the Twentieth Century: Innocent Beginnings, 1917–1950* (New York: Houghton-Mifflin, 2000), p. 372.

5. Arthur Sears Henning, "1936 Campaign Begins to Take Shape Rapidly," *Chicago Daily Tribune,* May 6, 1936.

6. Paul Krugman, "Jerking the Other Knee," *New York Times,* January 21, 2001.

7. Thomas S. Mulligan et al., "Collapse of Merger Pushes Enron to Brink of Ruin," *Los Angeles Times,* November 29, 2001.

8. Jon Carroll, "Missing Bill Clinton," *San Francisco Chronicle,* January 22, 2002.

9. Dan Morgan and Helen Dewar, "House Blocks FDA Oversight of Tobacco," *Washington Post,* October 12, 2004.

10. Martha M. Hamilton, "Industries Try for Federal Regulation," *Washington Post,* November 29, 1987.

11. Dan Morgan and Helen Dewar, "House Blocks FDA Oversight of Tobacco," *Washington Post,* October 12, 2004.

12. Walter Olson, "A Malleable Manufacturers' Lobby," *Wall Street Journal,* October 10, 1984.

13. David S. Broder, "Reagan Economics: From Ecstasy to Agony for Business Leaders," *Washington Post,* August 14, 1982.

14. Rowland Evans and Robert Novak, "Clinton's Corporate Dependents," *Washington Post,* March 1, 1993.

15. Timothy Noah, "Blaming Liberalism for Enron," *Slate,* January 21, 2002, http://www.slate.com/?id=2061023 accessed March 20, 2006.

16. John Carey, "Scott and Bill Went up the Hill," *Business Week,* March 16, 1998.

17. See note 16.

Chapter 2: The Parties of Big Business

1. Seth Lubove, "Stick to Your Knitting," *Forbes,* March 1, 2004.

2. Campaign finance data is from Federal Election Committee data compiled by the Center for Responsive Politics at http://www.opensecrets.org.

3. Rachel Abramowitz, "A Player in Every Sense," *Los Angeles Times,* July 3, 2002.

4. A. Abraham, "Ohio Group Sets The Table For Big Week," *Akron Beacon Journal,* July 24, 2004.

5. David D. Kirkpatrick, "Frist Sale Of Stock Spurs Inquiries Into Trusts," *New York Times,* September 24, 2005.

6. *Crossfire,* CNN, December 30, 2004.

7. Fairfax County Department of Tax Administration's Real Estate Assessment Information Site, http://icare.fairfaxcounty.gov/Main/Home.aspx, accessed March 21, 2006.

8. *Crossfire,* CNN, December 10, 2004.

9. "400 Richest Americans," *Forbes,* http://www.forbes.com/lists/2005/54 /Rank_1.html, accessed on March 20, 2006.

10. Isabella Geist, "Jackson Hole Hideaway," *Forbes,* November 8, 2004.

11. "Wyoming County Is Tops for Wealth," *Associated Press,* April 18, 2004.

12. All county election data is from CNN.com, http://www.cnn.com /ELECTION/2004/pages/results/president, accessed March 20, 2006.

13. Exit polls are from CNN.com, http://www.cnn.com/ELECTION /2004/pages/results/states/US/P/00/epolls.0.html and http://www.cnn .com/ELECTION/2000/results/index.epolls.html, accessed March 20, 2006.

14. Sean Loughlin, "Millionaires Populate U.S. Senate," CNN.com, June 12, 2003, http://www.cnn.com/2003/ALLPOLITICS/06/13/senators.finances, accessed March 20, 2006.

15. Quoted on "All Things Considered," National Public Radio, January 17, 2003.

16. Elizabeth Mehren, "Town Rocks 'Til Dawn with Nonstop Parties," *Los Angeles Times,* January 21, 1993.

17. Dennis Byrne, "Inauguration's Hoopla Is Grossly Insulting Display," *Chicago Sun-Times,* January 21, 1993.

18. Lloyd Grove, Elizabeth Kastor, Phil McCombs, Roxanne Roberts, and Martha Sherrill, "An Avalanche of Faith, Hope and Sincerity; Dinners Fit for a Republican: What's a Few Furs Among Friends?" *Washington Post,* January 19, 1993.

19. Inaugural committee data is from Center for Responsive Politics, http://www.opensecrets.org/clinton/inaugu.htm, accessed March 20, 2006.

20. Richard Miniter, "Clinton's Unlikely Boosters," *Insight,* March 14, 1993.

21. John Mintz, "GOP Right, Chamber in Bitter Feud: Clinton Victories Part Old Allies," *Washington Post,* April 2, 1993.

22. Phil Singer, "Senate Dems Trounce GOP Fundraising in 2005, Poised for Big Wins in 2006," Democratic Senatorial Campaign Committee press release, January 25, 2006.

23. Account of Rankin's vote is from: "Debate Lasted 16½ Hours," *New York Times,* April 6, 1917; "Seek to Explain Miss Rankin's 'No' " *New York Times,* April 7, 1917.

24. Roll Call vote 342, 107th Congress, first session.

25. Kent Wayne Snyder, "America's Congressman," Master's Thesis (Georgetown University, April 22, 2005).

26. H.R. 1050, 109th Congress.

27. http://www.billionairesforbush.com/story.php, accessed March 20, 2006.

Chapter 3: The History of Big Business

1. The account of the summer of 1792 is from: Thomas P. Slaughter, *The Whiskey Rebellion* (Oxford: Oxford University Press, 1986), pp. 114–117.

2. See note 1, p. 14.

3. See note 1, p. 121.

4. Quoted in Ron Chernow, *Alexander Hamilton* (New York: Penguin, 2004), p. 345.

5. See note 4, p. 345.

6. Charles A. Beard, *An Economic Interpretation of the Constitution* (New York: Macmillan, 1935), p. 102.

7. See note 6, p. 101.

8. See note 6, p. 101.

9. See note 6, p. 102.

10. See note 9.

11. See note 6, p. 330.

12. See note 6, p. 103.

13. Upton Sinclair, *The Jungle* (New York: Dover, thrift edition, 2001, originally published 1906), p. 112.

14. Book review, *Chicago Daily Tribune,* February 26, 1906.

15. "Jurgis Rudkus and 'The Jungle,'" *New York Times,* March 3, 1906.

16. Quoted in Gabriel Kolko, *The Triumph of Conservatism* (Chicago: Quadrangle Books, 1967), p. 103.

17. See note 16, p. 107.

18. "Packers Face Report Music," *Washington Post,* June 7, 1906.

19. See note 16, p. 106.

20. See note 16, p. 112.

21. See note 16, p. 2.

22. See note 16, p. 4.

23. See note 16, pp. 35–37.

24. See note 16, p. 37.

25. See note 16, p. 39.

26. Andrew Carnegie, "Control of Monopolies," *New York Times,* February 16, 1909.

27. See note 16, p. 174.

28. See note 16, p. 59.

29. See note 16, p. 78.

30. See note 16, p. 94.

31. See note 16, p. 96.

32. "Wilson Makes Defense Talk," *Los Angeles Times,* December 7, 1916, p. 13.

33. Murray Rothbard, "War Collectivism in World War I," *A New History of Leviathan* (New York: E.P Dutton and Company), 1972, p. 70.

34. Quoted in Paul A. C. Kostinen, "The 'Industrial-Military Complex' in Historical Perspective: World War I," *Business History Review,* Winter 1967, p. 381.

35. Quoted in Martin J. Sklar, "Woodrow Wilson and the Political Economy of Modern United States Liberalism," *Studies on the Left,* Fall 1960.

36. Grosvenor Clarkson, *Industrial America in the World War* (Boston: Houghton Mifflin Co., 1923), p. 63.

37. See note 33, p. 74.

38. See note 33, pp. 74–75.

39. See note 36, p. 313.

40. See note 37, p. 173.

41. See note 33, p. 81.

42. See note 33, p. 82.

43. See note 33, p. 78.

44. William E. Leuchtenburg, *The FDR Years: On Roosevelt and His Legacy,* "The New Deal and the Analogue of War" (New York: Columbia University Press, 1995), p. 67.

45. "F. D. Roosevelt Heads Construction Council," *Washington Post,* June 20, 1922.

46. Julius H. Barnes, "Herbert Hoover's Priceless Work in Washington," *Industrial Management,* April 1926.

47. Murray Rothbard, "Herbert Hoover and the Myth of Laissez-Faire," *A New History of Leviathan* (New York: E.P Dutton and Company), 1972, p. 123.

48. See note 47, p. 129.

49. See note 47, p. 136.

50. See note 47, p. 140.

51. W. David Lewis, *Airline Executives and Federal Regulation* (Columbus: Ohio State University Press, 2000), pp. 3–4.

52. Ida Tarbell, *Owen Young: A New Type of Industrial Leader* (New York: MacMillan, 1932), p. 228.

53. Arthur Sears Henning, "1936 Campaign Begins to Take Shape Rapidly," *Chicago Daily Tribune,* May 6, 1935.

54. Felix Bruner, "23 on Advisory Group Uphold Social Bill, NRA Extension," *Washington Post,* May 3, 1935.

55. Paul K. Conkin, *The New Deal* (New York: Thomas Y. Crowell Company, 1967), pp. 73–74.

56. William Domhoff, *The Higher Circles* (New York: Random House, 1970), p. 218.

57. See note 56, pp. 216–217.

58. John T. Flynn, "Whose Child Is the NRA?" *Harper's* Magazine, September 1934.

59. See note 55, p. 34.

60. Discussion of the Marshall Plan is from: Kim McQuaid, *Uneasy Partners* (Baltimore: Johns Hopkins University Press, 1992), pp. 36–47.

61. Stephen Slivinski, "The Corporate Welfare Budget Bigger Than Ever" (Cato Institute Policy Analysis, October 10, 2001, p. 5, Table 2).

62. See note 60, p. 74.

63. See note 60, p. 129.

64. Robert D. Hershey Jr., "Psychological Lift Seen," *New York Times,* August 17, 1971.

65. Vartanig G. Vartan, "Kaufman Opposes Ford's Tax-Cut Plan," *New York Times,* October 10, 1975.

66. Bill Nekirk, "Ford's Tax-Cut Proposal Leaves Executives Cold," *Chicago Tribune,* October 11, 1975.

67. Gene Smith, "Business Leaders Only Lukewarm to Program," *New York Times,* October 8, 1975.

68. See note 61, p 5, Table 2.

69. Press Release, "EPA Administrator Reilly Hails Signing of New Clean Air Act," Environmental Protection Agency, November 15, 1990.

70. Alan Sager and Deborah Socolar, "61 Percent of Medicare's New Prescription Drug Subsidy is Windfall Profit to Drug Makers" (Health Reform Program, Boston University School of Public Health), October 31, 2003, p. i.

Chapter 4: Robin Hood in Reverse

1. David McCally, *The Everglades: An Environmental History* (Gainesville, University Press of Florida), 1999, pp. 61–62, 89.

2. See note 1, pp. xviii, 90, 140.

3. Office of the Independent Counsel, "Referral to the United States House of Representatives pursuant to Title 28, United States Code, §595(c)" (September 8, 1998), sections II C and II D.

4. See note 3, section III D.

5. "Sugar's First Family," Center for Responsive Politics, www.opensecrets.org/pubs/cashingin_sugar/sugar08.html, accessed March 20, 2006.

6. See note 5.

7. Donald L. Bartlett and James B. Steele, "Sweet Deal: Why Are These Men Smiling? The Reason Is in Your Sugar Bowl," *Time,* November 23, 1988.

8. Brian M. Riedl, "Agriculture Lobby Wins Big in New Farm Bill," Heritage Foundation, Backgrounder #1534 (April 9, 2002).

9. Farm Service Agency Online, http://www.fsa.usda.gov/pscad/SelectLoan forfst.asp, accessed March 21, 2006.

10. USDA, Foreign Agriculture Service: http://www.fas.usda.gov/htp2/sugar /1999/november/prices.html, accessed March 20, 2006.

11. Organization for Economic Cooperation and Development, Agricultural Policies in OECD Countries, Monitoring and Evaluation 2005, http://www.oecd.org/dataoecd/44/6/35043935.xls, accessed March 20, 2006.

12. Karl Vick, "Big Sugar: A Sweet Deal Under Fire," *St. Petersburg Times,* May 15, 1994, p. 1A.

13. See note 7.

14. See note 1, p. 90.

15. Gene Barber, "The Way It Was: Historical Potpourri," *Baker County Press,* October 14, 1976.

16. http://www.rootsweb.com/~flbaker/history.html, accessed March 20, 2006.

17. Except where noted, Macclenny Wal-Mart information is from: Phillip Mattera and Anna Purinton, "Shopping for Subsidies: How Wal-Mart Uses Taxpayer Money to Finance Its Never-Ending Growth," *Good Jobs First,* May, 2004.

18. Roy Bernardi, "Statement of Roy A. Bernardi, Assistant Secretary for Community Planning and Development, U.S. Department of Housing and Urban Development, before the U.S. House of Representatives Committee on Financial Services Subcommittee on Housing and Community Opportunity," March 14, 2002.

19. Overseas Private Investment Corporation mission statement: http://www .opic.gov/Mission/DM_AtaGlance.htm, accessed March 20, 2006.

20. *Annual Report, 2001,* Overseas Private Investment Corporation, p. 18.

21. https://rezervasyon.bentour.com.tr/module.static/?page=hotel_info, accessed March 20, 2006.

22. Press Release, "OPIC Announces Indonesian Oil Projects," Overseas Private Investment Corporation, February 4, 2002.

23. Ian Vasquez and John Welborn, "Reauthorize or Retire the Overseas Private Investment Corporation?" Cato Institute Foreign Policy Briefing, September 15, 2003.

24. Overseas Private Investment Corporation, Request for Arbitration, November 4, 2004.

25. Milton Friedman, letter to Representative John R. Kasich (R–OH), chairman, Committee on the Budget, U.S. House of Representatives (September 5, 1996).

26. See note 23.

27. Steve Slivinski, "The Corporate Welfare Budget Bigger Than Ever," Cato Institute Policy Analysis, October 10, 2001.

28. United States Department of Agriculture, "USDA Budget Outlays" (2006) Budget Summary: http://www.usda.gov/agency/obpa/Budget-Summary/2005/OutlayTables.htm, accessed March 20, 2006.

29. See note 28.

30. United States Department of Agriculture, Foreign Agriculture Service "The Competition in 2002" (August, 2002), http://www.fas.usda.gov /cmp/com-study/2002/2002.pdf, accessed March 20, 2006.

31. Benjamin Stone and Dennis Kennelly, "Industry Suggests Improvements for Exports" *National Defense Magazine,* May, 2003, http://www .nationaldefensemagazine.org/issues/2003/May/Industry_Suggests.htm, accessed March 20, 2006.

32. Consolidated Appropriations Act of 2005, H.R. 4818.

33. USAID, "Summary of FY 2006 Budget and Program Highlights," Table 1.

34. "Power Marketing Administrations: Cost Recovery, Financing, and Comparison to Nonfederal Utilities," United States General Accounting Office, Report to Congressional Requesters (September, 1996), p. 30.

35. See note 34, p. 40.

36. Stephen Slivinski, "The Corporate Welfare Budget: Bigger Than Ever," Cato Institute Policy Analysis, October 21, 2001.

37. Chris Edwards, "Downsizing the Federal Government," Cato Institute Policy Analysis, June 2, 2004.

Chapter 5: Boeing's Bank

1. John F. Berry, "Ex-Im Chief Pushed Loan for Murdoch; Loan for Murdoch Pushed after White House Visit," *Washington Post,* March 19, 1980.

2. Dom Bonafede, "On the Eve of New Hampshire's Primary, Kennedy Is in the Make-or-Break Stage," *National Journal,* February 23, 1980, p. 317.

3. "Ex-Im Bank Skips Dividend," *Facts on File,* December 31, 1980.

4. The history of Ex-Im is from: William Becker and William McClenahan, *The Market, the State, and the Export-Import Bank of the United States, 1934–2000* (Cambridge University Press, 2003).

5. See note 4, p. 12.

6. *Budget of the United States Government* (FY 2007), p. 1143.

7. *2004 Annual Report,* Export-Import Bank of the United States, p. 26.

8. James Hess, Statement Before the Subcommittee on International Monetary Policy and Trade, House Committee on Financial Services, May 2, 2001.

9. Ian Vasquez, Statement Before the Subcommittee on International Monetary Policy and Trade, House Committee on Financial Services, May 8, 2001.

10. Original analysis by author from data compiled by National Journalism Center intern Joel Elliot from Export-Import Bank annual reports (1998–2004).

11. Sajid Rizvi, "UK to Give $850M to Boeing Rival," *United Press International,* March 13, 2000.

12. Thomas J. Downey, "Airbus Aid Distorts Market," *Financial Post,* July 25, 2005.

13. This section, except where noted, is from: Timothy P. Carney, "Boeing Takes More Than Half of Ex-Im Funds," *Human Events,* June 18, 2001.

14. See note 8.

15. Shelley Markham, "Nauru Seeks Help After Only Passenger Aircraft Repossessed," *Australian Associated Press Newsfeed,* December 19, 2005.

16. "Team Nauru not home for the holidays," *PacNews,* January 3, 2005.

17. CIA World Factbook, http://www.odci.gov/cia/publications/factbook/rankorder/2004rank.html, accessed March 20, 2006.

18. World's Richest People, *Forbes,* March 10, 2005.

19. http://www.state.gov/r/pa/ei/bgn/3584.htm, accessed March 20, 2006.

20. U.S. Department of Energy, Energy Information Agency, "World Oil Market and Oil Price Chronologies: 1970–2004," http://www.eia.doe.gov/cabs/chron.html, accessed March 20, 2006.

21. U.S. Department of Energy, Energy Information Agency, http://tonto.eia.doe.gov/dnav/pet/hist/mg_rt_usw.htm, accessed March 20, 2006.

22. James R. Kraus, "Chase Puts Together $1.9B Low-Risk Loan for Saudis," *American Banker,* December 3, 1999.

23. Center for Responsive Politics, http://opensecrets.org, accessed March 20, 2006.

24. Senate Office of Public Records, http://sopr.senate.gov, accessed March 20, 2006.

25. David Freddoso, "Mrs. Daschle, Big Business Lobbyist," *Human Events,* May 20, 2002.

26. Transcript, "Press Stakeout with Senate Majority Leader Tom Daschle (D-SD) Following Senate Policy Luncheons," June 4, 2002, Federal News Service.

27. Larry Makinson, "Outsourcing the Pentagon: Who benefits from the Politics and Economics of National Security?" The Center for Public Integrity, September 29, 2004.

28. Dan L. Crippen, Letter to Senator McCain Regarding Costs of Alternatives for Modernizing the Air Force Tanker Fleet (May 7, 2002).

29. Quoted by Mark Shields on *Capital Gang,* CNN, May 4, 2002.

30. Press Release, "Druyun Joins Boeing as Deputy General Manager for Missile Defense Systems" *Boeing,* January 3, 2003.

31. R. Jeffrey Smith, "E-Mails Detail Air Force Push for Boeing Deal," *Washington Post,* June 7, 2005.

32. Gary Washburn and Mickey Ciokajlo, "Chicago Snags Boeing," *Chicago Tribune,* May 11, 2001.

33. Press Release, "Tulsa, Oklahoma Passes Historic Economic Development Package," City of Tulsa, September 10, 2003.

34. "Is Washington State More Competitive in 2003?" Economic Development Council of Snohomish County, August 27, 2005.

35. Photo caption, "Otis Closes Door on Manufacturing" *Herald-Times,* March 31, 2005, p. A1.

36. Summary of Minutes of the Meeting of Credit Committee, Export-Import Bank of the United States, July 13, 2000.

37. See note 10.

38. Summary of Minutes of Meeting of Board of Directors, Export-Import Bank of the United States, February 18, 2005.

39. Bill Gertz, "China Nuclear Transfer Exposed; Hill Expected to Urge Sanctions," *Washington Times,* February 5, 1995.

40. Congressional Research Service Issue Brief, November 20, 2002.

41. Press Release, "Ex-Im Bank Approves $792 Million in Sales to China." The Export-Import Bank of the United States (November 19, 1996).

42. Campaign finance data from the Center for Responsive Politics' web site, http://www.opensecrets.org, accessed March 20, 2006.

43. Jeff Gerth et al., "The Arkansas Network: A Special Report," *New York Times,* February 14, 1997.

44. Press Release, "John Huang Pleads Guilty to Violating Federal Campaign Finance Laws," United States Department of Justice, August 12, 1999.

45. Bill Gertz, "Beijing Flouts Nuke-Sales Ban," *Washington Times,* October 9, 1996, p. A1.

46. R. Jeffrey Smith, "China Nuclear Deal With Iran Is Feared," *Washington Post,* April 17, 1995.

47. George W. Bush, "President Announced New Measure to Counter the Threat of WMD," Remarks by the President on Weapons of Mass Destruc-

tion Proliferation, Fort Lesley (J. McNair, National Defense University, February 11, 2004).

Chapter 6: Eminent Domain for Corporate Gain

1. Minnich's story, except where noted, comes from an interview at his Mahopac home in December of 2004.

2. Thomas J. Lueck, "Retail Center Is Proposed in East Harlem," *New York Times,* March 29, 1998.

3. Brody's story, except where noted, comes from an interview at his Bronx hardware store in November of 2004.

4. Jennifer Keeney, "Fighting City Hall," *Fortune,* May 13, 2002.

5. Terry Pristin, "On 125th S., a Plan for Shopping Center and 10-Screen Multiplex," *New York Times,* April 15, 1999.

6. WWOR News, I-Team, date unknown.

7. See note 6.

8. Douglas Montero, "Harlem's Being Built up at Little Guy's Expense," *New York Post,* August 6, 1999.

9. Alex Halperin, "Condemning (for) Private Business," *Gotham Gazette,* March 4, 2002.

10. Franz Leichter, "Give a Little, Get a Lot: Pataki's Economic Development Agency Resembles Political Slush Fund," paper issued by State Senator Leichter's office, 1996.

11. Campaign finance data from New York City Campaign Finance Board web site, http://www.nyccfb.info, New York State Board of Elections web site, http://nysboewww01.elections.state.ny.us/portal/page?_pageid=153,42096,153_4231 0:153_42314&_dad=portal&_schema=PORTAL, and the Center for Responsive Politics web site, http://www.opensecrets.org, all accessed March 20, 2006.

12. Charles E. Schumer and Robert E. Rubin, *Preparing for the Future: A Commercial Development Strategy for New York City* (Group of 35, June 11, 2001).

13. Editorial, "Helping New York Grow," *New York Times,* June 16, 2001.

14. David Lombino, "Owners Ousted from *Times* Site Awaiting Payout," *New York Sun,* January 9, 2006.

15. 348 U.S. 26.

16. *Kelo v. New London,* 125 S. Ct. 2655.

17. Telephone interview in January 2005.

18. http://www.nylovessmallbiz.com/quiz/taxes_regulations_insurance.asp, accessed March 20, 2006.

19. These examples are from the Castle Coalition web site, http://maps.castlecoalition.com, and from: Dana Berliner, *Public Power, Private Gain,* April 2003.

20. Dennis Coates and Brad R. Humphreys, "Caught Stealing: Debunking the Economic Case for D.C. Baseball," Cato Institute Briefing Paper, October 27, 2004.

Part III: Regulate Me!

1. George J. Stigler, "The Theory of Economic Regulation," *Bell Journal of Economics and Management Science,* Spring 1971, pp. 3–21.

2. Milton Friedman, "Regulatory Schizophrenia," *Newsweek,* June 29, 1981.

Chapter 7: Regulators and Robber Barons

1. The account of Daly's flights are taken from various news sources, particularly: Sam Jameson, "Ed Daly—He's a Believer," *Los Angeles Times,* April 3, 1975; and Cynthia Gorney, "King of the Cut-Rate Airways," *Washington Post,* June 25, 1980.

2. James Coats, "Babylift Hero Seeks OK for Cheap U.S. Flights," *Chicago Tribune,* April 14, 1975.

3. Richard Witkin, "Other Carriers Will Fight $89 Coast-to-Coast Flight," *New York Times,* April 3, 1975.

4. See note 2.

5. See note 2.

6. John W. Barnum, "What Prompted Airline Deregulation 20 Years Ago? What Were the Objectives of That Deregulation and How Were They Achieved?" Presentation to the Aeronautical Law Committee of the Business Law Section of the International Bar Association at its Annual Meeting in Vancouver, B.C., on 15 September 1998, accessed at http://library .findlaw.com/1988/Sep/1/129304.html, accessed March 20, 2006.

7. W. David Lewis, *Airline Executives and Federal Regulation* (Columbus: Ohio State University Press, 2000), p. 4.

8. Ernest Holsendolph, "Federal Controls on Airlines Seen Increasing Fares," *New York Times,* February 24, 1977.

9. George F. Will, "Feudalism in the Sky," *Los Angeles Times,* October 8, 1975.

10. Jack Egan, "CAB Keeps Prices High, Study Says," *Washington Post,* June 25, 1975.

11. See note 7, p. 17.

12. See note 7, p. 243.

13. See note 9.

14. Jack Egan, "Airline Officials Attack Efforts at Deregulation," *Washington Post,* March 20, 1975.

15. See note 14.

16. See note 14.

17. "What's This? Airline Chief Wants Continued Control," *Chicago Tribune,* November 21, 1975.

18. Carol Shifrin, "Degree of Change Needed in Airline Deregulation Disputed," *Washington Post,* December 2, 1976.

19. See note 18.

20. Robert Burkhardt, "Air Deregulation Bill Hit," *Journal of Commerce,* June 15, 1976.

21. Albert V. Casey, "Coming Down Hard on the Airlines," *New York Times,* November 8, 1976.

22. See note 8.

23. United Press International, "Deregulation Could Wreck Airlines, Eastern Warns," *Los Angeles Times,* March 30, 1977.

24. See note 6.

25. Weston Kosova et al., "Backstage at the Finale," *Newsweek,* February 26, 2001.

26. See note 25.

27. Food and Drug Administration Proposed Rule, *Federal Register* vol. 66, no. 12 (January 18, 2001), pp. 4706–4738.

28. FDA Docket # 00N–1396, vol. 276, c 7153.

29. FDA Docket # 00N–1396, vol. 277, c 7217.

30. See note 27, p. 4726.

31. See note 27, p. 4728.

32. Mary Wozniak, "Genetics are Altering the Way We Eat," *Fort Myers News-Press,* April 25, 2001.

33. FDA Docket # 00N–1396, vol. 261, c 6895.

34. See note 27, p. 4708.

35. See note 27, p. 4729.

36. See note 27, p. 4708.

37. See note 27, p. 4729.

38. See note 27, p. 4713.

39. Henry I. Miller and Gregory Conko, *The Frankenfood Myth: How Protest and Politics Threaten the Biotech Revolution* (Westport, CT: Praeger, 2004), p. 57.

40. See note 39, p. 60.

41. See note 39, p. 61.

42. Charles F. Dolan, "Statement of Cablevision Chairman Charles F. Dolan Regarding *A La Carte* Programming," December 1, 2005.

43. Reply Comments of Cablevision Systems Corporation, Federal Communications Commission, MB Docket No. 04-207 (August 13, 2004).

44. Sharon Theimer, "McCain Group Got Big Cable Donation While Senator Promoted Company Policy," *Associated Press,* March 7, 2005.

45. Sylvia Swanson, "Letter from the 1999 Staff President of the International Bottled Water Association," *Beverage Industry,* November 1, 1999.

46. *World News Tonight,* Peter Jennings, March 30, 1999.

47. John R. Emshwiller, "Shell-Breaking Machine Runs Afoul of Egg Producers," *Wall Street Journal,* October 19, 1989.

48. Julie Sloan, "Libertarians and Justice for All?" *Fortune Small Business,* June 1, 2004.

49. Valerie Bayham, "A Dream Deferred: Legal Barriers to African Hairbraiding Nationwide," Institute for Justice, http://www.ij.org/publications/other/national-hairbraiding.html accessed March 20, 2006.

50. See note 49.

51. Gary Rismiller's story and the account of the Arizona law come from a phone interview with Rismiller in January, 2006, and the Institute for Justice's Complaint in *Garrett Rismiller and Larry Park v. Arizona Structural Pest Commission et al.,* in the Superior Court of the State of Arizona in and for the County of Maricopa.

52. "Who Owns New York's Cabs?" *New York Magazine,* May 3, 2004.

53. See note 52.

54. Pamela G. Hollie, "World Airways' Battle Strategy," *New York Times,* July 26, 1980.

55. Cynthia Gorney, "King of the Cut-Rate Airways," *Washington Post,* June 25, 1980.

56. Ernest Holsendolph, "Low-Cost Airline Now Seeks Fares it Once Opposed," *New York Times,* March 10, 1982.

57. See note 54.

Chapter 8: The War against Tobacco

1. Complaint, *A. B. Coker et al. v. Charles C. Foti, Jr.,* In the United States District Court for the Western District of Louisiana, Shreveport Division.

2. Jack Elliott Jr., "Governor Sues Attorney General to Block Tobacco Lawsuit," *Associated Press,* February 16, 1996.

3. Mary Voboril, "New Legal Fight," *Newsday,* March 13, 1996.

4. John Schwartz, "For Tobacco Negotiators, Court Dates Are Looming," *Washington Post,* May 27, 1997.

5. Alison Frankel, "Smokin' Joe," *American Lawyer,* May 1998.

6. W. Kip Viscusi, *Smoke-Filled Rooms* (Chicago: University of Chicago Press, 2002), p. 4.

7. Martha Derthick, *Up in Smoke* (Washington: Congressional Quarterly Press, 2005), p. 172.

8. See note 6, p. 47.

9. See note 6, p. 7.

10. David Rice, "Senate Votes to Change Escrow-Fund Payments Small Tobacco Companies Say They'll Fight," *Winston-Salem Journal,* May 1, 2003.

11. See note 10.

12. Anne Paine, "Lawmaker Takes Aim at Little Tobacco," *Tennessean,* April 12, 2004.

13. William H. Sorrell, Mark E. Greenwold, Memorandum # 03-111, Re: Alert: Reduced Tobacco Settlement Payments and Request for Important Information, September 12, 2003. Available at http://www.timothypcarney .com/?page_id=224.

14. Walter Olson, "Puff, the Magic Settlement," *Reason,* January 2000.

15. See note 6, p. 38.

16. "President Clinton Announces Teen Smoking Initiative," ABC Breaking News, August 10, 1995.

17. "Nicotine in Cigarettes and Smokeless Tobacco Is a Drug and These Products are Nicotine Delivery Devices Under the Federal Food, Drug, and Cosmetic Act," *Federal Register,* August 28, 1996, pp. 44619–45318.

18. Sam Kazman, "Demonize, Then Pulverize," *Navigator,* November 2004.

19. *FDA v. Brown & Williamson Tobacco Corp.,* 529 U.S. 120 (2000).

20. Peter Hardin, "Senate Okays Buyout Deal, FDA Control," *Winston-Salem Journal,* July 16, 2004.

21. Peter Hardin, "No FDA Control a Setback for Altria," *Richmond Times Dispatch,* October 11, 2004.

22. Dan Morgan and Helen Dewar, "House Blocks FDA Oversight of Tobacco," *Washington Post,* October 12, 2004.

23. Samuel Loewenberg, "Why Is Philip Morris Supporting FDA Regulation of Cigarettes?" *Slate,* July 25, 2002, http://www.slate.com/?id=2068476, accessed on March 20, 2006.

24. See note 23.

25. *3rd Quarter Results,* Altria Group, Inc., November 10, 2005.

26. See note 7, p. 174.

27. "Tobacco Settlement: States' Allocations of Fiscal Year 2003 and Expected Fiscal Year 2004 Payments," General Accounting Office, March 2004.

28. See note 7, p. 193.

29. Transcript, "Regulation By Litigation: The New Wave of Government-Sponsored Litigation" (June 22, 1999), http://www.manhattan-institute.org/html/mics_1_b.htm.

30. Brooke Tunstall, "Orioles Won't Make a Pitch for Cuban Defectors," *Washington Times,* May 17, 2000.

31. See note 30.

32. Barry Meier and Jill Abramson, "Tobacco War's New Front: Lawyers Fight for Big Fees," *New York Times,* June 9, 1998.

33. Campaign finance data from Center for Responsive Politics web site, www.opensecrets.org.

34. http://www.oralcancerfoundation.org/tobacco/demographics_tobacco.htm, accessed on March 20, 2006.

Chapter 9: You Get Taxed, They Get Rich

1. James Dao, "A Governor's Hard Sell: Higher Taxes in Virginia," *New York Times,* January 20, 2004, Sec A, p. 12.

2. Virginia Department of Planning and Budget, Operating Budget, found at http://www.dpb.virginia.gov/budget/budget.cfm, accessed on March 20, 2006.

3. Editorial, "Gilmore's Highway Critics Aren't Quite on Target, Either," *Roanoke Times & World News,* August 26, 1999, p. A18.

4. See note 3.

5. "Governor's Panel Looks for Fixes Without Taxes," *Virginian-Pilot,* July 5, 1999.

6. James Dyke, "Improved Transportation Will Benefit All Virginians," *Richmond Times Dispatch,* August 20, 1999, p. A21.

7. See note 6.

8. Virginian Public Access Project, www.VPAP.org.

9. Kenneth Bredemeier, "Sales Tax? Road Kill: Business Community Licks Its Wounds, Regroups after Ineffective Campaign," *Washington Post,* November 25, 2002.

10. Coalition for Smarter Growth, et al., *The Sales Tax as Highway Robbery,* November 1, 2002, p. 2.

11. Editorial, "Interests," *Richmond Times Dispatch,* September 22, 2002.

12. Michael J. Lewis, "Referendum Is over, but Transportation Crisis Endures," *Washington Business Journal,* November 15, 2002.

13. Michele Clock, "Without Plan B, Area Scrambles To Make Up for Tax's Defeat," *Washington Post,* November 10, 2002.

14. Editorial, "Small Business and Big Virginia Taxes," *Washington Times,* January 8, 2004.

15. David Cay Johnston, "Dozens of Rich Americans Join in Fight to Retain the Estate Tax," *New York Times,* February 14, 2001, p. A1.

16. Remarks by President Clinton to Ministers' Leadership Conference, August 10, 2000.

17. Jonathan Rowe, "Every Baby a Trust Fund Baby," *American Prospect,* January 1–15, 2001.

18. John Berlau, "Buffetted: The Sage of Omaha Loves the Estate Tax—As Well He Might," *National Review,* August 23, 2004.

19. Frank Keating, "Reagan's Spirit: Alive and Well in Oklahoma," *The Tax Reformer,* Spring 2002.

20. "Keating is Shaping a New ACLI," *National Underwriter, Life & Health,* October 20, 2002.

21. Office of the President, "America's New Beginning: A Program for Economic Recovery," February 18, 1981, p. 16.

22. David S. Broder, "Reagan Economics: From Ecstasy to Agony for Business Leaders," *Washington Post,* August 14, 1982.

23. Timothy D. Schellhardt, "Chamber of Commerce Showdown Looms After Split on Tax Increases," *Wall Street Journal,* August 30, 1982.

24. Rowland Evans and Robert Novak, "Clinton's Corporate Dependents," *Washington Post,* March 1, 1993.

25. Eric Gelman and Ann McDaniel, "Two Inside Traders Go to Jail," *Newsweek,* May 20, 1985.

26. Doug Bandow, "A Corporate Lobby Pulls Its Punches" *Wall Street Journal,* July 23, 1986.

27. Paul A. Gigot, "Chamber Maids: Big Business Courts Clinton," *Wall Street Journal,* February 12, 1993.

28. Thomas McArdle, "Is Big Business Anti-Business," *Investor's Business Daily,* June 30, 1995.

29. William A. Smith, *Tax Crusaders and the Politics of Direct Democracy* (New York: Routledge, 1998), p. 149.

30. Michelle Fulcher, "Business Raising $250,000 to Fight Tax-Limit Plan," *Denver Post,* October 19, 1988, p. 11A.

31. Jim Hughes, "Chalk Up Win to Money, Organization," *Denver Post,* November 2, 2005.

32. All 2005 Colorado campaign finance information comes from the web site of the Colorado Secretary of State, Elections Division. The data comes from the filings of the "Vote Yes on C & D" Committee.

33. See note 29, p. 187, n 161.

Chapter 10: Environmentalism for Profit

1. The account of the Unocal case, except where noted, comes from: Federal Trade Commission, Complaint in the Matter of Union Oil Company of California (March 4, 2003).

2. Patent No. 5,288,393.

3. "California Refinery Calls Halt to Processing," *Oil & Gas Journal,* June 12, 1995.

4. Elizabeth Douglass and Gary Cohn, "Refiners Maintain a Firm but Legal Grip on Supplies," *Los Angeles Times,* June 18, 2005.

5. See note 4.

6. Capital Research Center online database at http://capitalresearch.org/search /search.asp, accessed March 21, 2006.

7. "Welcome to Kyoto-Land," *Economist,* October 9, 2004.

8. Rob Routliffe, "Participation in GHG Markets: The DuPont Experience" Business Roundtable Presentation, September 24, 2004.

9. "New Market Shows Industry Moving Forward on Global Warming," *Associated Press,* January 16, 2003.

10. DuPont Canada, Inc., Submission for Voluntary Challenge & Registry, Inc., "Action Plan" (October 2002).

11. Lauren Miura, "Climate Change: Market Inconsistencies Inhibit Carbon Trading," *Greenwire,* March 17, 2003.

12. Nick Doak, "Greenhouse Gasses are Down," *Chemistry and Industry,* December 2, 2002.

13. Office of Public Records, *Year End Report,* Secretary of the Senate (2004).

14. Charles River Associates, "The Post-Kyoto Climate—Impacts on the U.S. Economy" (1999).

15. Paul Anderson, "Taking Responsibility," *Charlotte Business Journal's* 10th Annual Power Breakfast (April 7, 2005).

16. "Duke to sell some power generation assets to LS Power for about $1.5 billion," *Associated Press,* January 9, 2006.

17. Press release, "State Regulators Approve Cinergy/PSI Rate Increase," *Cinergy,* May 18, 2004.

18. The story of the launch of "ecomagination" comes from: Amanda Griscom Little, "It was Just my Ecomagination," *Grist,* May 10, 2005.

19. Juliet Eilperin, "World Leaders to Discuss Strategies for Climate Control," *Washington Post,* November 27, 2005.

20. Center for Responsive Politics, online database at http://www.opensecrets.org, accessed March 21, 2006.

21. Capital Research Center online database at http://www.capitalresearch.org, accessed March 21, 2006.

22. *Public Papers of the Presidents of the United States,* 672.

23. Jerry M. Flint, "G.M. Sees Autos Fume-Free by '80," *New York Times,* January 15, 1970.

24. See Chapter 13 for more discussion of leaded fuel.

25. See note 23.

26. Michael Weisskopf, "Catalytic Converters: Smog Debate Revisited," *Business Dateline,* March 26, 1990.

27. "Ethyl Corp. Disclaims Rap at GM," *Washington Post,* January 18, 1970.

28. Review & Outlook, "Chrysler Squeaks," *Wall Street Journal,* March 3, 1978.

29. Peter Hong, "Honk if you Hate the EPA," *Business Week,* July 27, 1992.

30. Center for Responsive Politics, online database at http://www.opensecrets.org, accessed March 21, 2006.

31. Ken Ward Jr., "Getting Tough on Valley Fills," *West Virginia Gazette,* March 31, 1998.

32. Martin Kady II and Samuel Goldreich, "Industry-Friendly Energy Bill Faces Difficult Negotiations Ahead in Senate," *CQ Today,* April 14, 2003.

Chapter 11: Enron

1. The account of the first game at Enron Field is compiled from various news stories from April 8, 2000: Mark Rosner, "Astros Christen Enron with Loss," *Austin American-Statesman*; Michael A. Lutz, "Phillies 4, Astros 1" *Associated Press*; Fran Blinebury, "All's Well, Even if it Didn't End Well at Enron" *Houston Chronicle*; W.H. Stickney, "Gant, Phillies, Spoil Astros' Festive Mood," *Houston Chronicle.*

2. The stories of eminent domain takings for Enron Field are from: Richard Connelly, "Make Way for McLane," *Houston Press,* December 4, 1997.

3. Richard Connelly, "Sports Afield," *Houston Press,* November 20, 1997.

4. Bob Deans, "Lindsey Led Enron Review, White House Discloses," *Cox News Service,* January 16, 2002.

5. Bethany McLean and Peter Elkind, *The Smartest Guys in the Room: The Amazing Rise and Scandalous Fall of Enron* (New York: Portfolio, 2003).

6. Editorial, "The Real Scandal," *St. Louis Post-Dispatch,* January 22, 2002.

7. See note 5, p. 173.

8. Thomas S. Mulligan et al., "Collapse of Merger Pushes Enron to Brink of Ruin," *Los Angeles Times,* November 29, 2001.

9. John Schwartz, "Enron's Collapse," *New York Times,* January 13, 2002.

10. Allan Sloan, "Who Killed Enron?" *Newsweek,* January 21, 2002.

11. Jon Carroll, "Missing Bill Clinton," *San Francisco Chronicle,* January 22, 2002.

12. John Kampfner, "Collapse of the US Energy Giant Questions the Morality of Making a Fast Buck," *Express,* January 28, 2002.

13. H. Josef Hebert, "Cabinet Members Say They Didn't Inform Bush About Enron Calls for Help," *Associated Press,* January 13, 2002.

14. See note 13.

15. Jerry Taylor, "Enron Was No Friend to Free Markets," *Wall Street Journal,* January 21, 2002.

16. Al Gore, "The Selling of Energy Policy," *New York Times,* April 21, 2002.

17. Dan Morgan, "Enron Also Courted Democrats," *Washington Post,* January 13, 2002.

18. Kenneth L. Lay, "For Prevention's Sake, Focus on Climate Solutions," *Austin American-Statesman,* December 8, 1997.

19. Robert D. Novak, "Enron's Secret Energy Plan," *Chicago Sun-Times,* January 17, 2002.

20. See note 17.

21. See note 19.

22. Bill Lickert and Christopher Morris, "The Truth About Bush & Enron," *National Review Online,* February 8, 2002.

23. See note 15.

24. Capital Research Center database, http://capitalresearch.org/search /gmdisplay.asp?Org=470615943.

25. http://www.undueinfluence.com/nature_conservancy.htm, accessed March 21, 2006.

26. Timothy Noah, "Who Turned Dubya Briefly Green," *Slate,* March 15, 2001.

27. Wendy Zellner, Christopher Palmieri, Peter Coy, Laura Cohn, "Enron's Power Play," *Business Week,* February 12, 2001.

28. James L. Sweeney, "Lights Out," *Hoover Digest,* Fall 2002.

29. See note 28.

30. Patrice Hill, "Enron Got Clinton Help in California," *Washington Times,* February 26, 2002.

31. Special Agent Steven C. Coffin, affidavit accompanying criminal complaint in *United States of America v. John Forney,* p. 12 ¶ 37, May 30, 2003.

32. See note 15.

33. Kenneth L. Lay, prepared testimony before the Committee on Appropriations, Subcommittee on Foreign Operations, U.S. House of Representatives, March 23, 1995.

34. Quoted in: Richard A. Oppel Jr., "The 2000 Campaign: The Donor," *New York Times,* June 30, 2000.

35. See note 5, p. 110.

36. See note 5, p. 77.

37. Linda F. Powers, testimony before the Subcommittee on International Economic Policy and Trade, Committee on International Relations, U.S. House of Representatives, March 18, 1997.

38. Sustainable Energy and Economy Network, *Enron's Pawns,* March 22, 2002, p. 15.

39. See note 5, p. 78.

40. Arundhati Roy, "Shall We Leave it to the Experts?" *Nation,* February 18, 2002.

41. See note 5. Except where noted, the story of Dabhol comes from McLean, pp. 79–83.

42. David E. Sanger, "How Washington, Inc., Makes a Sale," *New York Times,* February 15, 1995.

43. Robert D. Novak, "Enron's Corporate Welfare," *Chicago Sun-Times,* April 29, 2002.

44. Overseas Private Investment Corporation, Request for Arbitration, November 4, 2004, p. 10.

45. Bruce Rich, Statement before the House Committee on International Relations, June 10, 2003.

46. Quoted in: "Enron's Pawns," Institute for Policy Studies, March 22, 2002, p. 8.

47. See note 46, pp. 15–16.

48. See note 43.

49. Export-Import Bank of the United States, Summary of Minutes of Meeting of Board of Directors (September 13, 2000).

50. See note 43.

51. Peter S. Goodman, "China Invests Heavily in Sudan's Oil Industry," *Washington Post,* December 23, 2004.

52. Press release, "U.S. Commerce Secretary Daley Completes Successful First Day of Infrastructure Mission to China," U.S. Department of Commerce, March 29, 1999.

53. See note 38, p. 3.

54. Daniel Bayly's story is from: Landon Thomas Jr., "Deals and Consequences," *New York Times,* November 20, 2002.

55. See note 5, p. 132.

56. See note 5, p. 202.

57. See note 54.

58. Tony Freemantle, "Mayor Says African Trip Was Success in Marketing for City," *Houston Chronicle,* December 2, 1999.

59. Pat Reber, "U.S. Commerce Secretary Starts Trade Talks in South Africa," *Associated Press,* November 30, 1998.

60. See note 38, p. 34.

61. See note 5, pp. 39–42.

62. See note 5, p. 41.

63. Calpers web site, http://www.calpers.ca.gov/index.jsp?bc=/about/home .xml.

64. Press release, "Calpers Investment Fund Tops $200 billion," *Calpers,* December 12, 2005.

65. The story of Calpers and Jedi comes from: William C. Powers Jr., Raymond S. Troubh, and Herbert S. Winokur Jr., "Report of Investigation by the Special Investigative Committee of the Board of Directors of Enron Corp" (February 1, 2002); note 5, p. 67, and elsewhere.

66. Footnote 10 in the Enron "Report of Investigation," reads: "It is presently common knowledge among Enron Finance employees that Kopper and [Michael] Dodson are domestic partners. We do not have information concerning their relationship in December 1997 or what, if anything, Enron Finance employees knew about it at that time."

67. See note 65, p. 41.

68. Mike Wise, "Forgotten Team Gives U.S. Gold in the Bobsled," *New York Times,* February 20, 2002.

69. "Enron Fall Creates Race to Regulate," *New York Times,* February 10, 2002.

70. "Damaged Goods," *Economist,* May 21, 2005.

Chapter 12: Ethanol and Archer Daniels Midland

1. Memorandum from Paul R. Michel, Watergate Special Prosecution Force (February 7, 1975).

2. Peter Carlson, "Chairman Across the Board" *Washington Post Magazine,* July 14, 1996.

3. See note 2.

4. See note 2.

5. See note 2.

6. See note 2.

7. See note 2.

8. Compiled from Federal Election Commission data.

9. George Anthan, "Gore's Farming Credentials: His Vote for Ethanol," *Des Moines Register,* March 28, 1999.

10. *Meet the Press,* NBC, August 1, 1999.

11. 103rd Congress, Second Session, roll call vote # 255.

12. 108th Congress, First Session, roll call vote # 203.

13. *Annual Report,* Archer Daniels Midland (2004).

14. Press release, "Ethanol Fuel from Corn Faulted as 'Unsustainable Food Burning' in Analysis by Cornell Scientist" Cornell University (August 6, 2001).

15. Brent Yacobucci and Jasper Womach, "Fuel Ethanol: Background and Public Policy Issues," Congressional Research Service Report for Congress (updated December 17, 2004).

16. See note 2.

17. James Bovard, "Archer Daniels Midland: A Case Study in Corporate Welfare," *Cato Institute Policy Analysis,* September 26, 1995.

18. "Gasohol Loan Guarantees Announced," *Associated Press,* October 10, 1980.

19. See note 17.

20. Michael Isikoff, "USDA Starts Major Gasohol Subsidy Plan," *Washington Post,* June 3, 1986, p. D1.

21. See note 20.

22. See note 17.

23. Dan Carney, "Dwayne's World," *Mother Jones,* July/August, 1995.

24. Ben Evans, "2005 Legislative Summary: Energy Policy Overhaul," *Congressional Quarterly Weekly,* December 30, 2005.

25. "Implications of Increased Ethanol Production for U.S. Agriculture," report prepared by the Food and Agricultural Policy Research Institute (University of Missouri, August 22, 2005).

26. General Accounting Office, "Tax Policy: Effects of the Alcohol Fuels Incentives," report to the Chairman of the Committee on Ways and Means, March, 1997.

27. *Moneyline,* CNN, January 26, 1993.

28. David Pimentel and Tad Patzek, "Ethanol Production Using Corn, Switch-grass, and Wood; Biodiesel Production Using Soybean and Sunflower," *Natural Resources Research,* March 2005, pp. 65–76.

29. Society of Automotive Engineers (Warrendale, PA, 2000).

30. Marcelo E. Dias de Oliveira, Burton E. Vaughan, and Edward J. Rykiel Jr., "Ethanol as Fuel: Energy, Carbon Dioxide Balances, and Ecological Footprint," *BioScience,* July 2005.

31. Most information on the Reg-Neg story comes from: Migdon Segal, "Ethanol and Clean Air: The 'Reg-Neg' Controversary and Subsequent Events," Congressional Research Service Report for Congress, June 22, 1993.

32. Michael Arndt, "Bush Wrestles with Ethanol Issue; His Dilemma: Farm Vote vs. Clean Air Rule," *Chicago Tribune,* September 9, 1992.

33. Chart "Who Gave How Much," *New York Law Journal,* December 11, 1995.

34. See note 32.

35. Barbara Demick, "Behind the Inaugural Facade-Power Brokers Picking up the Tab." *Tacoma Morning News Tribune,* January 20, 1993.

36. "An Avalanche of Faith, Hope and Sincerity; Dinners Fit for a Republican: What's a Few Furs Among Friends?" *Washington Post,* January 19, 1993.

37. Maureen Lorenzetti, "U.S. Appeals Court Rejects EPA Ethanol Mandate," *Platts Oilgram Price Report,* May 1, 1995.

38. "Ethanol Firms to Reduce Pollution," *Energy Conservation News,* October 2002.

39. Gerald Karey, "Sierra Club to Sue Two U.S. Midwest Ethanol Plants," *Platts Oilgram News,* September 30, 2002.

40. See note 30.

41. See Hemant K. Roy, James M. Gulizia, William J. Karolski, Anne Ratashak, Michael F. Sorrell, and Dean Tuma, "Ethanol Promotes Intestinal Tumorigenesis in the MIN Mouse," *Cancer Epidemiology Biomarkers and Prevention,* November 2002.

42. See note 17.

43. Office of Energy, "Fuel Ethanol and Agriculture: An Economic Assessment," U.S. Department of Agriculture, Agricultural Economic Report no. 562 (August 1986).

Index